The Irony of Early School

MICHAEL B. KATZ

The Irony of
Early School Reform

EDUCATIONAL INNOVATION
IN MID-NINETEENTH CENTURY MASSACHUSETTS

BEACON PRESS   BOSTON

Copyright © 1968 by the President and Fellows of Harvard College
All rights reserved
International Standard Book Number: 0–8070–3187–9
First published as a Beacon Paperback in 1970 by arrangement with
  Harvard University Press
Beacon Press books are published under the auspices of the
  Unitarian Universalist Association
Printed in the United States of America
Second printing, May 1972

For my mother and father

Preface

The study from which this book emerged began as a purely analytical attempt to determine the relationships between educational innovation and urban-industrial development in ante-bellum Massachusetts. It was Professor Daniel Calhoun who forced me to recognize the fact that implicit in my first complete draft was a critical commentary on the origins of contemporary aspects of urban education. I rewrote the manuscript to emphasize these connections between, as I see them, past mistakes and the present disastrous state of formal education in our cities. Thus this book tries at once to be a scholarly historical study and a piece of social criticism. It has become a very personal document; since I have not been able to escape my biases, I have tried at least to make them explicit. For the often partisan nature of my argument I offer no apologies; the crisis in our cities must arouse a passionate response in all those who care about the quality of American life. My hope is that this book may in some way help contemporary reformers gain more perspective on the staggering social ills with which they contend.

M.B.K.

Toronto
March 1968

Acknowledgments

This study was made possible by the grant of a contract from the United States Office of Education (Cooperative Research Program, Project S-085). For this award I am deeply grateful. The statistical work involving a computer was supported by a National Science Foundation grant. For allowing me time under the grant I would like to thank Professor John B. Carroll. Throughout my stay at the Harvard Graduate School of Education, where this study was first submitted as a doctoral dissertation, the administration provided tolerance, freedom, interest, and very considerable financial support, and it did so with the graciousness and generosity characteristic of its dealings with students. My thanks go especially to Associate Dean Edward Kaelber.

The financial assistance and encouragement necessary to revise this study for publication have been generously and unhesitatingly provided by my present colleagues at the Ontario Institute for Studies in Education; in particular, I must thank Dr. Willard Brehaut, chairman of the Department of History and Philosophy of Education. Mrs. Caroline Miller, my research assistant, meticulously checked footnotes and assisted with the proofreading of the revised version. Mrs. Anne-Marie Oraw Hodes has also been of great assistance in proofreading and the preparation of the manuscript for publication.

The librarians and school officials whose assistance I sought have been almost unfailingly helpful. In particular, I would like to thank Miss Ruth Hill of the Beverly Historical Society, whose eagerness to help scholars use the Society's fine collection should be imposed upon more often. Many friends and colleagues have patiently listened to me think out loud about this study over the past four years; a number have read drafts and sections and made extremely helpful comments. Dr. Allan Ellis provided the guidance and instruction in statistical and computer matters that made the quantitative sections of this study possible. Also, my special thanks go to Drs. Robert Dreeben, Stephan Thernstrom, and David Tyack. My advisor was Dean Theodore R. Sizer; the profitableness and pleasantness of my residence at H.G.S.E. were due in no small part to his consideration and assistance. This study started as a paper in the seminar of Dr. Daniel Calhoun. He has since read many versions and, indeed, almost every draft of each section; he has, as well, spent many hours discussing the study with me. His always penetrating and stimulating comments have given this study much of whatever merit it possesses. For all the help I have received I am most grateful. Of course, all errors, misinterpretations, and other blunders or barbarisms that remain are entirely my own responsibility.

For permission to quote from unpublished material I should like to thank the Beverly Historical Society, the Massachusetts Historical Society, and the Essex Institute.

Contents

The Irony of Early School Reform

I think we may fairly regard the year 1837, when the
Massachusetts Board of Education was established, and
Horace Mann appointed as its first secretary, as the
commencement of the modern epoch of education in
this country.

Barnas Sears, 1880

Introduction. Educational Reform: The Cloud of Sentiment and Historiography

Americans share a warm and comforting myth about the origins of popular education. For the most part historians have helped to perpetuate this essentially noble story, which portrays a rational, enlightened working class, led by idealistic and humanitarian intellectuals, triumphantly wresting free public education from a selfish, wealthy elite and from the bigoted proponents of orthodox religion.[1] Much current historical writing disputes this interpretation. More and more in recent years historians have attacked the notion that fundamental social controversy provided the dynamic of national development. Instead, they argue, the apparently opposing sides in past controversies represent but variations of a consensus on fundamental principles.

But a consensus viewpoint applied to education is no more satisfactory than the older conflict version.[2] A hard look at the myth of popular education and at realities that are common knowledge produces some glaring discrepancies and paradoxes. Everyone knows that for many years only a tiny proportion of eligible children went to high school. Yet the founding of the high school, in the conventional version, was a great achievement of popular democracy. Could there have been a ready consensus to establish expensive, minority institutions? Popular education, so the story goes, was an outgrowth of working-class aspiration, but the estrangement between the culture of the school and the working-class community has been lamented at least since the time of Dewey. Such an estrangement implies the existence of a deep cultural division throughout society. It seems to provide evidence to support the theories that stress social controversy, but it also runs counter to the idea of an education-hungry working class.

Popular education, according to the myth, started in a passionate blaze of humanitarian zeal; but most large urban school systems since the later nineteenth century have been cold, rigid, and somewhat sterile bureaucracies. Could a truly humanitarian urge to help realize widely diffused aspirations have turned so quickly into the dispassionate ethos of red tape and drill? How are we to account for the discrepancies between myth and actuality? Are parts of the myth valid, parts untrue? To answer these questions and brush aside the cloud of sentiment and historiography that covers the origins of mass popular education we can start by asking a few direct and important questions: Were educational reform and innovation the product of working-class demands? Were the more prominent supporters of popular education motivated by humanitarian and democratic concerns? Did educational reform entail fundamental social controversy?

I have asked these questions, which test the myths surrounding the origins of popular education, because I hope to suggest answers to larger questions that have relevance for educational reformers of our own time. Did the nature of the origins of popular education have lasting consequences for American society? Were these consequences, if any exist, beneficial or harmful? By coldly evaluating the reform movement of the mid-nineteenth century, can we learn anything of use to that of the mid-twentieth? Questions of influence and significance are the most dangerous for the historian; they are also the most fascinating and important. Certainly this study cannot hope to prove, in a hard and empirical sense, its conclusions regarding the impact of educational reform. Yet the results of a study of the mid-nineteenth century strongly suggest that the way in which popular education started — its social base, its ideology, its pace — had permanent consequences.

My interpretation and conclusions generally differ sharply from those of the mid-nineteenth century commentators, who first propagated that popular version of educational reform that rests uneasily in the borderland between history and myth. "It is a double decade more distinguished than any since the revival of letters for the diffusion of knowledge generally among the masses of men," George Boutwell wrote of the twenty years since the 1837 founding of the Massachusetts Board of Education.[3] In the last twenty-five years, asserted Judge Emory Washburn in 1864, "A new life . . . has been infused into the whole system of popular education here."[4]

As told by these commentators the story was straightforward. "For nearly two hundred years our system of free schools was sustained directly by the people, without special care or direct aid from the government," the Board of Education reminded readers of their twentieth report in 1858. The enlightened consensus of pre-industrial society sustained popular education. "The people were then homogeneous; the sentiment in favor of education was universal; deficiencies in the schools, when they existed, were often supplied by instruction in the family." The schools were not without faults; "there was little completeness of system or perfection of detail, yet the results were worthy of all praise."[5]

But the onset of urban industrial growth destroyed the social basis of popular education; "a foreign and a manufacturing population came in; the labor of children became more valuable; in connection with the increase of population, the concentration·of wealth, and the division of sects and of classes, numerous private schools sprang up, and it was found that the public schools were losing their efficiency, and the system itself its vitality." The decline of public education "alarmed patriotic and good men, and gave rise . . . in 1837, to the Board of Education." With zeal the Board and its secretaries, assisted by the legislature, "labored to break up the former torpor, to introduce arrangement and system, and to secure for the subject of education that place and interest which it must have among a free people, if their institutions are to be either enjoyed or perpetuated." [6]

Most contemporary chroniclers and later historians generally have agreed that the "revival" of education was a great success, that the fourth, fifth, and sixth decades of the nineteenth century in Massachusetts witnessed the true beginning of the remarkable and continuous growth of mass popular education in America. But the interpretation of the cultural context of this reform is still a matter of historical controversy. As recent historical studies have revealed, this movement is by no means as unambiguous as it first seems. Underlying the extension of democracy symbolized by the election of Andrew Jackson, the nobility of the anti-slavery crusade, the remarkable transformation of an agrarian economy, the belief in the goodness of man and the reality of progress allegedly symbolized by Emerson: underlying these phenomena were haunting doubts, pervasive value conflicts, and severe social tensions. [7] The movement for educational reform reflected the complexity of social development; for, as the Board of Education itself observed, education was deeply intertwined with the rest of society. To unravel the most important threads, to explicate the relationship between education and society, is one goal of this study.

The Board of Education connected educational change with the building of factories, the growth of cities, and the waves of immigration; but they left the nature of the connection vague. Was it that industrialism had destroyed public education by dissolving its social basis? If so, what did educational leaders substitute for an enlightened, homogeneous, agrarian population? Did education itself play no part in the economic transformation of the commonwealth? Were schoolmen only "patriotic and good," purely altruistic? Were the ends of education solely the enjoyment and perpetuation of democracy? Did the creation of new institutions and the rekindling of interest mean that the educational reform movement was a success? What was the relationship of goals to results? To begin to answer these questions, we must look more closely at the context in which reform flourished; for the goals of educational reform were declared amidst a profound change in the conditions of human experience within Massachusetts, and it is against the backdrop of this change that all questions concerning the relation of education and society must be formulated.

I. THE NEW SOCIETY

"Industrialization" and "urbanization" are such common terms, they have so permeated discourse, that they have become concepts, abstractions almost devoid of power, more often conjuring images of dull textbooks rather than the pains and tensions of human beings caught up in the creation of a new world. But to assess the significance of events in mid-nineteenth century Massachusetts, we must consider quantitative measures of economic and social change not as abstractions, but as expressions of a profound alteration in human experience. Statistics should serve as reminders that a generation, the very generation of educational reformers, watched the contours of society propelled, twisted, and bent into radically new shapes, shapes that brought new forms to all aspects of the life of men, to their every relation.

Consider what happened during the life of Horace Mann, the most famous educational reformer of the time.[8] He was born in 1796, in the year John Adams was elected president; throughout his youth and young manhood about two-thirds of the population of Massachusetts lived in rural communities of less than three thousand people scattered throughout the state. When he was fourteen years old, Massachusetts contained less than half a million people; between his fourteenth and thirty-fourth birthdays population increased slowly, by little more than a quarter.[9] Immigration was slow, the population ethnically homogeneous. Urban merchants financed trading operations covering much of the world.

Farming was carried on as it had been for decades, clothes were made in the home, and the products of independent craftsmen supplemented the work of farming families. Throughout the state and nation most people assumed that the Massachusetts economy would continue to rest on commerce and agriculture.[10]

But Mann saw all this change. During the 1840's, throughout most of which he was secretary of the Board of Education, the population leaped by more than 30 percent; by the year following his death, 1860, Massachusetts had nearly a million and a quarter inhabitants. Mann watched the hordes of immigrants pouring into the commonwealth. In the year that he was thirty-five slightly less than fifteen hundred aliens landed at Charlestown; nine years later the number had multiplied almost four times, fourteen years later almost eight times, eighteen years later almost nineteen times. Most of the newcomers, over seven out of ten in fact, were from Ireland; they brought new, strange, and disturbing ways to the commonwealth.[11] Under a swelling Celtic wave the homogeneous land of Yankees disappeared forever. Mann himself had moved from a small town to the city, and many of his contemporaries did likewise. In southern New England the proportion of the population living in towns with fewer than three thousand residents declined from 67.1 percent in 1810 to 52.1 in 1840 to 30.1 in 1860. Throughout the same period the proportion of the population living in towns and cities with more than 10,000 inhabitants grew from 6.9 to 18.5 to 36.5 percent.[12]

In Mann's youth merchants used the profits from their ventures to buy more ships, to invest in new trading enterprises. But the embargo imposed on foreign goods prior to the War of 1812 both fostered a shortage of manufactured goods, which had previously been imported, and reduced drastically the opportunity for investment in foreign trade. The combination of demand and the availability of capital stimulated the growth of native industry, particularly the manufacture of cotton cloth.[13] Throughout a large part of Mann's life, then, manufacturing grew in Massachusetts; but many of the early ventures, generally small and started without sufficient capital, failed by 1820. The years of most marked progress, the real onset of industrial growth, began around 1830, and the three decades from 1830 to 1860 saw the transformation of the economy of the state.[14] By the time Mann had been secretary of the Board of Education for eight years, in 1845, the value of the agricultural produce of the state was only 34 percent of the value of manufactured goods. Ten years later that figure had been halved. The early forties to the mid-fifties was, indeed, a period of remarkable growth in manufacturing as well as in population and immigration. From 1845 to 1855 the yards of cotton cloth manufactured rose from 175,862,919 to 314,996,567; and their value, corrected for changes in price, rose likewise from nearly ten to nearly twenty-one million dollars.[15]

Manufacturing had its first great impact on the family. For generations New England girls had remained with their families until marriage. Now large numbers of farm girls left home to work in the mills of Lawrence, Lowell, and other places. Whole families moved to manufacturing areas and worked in the mills in the southern part of the state. Immigration changed this pattern. The immigrants swelled the labor force and fostered competition for jobs, and the consequent lowering of wages tended to discourage native girls from working in the factories. The supply of native girls was diminished further by the westward migration of entire farm families. Moreover, as large numbers of Irish entered the mills and factories, natives, who found the Irish repugnant, often left.[16] By the 1860's the unskilled work in the new large industries was mainly the province of immigrants. In Horace Mann's lifetime Massachusetts had acquired a proletariat.

The development of industry was fostered by technological innovation as well as by the increasing supply of labor; with this technology came a new conception of work and a heightened sense of man's power to transform his environment. In the cotton industry the introduction of the power loom in 1824 initiated a shift from the small yarn mill to the large factory in which all the stages of the manufacturing process were gathered under one roof;[17] and after 1840 the introduction of the turbine provided the first big innovation in the source of power for the mills. In 1826 the production of wool was stimulated by the invention of the Goulding condenser, a device for transferring the filaments of wool to the different machines in the manufacturing process; and the introduction of "self-acting mules" after 1840 increased the productivity of wool manufacture still further. Similarly, the shoe industry was revolutionized: "first came mechanical devices for cutting and rolling leather, then pegging machines, and finally sewing machines — all introduced between 1840 and 1860." [18] With the new machines one man could do the work of scores using the old methods of production; "Indeed it would almost seem as though [man] were now but just entering on that dominion over the earth, which was assigned to him at the beginning." Man "is indeed, 'lord of creation'; and all nature, as though daily more sensible of the conquest, is progressively making less and less resistance to his dominion." [19] Unskilled labor and powerful machines were combined in manufacturing processes based on the division of labor. For many, work no longer remained a craft, an acquired skill, an important part of a man's life; instead men began to be alienated from their work, increasingly re-defined as the repetitive operation of a machine, the making of a motion that was only one small part of the production of a shoe, a piece of cloth, a rifle, or a watch.

Transportation as well as the machine revealed man's new power over nature: "Steam is annihilating space . . . Travelling is changed from an isolated pilgrimmage to a kind of triumphal procession . . . Caravans of voyagers are now winding as it were, on the wings of the wind, round the habitable globe. Here they glide over cultivated acres on rods of iron, and there they rise and fall on the bosom of the deep, leaving behind them a foaming wheel-track like the chariot-path of a sea-god." [20] It was the railroad rather than the steamship that immediately affected the life and economy of Massachusetts. Until Horace Mann was nearly forty years old no railroads existed in Massachusetts. Indeed, his work in the Massachusetts legislature helped to spur their advent. By the time he died, 1,264 miles of tracks crisscrossed the state.[21] Railroads carried raw materials to the new industries and marketed their finished products. They stimulated the development of suburbs, a new residential pattern. Within ten miles of Boston, where the commuting fare was economical, some places like Saugus were virtually created while others, like Lynn, grew phenomenally.[22]

No aspect of life in Massachusetts remained in 1860 as it had been in Horace Mann's youth. The growth of cities stimulated a shift from domestic to commercial farming, a trend reinforced by the introduction of canals and railroads. Innovation marked agriculture as well as industry; farmers adopted new tools, like the iron plough, and substituted horses for oxen as draft animals. However, the Erie Canal and, after 1840, the introduction of the railroad ruined some of the developing commercial specialties, like wool-growing and beef-fattening, because wool and cattle could be obtained more inexpensively from the West. Yet some produce remained very profitable, especially vegetables, fruit, and milk, which could not be transported long distances without refrigeration, and farmers utilized the growing number of branch railroad lines to market their goods.[23]

Their domestic manufactures supplanted by the products of machines, farm women cast about for a new means of supplementing their incomes. Some left home to work in the new factories and mills or to teach, others turned to new domestic occupations, such as raising silk worms, a brief and abortive fad.[24] Still, labor for carrying on the work of farming itself was not always easy to find, for the lure of the city penetrated to rural Massachusetts. As a writer in the *New England Farmer* complained: "Every farmer's son and daughter are in pursuit of some geneteel mode of living. After consuming the farm in the expenses of a fashionable, flashy, fanciful education, they leave the honorable profession of their fathers to become doctors, lawyers, merchants, or ministers or something of the kind." [25]

The conduct of business altered with the changes in manufacturing and agriculture. "By 1860," writes Thomas Cochran, "business had assumed almost all the varied forms and functions with which we are familiar in the twentieth century." Managers had learned how to coordinate "big office staffs, particularly in finance and transportation," and a class of business executives had been created. No important monopolies had been formed, but "managers had experimented with almost all the modern techniques of limited competition." [26] Horace Mann and his contemporaries in the state legislature had helped to accelerate the emergence of the new economy within their own lifetime. Between the late eighteenth and mid-nineteenth centuries the Massachusetts state government discarded an almost mercantilist conception of its function and a suspicion of industrial growth. Their new, more liberal formulation stressed as little governmental interference with the economy as possible and a granting of privileges such as incorporation on a general rather than a selective basis. Moreover, direct assistance through innovations like limited liability and the guaranteeing of the security of loans for railroad construction helped to make possible the economic transformation of the state. [27]

Horace Mann's adult life encompassed the most remarkable changes in the economy of the state in the years before the end of the Civil War. In the half decade after his death in 1859 the growth of the Massachusetts economy slackened considerably. For instance, between 1850 and 1855 the population increased 15 percent, between 1855 and 1860 it grew 8 percent, and between 1860 and 1865 only 3 percent. [28] The difficulty of obtaining raw material during the Civil War fostered a marked decline in the number of hands employed in the cotton industry and in the amount of goods produced. Likewise, the pace of industrialization slackened; between 1845 and 1855, as noted earlier, the value of agricultural products dropped from 34 to 17 percent; from 1855 to 1865 it declined only from 17 to 14 percent. Between 1845 and 1855 the number of hands employed in manufacturing rose 69 percent; in the next ten years it increased but 10 percent. Business, however, was apparently more profitable than ever. In 1845, $.65 worth of cotton goods were produced for every dollar of investment in the cotton industry; by 1855 the figure had increased to $.81; by 1865 it had skyrocketed to $1.63.[29] Probably the decline in output during the Civil War caused a shortage, rising prices, and increased profit. The rise in prices and the inflation during the Civil War were phenomenal. If 1913 is taken as a standard, representing 100, then the cost of living in 1840 was 60, in 1861 it was 61, in 1865 it was 102.[30]

When Horace Mann was born in 1796, almost no one would have predicted that within one lifetime the landscape of the commercial and agrarian yankee commonwealth would be spotted by foul Irish slums, scarred by iron tracks, disfigured by mills and factories. Even the most farsighted did not expect that more children would be growing up in cities and urban areas than on farms or that women and children would be working in factories, operating machines that replaced the labor of scores of men and destroyed the traditional crafts of the home. Within the lifetime of one man a new society was born, a society that smashed old expectations with the force of steam, that ripped apart and restitched the web of relationships composing the experience of men.

2. THE NEW EDUCATION

As a new society emerged within Massachusetts, the shape of public education expanded into new forms. The educational reform movement that arose examined and transformed every aspect of schooling, from administration to pedagogy, from finance to the sex of teachers.[31] An expansion of public schooling accompanied the leap in population. Between 1840 and 1865 the number of pupils enrolled in winter schools increased 53.8 percent, and the number of schools 54.5 percent. Yet the number of teachers increased 74.4 percent, 20 percent more than the number of pupils; the number of pupils assigned to each teacher was decreasing. Augmented teacher salaries accompanied the expansion of educational facilities. From 1840 to 1865 the average salary of male teachers increased 65.5 percent, that of female teachers 71.1 percent. Until the inflation of the 1860's these increases represented real gains because the cost of living remained relatively stable. A decreasing pupil-teacher ratio and rising teacher salaries helped increase per-pupil expenditure more than two and one-half times during this period. The school tax rate, however, changed but little, and the state multiplied its total and per-pupil expenditure without allocating proportionally more of its resources to schools. A rise in property values, the basis for school taxes, made possible this fortunate situation. Indeed, between 1840 and 1865 the value of the commonwealth's real estate more than tripled.

The face of public education altered in other ways, too. Teaching became a predominantly female occupation; in 1840, 61 percent of Massachusetts teachers were men; by 1865 the proportion had dropped more than three and one-third times to 14 percent. Public schools, moreover, were educating proportionally more of the state's children. The number of children attending incorporated academies remained relatively stable, but the number attending the more numerous, less prestigious, and often ephemeral unincorporated academies and other private schools dropped markedly. In 1840, 22 percent of Massachusetts school children attended private schools; by 1865 the proportion was halved. The creation and spread of a new type of school, the public high school (defined in detail in Appendix B) accompanied the decline in academy attendance. The first, the Boston English High School, was founded in 1821. In 1840 there were but 18 high schools in the state; in 1865 there were 108.[32]

Presiding over the transformation of public education was the state government. As it abandoned mercantilist tendencies for a more liberal, non-interventionist approach to economic life, its attitude toward education changed in the opposite direction. The state took a far more active and positive role than before in the promotion of public education. In 1837 the legislature created the Board of Education. Although the Board lacked coercive power, its secretaries used their annual reports to disseminate comparative educational statistics and educational theory as well as to advocate reform. During this period the legislature also voted to establish the first state normal schools in the United States[33] and, in 1852, passed the first compulsory school law.[34] The most effective sanction the state could use against a town was to withhold its portion of the state school fund, first distributed in 1834. In 1865 it used this weapon to coerce recalcitrant towns to meet their legal obligations to establish high schools.[35] The state sponsored and encouraged other innovations. It disbursed money for school libraries to districts and even commissioned a controversial set of books. The legislature permitted the towns to abolish the district system (defined and discussed in Part I), and the secretaries of the Board of Education encouraged them to do so. The state permitted the appointment of paid local superintendents. Secretaries encouraged the use of better styles of school architecture, new pedagogical techniques, and different methods of school management and discipline.[36] Local school reports reveal that many of these innovations were adopted; the process of education itself was changed.

Within Massachusetts the most remarkable period of economic expansion had ended by 1860; during the half decade from 1860 to 1865 there was little change; the same is true of educational expansion. Some measures of education were even marked by retrogression. The increase in enrollment, the number of schools, and the number of teachers slowed considerably. Salary increases were slight; indeed, the rise in prices far outstripped the gains in the salaries of teachers, whose financial condition deteriorated badly during the Civil War. Likewise, the rise in property valuation slowed, and the 12 percent rise in per-pupil expenditure could hardly keep pace with inflation. Public schools even lost some of the inroads they had made on private education. The proportion of students attending academies rose slightly, and the number at unincorporated academies grew markedly. In the mid-nineteenth century a new society and a new education emerged within Massachusetts, and their growth patterns were remarkably similar.

Thus, to explore the origins of mass popular education is, to a large extent, to try to relate the new society and the new education. The attempt here is to establish, on the one hand, the relation between reformers' ideology and their style of reform and, on the other hand, to see both in the context of fundamental alteration in the conditions of life in Massachusetts. By ideology, I mean substantially the same thing as Merrill D. Peterson, who writes, "the term ideology is given to that synthesis of ideas and representations designed to state an ideal and to motivate action. It may be true in some of its parts; but it is a gross oversimplification both of history and of the existing situation, the true recognition of which would not be an accord with the feelings and interests of the men who advance the ideology." [37] My frame of reference, it should be evident, differs from the prevailing trend in the study of the relationship between education and economic development. This trend rests, for the most part, on overly simplistic and mechanistic assumptions about human behavior.[38] I am concerned not with the contribution of education to ante-bellum economic growth and gross generalizations about "human resource development," or relations between "levels" of education and "levels" of industrialization, but with the often subtle interplay of factors in a complex situation, with the pattern of interaction formed when major alterations in the conditions of life, mediated by the tensions and values of men, provoke innovations in social policy. The concern here, as well, is with the irony and problems that arise when ideologically treasured innovations confront social reality. What, in short, were the results, the consequences of reform?

At the outset the reader should realize that this exploration of relationships is neither narrative nor descriptive history. Instead this study focuses on small, concrete situations, which it tries to examine thoroughly. The intent is not to be narrow; rather it is to start with the concrete and through careful analysis to work outward to conclusions of broad cultural significance. This approach requires the use of some techniques more often found in disciplines other than history. Interpretation of specific, complex, and frequently puzzling phenomena requires the use of ideas developed by social psychologists. I have tried not to encumber the text with social scientific theory, but my conclusions about motivation have been pondered and revised in the light of current theories, particularly those concerned with the role of ambivalence in motivation. Similarly, certain very empirical questions, such as ones about the social composition of high schools, and the kinds of areas in which innovation occurred, are crucial to the analysis. To answer these I have had to use some fairly elaborate statistical techniques. In general, I have included the technical information about the handling of the data and most tables in the appendixes and used the conclusions of the statistical analyses in the text as they are relevant.

To approach the issues with which this study is concerned I have focused on three important events or situations that seemed significant and somewhat surprising. The first is the abolition of Beverly High School in 1860; the second is the attack of the American Institute of Instruction on a respected colleague, Cyrus Peirce; the third is the criticism of the state reform school offered by some of the state's leading reformers, who should, by all expectations, have been its champions. From each situation I have tried to build outward, seeing it in the context of state-wide reform and assessing its general significance for the time and its implications for the future.

However, I should make clear again that in no sense is this study intended as a complete history of the educational reform movement. It makes no effort to provide a thorough or even balanced description of the remarkable development of public education within Massachusetts. Little attention is paid to political parties, to religious controversies, or to foreign influences. This is not to say that politics, religion, and foreign influences are not important; they certainly are, but other scholars have investigated these topics, which are the traditional emphases of the historians of education concerned with this period.[39] This study hopes to provide a different and a new perspective. Indeed, it is my feeling that the attention paid to the more traditional categories has helped obscure the underlying dynamics of the reform movement, and it is precisely these dynamics that this study hopes to illuminate.

Readers may feel that throughout this study I disparage older interpretations but do not treat them in specific enough detail to support my points. I have not done so quite purposely. For one thing, the weaknesses of the older studies are widely recognized and have been ably discussed elsewhere. Professor Lawrence Cremin, for one, himself the author of an earlier account, has criticized his own as well as other interpretations of the educational reform movement of the mid-nineteenth century. Professor Cremin has also offered a persuasive version of the circumstances surrounding the origin and perpetuation of the standard account of this period.[40] In general, the older versions suffer from the same weaknesses as the books on the Jacksonian period written about the same time. Through an equation of the term working man with working class, in our modern sense, they have overstressed the role of labor in political and social reform. The works of Lee Benson, Marvin Meyers, and Walter Hugins, to name but a few, have yet to make much impact on educational historiography. The earlier interpretations also reflected the then current historiographical emphasis on the impact of suffrage extension, but we now can be pretty well certain this took place before the "Age of Jackson," the actual passing of suffrage legislation and the educational revival.[41] Thus, educational historians have been slower than their colleagues in other fields in offering more modern and sophisticated versions of this crucial period. Yet, these older works should not be simply dismissed; to the discerning and judicious reader, reasonably well-versed in present historiography, they offer much of value: Frank Tracy Carlton rightly saw and stressed the importance of industrialization; Sidney Jackson offered excellent insights into the role of the wealthy who sometimes used education as a counterforce to social trends that distressed them and whose style of reform was pure imposition; Lawrence Cremin has provided an exceptionally lucid delineation of the conception of the common school.[42] Because the weaknesses of these older books are, significantly, those of a generation of historical writing and because the general weaknesses of this interpretation of the period and of these books in particular have been recognized, it seemed ungenerous and unnecessary to offer detailed criticisms of older works. It seemed, rather, more to the point to concentrate on presenting a new version.

The very success of the public school tended to remove it further from the very class of children for whose benefit it was originally established. Theoretically, the public school is for all; practically, it is conducted with less regard to the very lowest stratum of society than is desirable. Our public schools are now the best schools to be found, but they are surrounded by a set of rigid rules, customs, and traditions which have a tendency to keep out the very children that these schools were established to educate.

M. A. Newell, 1883

The system [of public education], to be beneficial, must enlist the sympathies of the middle class, which it will accomplish only when it becomes identified with their hopes and ambition.

B. G. Lovejoy, 1881

Part I.   Reform by Imposition: Social Origins of Educational Controversy

I. THE ABOLITION OF BEVERLY HIGH SCHOOL

At the Beverly town meeting in March 1860, clerk John I. Baker called the roll of the eligible voters on a motion of Joseph Thissell to abolish the two-year-old high school, redistribute the money already appropriated among the school districts, and challenge in the supreme court the state law requiring towns of a certain size to maintain a high school. Numerous citizens, unable to make up their minds, stayed silent when Baker called their names. But 392 did vote, 143 against the motion to abolish, 249 in its favor.[1] Contrary to the myth that views public secondary education as the fulfillment of working-class aspirations, the Beverly vote revealed the social and financial leaders of the town, not the least affluent citizens, as the firmest supporters of the high school.

Beverly was not an important town, and the abolition of its high school was not, in itself, of significance for the development of American education. However, the vote is of first-rate importance because it suggests answers to critical and largely unanswered questions concerning mid-nineteenth century educational reform. Heretofore assertions about the supporters and opponents of educational innovation and generalizations about the conflict involved in the reform process have been based on strikingly little empirical evidence. The Beverly incident provides concrete data about the dynamics of the reform process.

Analysis of these data suggests specific answers to the basic questions of who supported and who opposed reform and what sorts of conflicts arose. Although Beverly was in some ways unique, developments in the town, as we shall see, represented a particularly explicit manifestation of the problems inherent in the impact of technological progress upon ante-bellum communities; and consequently the abolition of the high school poses questions of relevance to an understanding of the relationship between educational innovation and social progress throughout the state.

Because the high school issue was so important within Beverly, clerk Baker, most unusually, recorded the name of each individual who voted and the nature of his vote. Tax books and the manuscript census of 1860 furnish information about the residence, occupation, wealth, age, and number of dependents of 343 of the 392 voters.[2] (This information is presented in tabular form in Appendix D.) First of all, consider the people who opposed abolition of the high school. Most of them lived in the two most populous, dense, and centrally located districts, the Grammar and the South.[3] Supporters included those in the most prestigious occupations: 17 of the 19 professionals and public employees, 8 of the 9 sea captains and master mariners, and all 4 "gentlemen." The vote of the businessmen was less decisive, but a significant majority of this heterogeneous category, including everything from wealthy merchant to shopkeeper, were among the supporters of the high school. Moreover, most of the businessmen who lived in the Grammar and South districts supported the high school as did most of the wealthiest ones. Throughout the town the vote of the artisans was split, but those who lived in the Grammar and South districts and those with children generally favored the high school. The wealth of the town was clearly on the side of the high school. Those who opposed abolition had an average personal estate, real estate, and total estate much higher than those who favored it. Of those in the top category for each kind of valuation, over $5,000, high school supporters predominated. Sixteen of 26 with real estate in this category, 18 of 24 with personal estate, and 33 of 49 with total estate were among those who stood out against the abolition of the high school.

Most of the men who favored abolition lived in the outlying districts, which were sparsely populated. The Cove district, where only 5 out of 57 voters supported the high school, was the only district untouched by the railroad. Moreover, those in the least prestigious occupational categories were as solidly opposed to the high school as the prominent were in favor. Voting to abolish were 37 of the 44 farmers, 80 of the 109 shoemakers, 21 of the 24 mariners and fishermen, and all 10 laborers. The businessmen who opposed the high school generally had less wealth than the ones who supported it, and more lived in the outlying districts. As for the artisans, fewer of the ones who voted for abolition had children of school age than did those who supported the high school. Indeed, dependency was an important characteristic. Of 171 voters with no children of school age, 120 voted to abolish the high school. However, no significant differences existed between groups of voters in number of children of high school age or in number of teenage children attending school. Finally, the people who voted to abolish the high school were the least wealthy on every measure. Not only that, but the distribution of the wealth they did have was different. Whereas those who supported the high school generally had an estate balanced fairly evenly between real and personal property, those who voted for abolition had more valuable real than personal holdings. That is, opposition to the high school came not only from the least wealthy but also from those whose holdings in land and buildings exceeded their personal property.

None of these characteristics, of course, is truly independent of the others. Yet there were two sorts of dominant groupings in the vote on the high school issue. First of all, people with no school-age children were protesting the continuation of an institution that increased their tax bill. Beyond this was a clear social division that encompassed many, though not all, the voters. Those in prestigious occupations and those most wealthy were supporting an innovating addition to the educational system, even though they were the ones who would pay the highest taxes. Opposition came from the working class:* fishermen, farmers, shoemakers, and laborers. These groups were almost as unanimously opposed to the high school as the former were in favor. A third important element was the business and artisan groups among which few differences in wealth could be discerned. In fact, it was again the wealthier businessmen, who would be more highly taxed, who voted more often for the high school. For the business and artisan groups, concerns other than taxation probably were important. The association between vote and residence provides a clue here since these people were engaged in retail work; they were dependent upon their neighbors for a livelihood, and it is reasonable to infer that both the prejudices of their neighborhood and the desire to avoid offending customers were relevant factors in their vote.

Still, we must ask, were there other reasons for these more middle-class townsmen to support the high school? Indeed, the explanation of the vote to abolish Beverly High School is far from clear. Opposition did not come from vested interests, and it came only partly from the traditional bane of educational innovators, parsimonious people with no children of school age. Why did the wealthy and prestigious favor a high school? Why did the working class oppose? To answer these questions concerning the motivation of the vote on Beverly High School the rest of Part I considers in more depth a number of factors: the ideology of reform, the interests and situation of education promoters and their antagonists, the nature of local controversy, and the key features of educational

---

* I use the term working class throughout this study to mean people in the lowest socio-economic categories. Thus, I am using the term in its current sense. I do not mean "workingman" in the sense the term was employed in the mid-nineteenth century, since this covered a much broader range of social groups, including people we would today term middle and upper middle class. On the term workingman see Walter Hugins, *Jacksonian Democracy and the Working Class* (Stanford, 1960), p. 52.

innovation. To begin the inquiry, a closer look at an individual supporter of Beverly High School helps refine our questions.

One of the most prominent high school promoters in Beverly was Robert Rantoul, Sr. His son, Robert Rantoul, was the famous Democratic senator who helped found the Free Soil Party and whose early, tragic death evoked an ode from Whittier. Rantoul, Sr., was one of the first citizens of both Beverly and Massachusetts.[4] Born in 1778 in Salem, Rantoul was the son of a Scottish immigrant drowned at sea when his son was still quite young. In spite of severe financial difficulties Rantoul attended, successively, a dame school, a private writing school, the town grammar school, and, occasionally, a Latin school. At the age of fourteen he left school and was apprenticed to a doctor-apothecary. Rantoul, a quick learner, was soon managing the shop; and his successful experience enabled him to raise the money to buy a vacant apothecary shop in Beverly when he was but seventeen and a half years old. Rantoul continued his success as an apothecary and began his rise to eminence as a local merchant. Most likely with an eye toward his political future, Rantoul by himself studied law and learned enough to practice and to become a local judge. He signified his arrival at the top of Beverly society by providing his son with one of the most prestigious educations Massachusetts could offer. Robert Rantoul, Jr., attended Phillips Andover Academy and upon graduation in 1820 entered Harvard College. Another sign of Rantoul's social arrival was his prominent position in important town financial ventures. He was founder of the Marine Insurance Company in Beverly and an active director of the local bank. These activities, as well as a legacy including a complete set of *Hunt's Merchants Magazine,* indicate that Rantoul was a promoter. The extent of Rantoul's holdings and his involvement with commercial life and industrial development are revealed by his estate. Rantoul left $16,350 in real estate and $28,326.45 in personal estate. His stock holdings were distributed among railroads, steam cotton mills, turnpikes, banks, and insurance companies. The uncollected debts he left indicate that he was also a moneylender, and the bequeathed rents on a number of properties show that he was likewise a realtor.[5]

Rantoul's public speeches and private writings offer no clue that he was a promoter; rather they are designed, it would seem deliberately, to present a rather different impression. To Rantoul no value deserved more attention than social unity; nothing was more repugnant than communal conflict. Throughout his speeches and his autobiography runs a real longing for a truly unified society, which he locates somewhere in the past. When Rantoul lectured on "economy" at the Lyceum in 1835, he stressed that he would say "nothing to encourage that miserable spirit of envy and jealousy, which finds its highest gratification in planting and fostering the most bitter feelings of opposition and hatred between those in the different classes into which society is divided." Instead, he stressed "mutual dependence." [6] Elsewhere he commented with nostalgic regret on the demise of voluntary fire fighting, which had provided a "favorable influence upon the mass of the community, provoking a generous desire to aid one another by personal efforts and sacrifices." Unfortunately, the termination of voluntary fire fighting represented one phase of a misguided "lessening of sympathy for our fellow beings." Similarly, the high point in the history of Beverly, according to Rantoul, was the united community action in response to an 1832 cholera threat, united action that would not have been possible, he lamented, a few years later.[7]

Other observers noted the earlier social unity in Beverly. Historian Joseph Ober saw harmony as a product of kinship and portrayed Beverly as a large family, almost a clan. Throughout generations the people of Beverly "had contentedly tilled the soil and ploughed the sea, leaving their ancestral homes only to participate in the business affairs of the town or when summoned by the imperative calls of war." Intermarriage had united the people in the different sections of the town, and they "were individually members of one and the same great family; their interests and their traditions were identical." [8] Edwin Stone, another historian, noted in 1842 that lawyers in Beverly found it impossible to make a living by fees alone. A "distinguished member of the Essex bar," he wrote, had remarked "as a singular fact in his experience, that during a practice of nearly forty years, he had never known a native of Beverly convicted of any heinous crime." [9]

To Ober, the destroyer of the happy family was the summer boarder, whose arrival with the railroad around 1840 introduced a "new element" into the town.[10] As for Stone's comments on the law-abiding nature of Beverly citizens: among the seventy-nine arrests in the town during 1864, one was for murder, seventeen were for assault, eighteen for larceny, one for keeping a "disorderly house," and two for "night walking." Two, likewise, were of "stubborn children"; four were for adultery. In 1863 the newspaper reported with horror that one Stackpole, an example of the "fast young men" who infested the town, had killed his sister and attempted to murder his parents. Nor were the recent immigrants always placid, as indicated by the town paper's disgusted account of the stabbing of one Irishman by another on Water Street.[11]

Rantoul perceptively connected the demise of social unity with the changes that were overtaking the commonwealth and the town of Beverly. "The introduction of shoemaking as a general employment" had "gradually changed the habits, manners and morals of the mass — from a fishing, sea-faring and farming population" into "a manufacturing population in the main." [12] Farming, Rantoul told a local audience, was better than trade as an occupation. In itself mercantile life, the distribution of products and luxuries over a wider area, was a fine activity; but, unfortunately, trade had some unlovely aspects: "too many mean artifices and tricks, too much overreaching and even gross atrocious frauds, and a reckless sacrifice of health, morals, comfort and of the vast number of lives . . ." On the whole then, agriculture provided a better life than trading. Massachusetts soil was not the most fertile, but "labor, intelligently and skillfully applied in the cultivation of the ground," offered an "ample reward." No farmer could grow as rich as a merchant or a manufacturer; there was no hope of sudden or spectacular accumulation; but an "active and industrious" man would obtain a "comfortable subsistence" and have a bit left over. And how much superior was the idyllic life on the farm to the uncertainties and questionable morality of trade. It was unfortunate that the country had suffered already from the "large and disproportionate number . . . withdrawn from the laborious and productive classes in rural life, to engage in the unproductive pursuits of trade . . ." [13] Thus spoke Robert Rantoul, merchant, lawyer, promoter: a man who never was a farmer, who grew up in a city, who directed a bank, who sent neither son nor grandson to a farm, who subscribed faithfully to that agent of the mercantile spirit, *Hunt's Merchants Magazine*.

In 1854 Robert Rantoul formally retired from town affairs. But three years later he returned to the annual spring town meeting. One purpose, claimed the aging patriarch, was to bid farewell and thanks to the townspeople; the other was to speak in favor of the proposed town high school. In his nearly completed autobiography Rantoul commented, "This subject I deem to be very important and have come to speak and vote in favor of such a school. I spoke at some length but by the result of the vote with very little effect as there was a large majority against the measure." Yet, some citizens drew up an indictment against the town for not complying with the state law requiring towns of its size to have a high school. This action precipitated another town meeting. Again Rantoul attended; this, however, was the last time. [14] By his side were his grandsons, who also argued for the high school. One grandson was Robert S. Rantoul, a lawyer, later president of the Essex Institute. In his papers exist the fragments of a speech listing citations of court cases, which were apparently chosen to show the town that the law was clearly on the side of the state. Surely, he must have told the townspeople, they would lose the ensuing legal battle if they persisted in their defiance. [15] The high school, started in 1858, was abolished in 1860; by then Rantoul was dead, but one of those who stood out against its destruction was the wealthy druggist, William Endicott, one of the grandsons who had been at Rantoul's side in 1857.

Why did Rantoul support a high school? Is there a relation between his activities as a promoter, his longing for social harmony, his disingenuous or incongruous remarks on the virtues of farm life and his activity on behalf of education, especially a high school?[16] Rantoul left no direct answers to these questions, but his perception of his society and the values he extolled were representative of leading schoolmen and high school promoters throughout the state. If we look at the attitudes and arguments of these men, we can better understand both Robert Rantoul and the abolition of Beverly High School.

2. EDUCATIONAL PROMOTERS AND THE HIGH SCHOOL

Massachusetts educational promoters proudly argued that education had fostered the impressive economic progress of the commonwealth. The relation between education and the creation of wealth was, in fact, the thesis of Horace Mann's fifth report, in which he elaborated at length his contention that the progress and prosperity of a manufacturing economy were dependent upon the education of the entire population. Elsewhere, he claimed that "education is not only a moral renovator, and a multiplier of intellectual power, but . . . also the most prolific parent of material riches." Education, therefore, should "not only be included in the grand inventory of a nation's resources," but should "be placed at the very head of that inventory." [17] The connection between education and industrial prosperity and the enthusiasm with which schoolmen welcomed economic transformation were well illustrated in the first report of George Boutwell, third secretary of the Massachusetts Board of Education.[18]

Boutwell stressed that education had been of the utmost importance in the development of Massachusetts into an industrial state. The role of the schools was increasingly potent since "labor," in its "leading characteristics," had been previously a "manual process," but now had become, "in its force and value, essentially intellectual." The fruits of intelligence were harvested in improved agricultural production and especially in industry. "The prosperity of the mills and shops is based quite as much upon the intellectual vigor as upon the physical power of the laborers." In his rapturous description of the qualities of intellectualized industry Boutwell demonstrated one side of the ambivalence of Massachusetts educators to industrial society:

> Labor is not imitative merely, — it is inventive, creative. The laborer is no longer servile, yielding to laws and necessities that he cannot comprehend, and therefore cannot respect, but he has been elevated to the regions of art and works by laws that he appreciates, and aspires to a perfection as real, at least, as that of the sculptor, painter, or poet . . . The laws of labor are the laws that exist and are recognized in art, eloquence and science. The great law of these latter unquestionably is, that every student shall be at the same time an original thinker, investigator, designer and producer.

The artist-laborer had a central role to play in the state since, claimed Boutwell, "Massachusetts, from its history and position, is necessarily a manufacturing and commercial state." Manufacture and commerce, he continued, require intellectual cultivation and "a high order of learning." Consequently, the industrial and commercial success of Massachusetts depended "for the materials of its growth and prosperity on the intelligence of the laboring classes upon the land and in the shops and mills. Thus we connect the productive power of our state with its institutions of learning." [19]

"Now the increased means for education for the last sixty years," wrote Horace Mann to J. A. Shaw in 1840, "have not kept pace with the increasing obligations, duties, and temptations of the community." [20] Here Mann sounded a widely echoed theme. In the past, educators argued, the common schools had made Massachusetts prosperous, but the educational institutions sufficient for the needs of a simple agrarian commonwealth would not meet the demands of an urban-industrial society. As the Winchendon school committee proclaimed: it was a "fixed point" that all should receive a good education but the term "good" itself was "movable." In educational requirements the "tendency was upwards." The occupations previously open to a boy with only an elementary common school background now required a secondary education.[21] In every variety of work "rapid progress," commented the Brookline school committee in 1855, called for a "corresponding expansion . . . in education." "Modern commerce" required the "young merchant" to have "a more adequate knowledge of the great globe he dwells on than can be acquired from the pages of a Grammar School textbook"; the farmer could not "much longer dispense with some scientific knowledge of the soil he cultivates." Similarly, "the ships, the mills, and warehouses we need can no longer be built by the 'rule of thumb' of an ignorant mechanic." In short, "whole classes in our community who, not a generation ago, would have been content to earn their living by unskilled labor, are now thrust from that lower market, and forced to add knowledge and intelligence to the labor of their hands." The answer, to the committee, was "not to regret this state of things, but . . . to provide for it." [22] And provision to them meant a high school. Similarly, Rantoul may have had a high school in mind when he complained that some parents scoffed at the newer, more advanced subject matter of education with the attitude "that as they did not attend, when young, to those studies, therefore it is not important for their children to attend to them." But this was a fallacy "inasmuch as their children come into life in a community much better taught than was the society in which their parents began life." [23]

Intertwined with the arguments relating the necessity of improved education, especially a high school, to the economic requirements of an industrializing society are contentions stressing the relationship between the high school and social mobility. The Winchendon committee argued that the availability of foreigners to perform the "least desirable" sorts of work enabled "our sons to rise to other employments." To seize the new opportunities for its children a town required an advanced educational system, especially a high school; there was no other alternative if parents desired their children to rise on the economic and social scale. "Shall we," asked the committee, "stand still, and see our children outstripped in the race of life, by the children of those who are willing to pursue a liberal and far-sighted policy?" [24]

The relation between the high school and both communal prosperity and mobility was driven home to the people of Beverly by Rufus Putnam, part-time superintendent and principal of a high school in neighboring Salem. He informed the town that there was a direct correlation between educational facilities and the wealth of a community. He told the citizens of Beverly that to develop their economy they would have to develop their schools, and, he maintained, no improvement was more crucial than a high school. "The best educated community" will "*always* be the most prosperous community . . . nothing so directly tends to promote the increase of *wealth* of a community as the thorough mental training of its youth." [25] When he had taken charge of the Bowditch (English) High School in Salem, Putnam told the people of Beverly in 1853, parents had difficulty finding employment for children who had attended. But technological change had completely altered the situation: "the introduction of Machinery in the arts had increased the demand for education inasmuch as there was more mind required in the use of machinery than without it . . . and an increase in a greater proportion of mental process to produce the increased results called for more education." In fact, "there was such a demand for well educated boys that some were induced to leave school before they had completed their regular course of study." [26]

The argument that a high school would foster mobility probably appealed to parents of limited or moderate means, for they are the ones who would not be able to provide their sons with the capital or influence that might make a good education less necessary. It is likely that these arguments influenced many of the artisans and less wealthy businessmen who voted for the retention of Beverly High School. Similarly, it is likely that the affluent supporters were influenced by the appeal to communal wealth, since as owners of real estate and as investors they stood to gain the most from urban and industrial development. But would the arguments concerning mobility appeal to them? Had they an interest in paying taxes to develop competition for themselves and their children? Another prominent high school promoter from Beverly helps answer these questions.

Dr. Wyatt C. Boyden, next-door neighbor of Robert Rantoul, was the leading town physician. The two promoters did not always agree. Boyden was a Whig, a friend of Rufus Choate, an admirer of Webster. Rantoul was a Democrat. In 1836 Boyden was one of four physicians whose united raising of fees evoked a petition from a town meeting, a petition urged by Rantoul.[27] Both Rantoul and Boyden were charter members of the Beverly Academy, which flourished from the 1830's to the mid-50's, but a fight between the trustees and proprietors led to Rantoul's resignation. The fight had been over the appointment of a teacher, one James Woodbury Boyden, the doctor's eldest son.[28] However, the two men must frequently have submerged their differences. For nearly two decades they served together on the town school committee; and both were among the ten original members of the Republican party in Beverly.[29] The cooperation of Boyden, the Whig, and Rantoul, the Democrat, underlines the fact that on the local level partisan politics was simply irrelevant, in this period, to educational reform.

The son of a financially struggling country doctor, Boyden was born in Tamworth, New Hampshire, in 1794. A combination of common schools, a brief spell at an academy, and private tutoring by a local minister prepared Boyden for Dartmouth, which he entered in 1815. In 1819 he became the first Tamworth resident to receive a Dartmouth A.B. From 1815 to 1826 Boyden alternated going to college with school teaching and, finally, studying medicine at Dartmouth. As was common in that period, he actually started to practice before he had received his degree. During one term Boyden taught school in Beverly Farms, where he met Elizabeth Woodbury. They married in 1821 and settled in New Hampshire until pressure from Elizabeth's parents and the offer of an attractive junior partnership in a flourishing practice attracted them back to Beverly.[30]

Unlike his father, Boyden was a prosperous doctor. "During the healthy and active part of my life," he wrote, "I have had a leading and somewhat lucrative business . . . My yearly income has from the beginning more than supported me." [31] Boyden's financial status was not, however, solely the result of his income from fees. With considerable shrewdness he early perceived the future of the shoe business in Lynn, and his considerable investments there, claimed his grandson, "have proved of substantial benefit to the family." Boyden also provided his sons with capital. "When he found that his son Albert was a shrewd and safe man," wrote Boyden's grandson, "he entrusted money to him for investment in Illinois farm-mortgages at rates of interest which, though normal for their times, seem fancifully high in our days of cheap money." Dr. Boyden died in 1879 and left an estate valued at $75,000, "this sum being almost entirely the result of his own earnings, savings and investments." [32]

This physician-promoter also engaged actively in the affairs of Beverly. Boyden's learning and his love of the classics made him a leader in educational matters; and he served for twenty-four years as a member of the school committee. He was also, as has been noted, a charter member of the Beverly Academy. According to his grandson, he was the town's most active and influential exponent of graded schools. Despite his long interest in education, the decision to vote for the high school was not an easy one for Boyden to make. In a fragment of a letter, perhaps never sent, Boyden admitted his unwillingness to increase "the high rate and pressure of our Town Expenses — for schools, and all other purposes. I confess I have had some reluctance to add to them the expense of a high school." [33] But Boyden's fundamental assumption regarding education was that "the prosperity of the country — and the permanence of our civil, political and religious Institutions . . . depend on the intelligence and virtue of the people." To insure these conditions the founders of New England, Boyden explained, had established free common schools open to all and a college generously aided by public funds. But, he continued, "There was still a course of education wanted, intermediate between the common school and the college." The "academies . . . private schools and private tuition" hardly met this need and, moreover, served the rich rather than the "middling and poorer classes." The lack of higher educational opportunities for the poorer class was a serious situation: "The State had an interest in the education of the best talent of the community. And this talent was as often found among the middling and lower classes as among the rich — perhaps oftener. For the rich are apt to become luxurious, indolent and lazy. They have not the stimulus of necessity — which is not only the mother of invention — but of diligence — of great effort and progress." Because academies and private schools proved "unacceptable to the people at large, by reasons of distance and expense . . . our Legislature established the high school system." The purpose of the high school system, he emphasized, was to make available "preparation for college and the higher branches of learning . . . to distinguished industry and talent, in whatever condition and circumstances it might be found."

Boyden made it clear that his vote for the high school, should he so cast it, would not be on his "own account" because he could afford to educate his own children. Nor would he vote for one "to supply the rich. They can supply themselves with the means of education." His vote, rather, would be, first, for those individuals "who have not the means of a higher education within themselves." His motivation for providing that means was his conception of "the public good"; "for the interest of the State . . . the best talent of the community should be educated, wherever it may be found." Ironically, the very people for whose good Boyden eventually supported a high school had not the enlightened self-interest to accept his graciousness.

But who would a high school educate? Would all attend? Boyden neither advocated nor believed in a democracy of intellect, and his social convictions become even clearer from his remarks on the distribution of ability. Some had not the "capacity" to learn the "higher branches"; others would have no opportunity; many would not want to; and a number would not find the higher learning in "their interest." To imagine that all could learn the higher branches was, in fact, a dangerous illusion: besides being untrue, it threatened to alter a delicate social balance, which required hewers of wood and drawers of water. Society needed learned men, "preachers, teachers and authors," but it also required "food, shelter and clothing." And food, shelter, and clothing were "not the higher branches of learning." Neither was higher learning "merchandise" which could be bought and sold. In fact, those who had not the need for higher learning had better avoid it: "As a little learning is a dangerous thing — 'drink deep or taste not the Pierian Spring.'" Only common school education was "fundamental . . . for practical life and it should be made as universal and practical as possible." Indeed, "knowledge of the common branches is about as much as the mass of scholars can acquire during the period of their childhood and youth." [34]

In proper doses education was a fine tonic. Too little and prosperity faltered while deserving talent went unrewarded. Too much and the intricate social organism no longer functioned properly. Dr. Boyden, essentially, prescribed a meritocracy which would absorb and assimilate the bright, ambitious, hard-working boy, as he himself had been. But he had no desire to alter the hierarchy which made a social ladder necessary, and with more than a little of the smugness of the man who had made it the hard way, he wanted the ladder itself neither easy to climb nor wide.

As in Beverly, school promoters throughout Massachusetts were people intimately connected with the economic transformation of the state. On the state level James Carter, the first great advocate of school reform, based an argument for extended education on the fact that Massachusetts had to industrialize in order to survive.[35] Horace Mann helped push through the Massachusetts legislature bills supporting and assisting railroad construction. George Boutwell was a merchant. In Lawrence, Henry K. Oliver, the most vocal school promoter and a leading candidate for appointment as the third secretary of the Board of Education, was agent for one of the largest cotton mills in the state.[36] This was the former occupation of Joseph White, fourth secretary of the Board of Education. School committeemen had to represent the most educated citizens; for they had to be able to examine intelligently teachers, inspect schools, and write reports. Often the ministry played an active role, but in most towns lay participation was important and critical. For many years one of the most active educational reformers in Beverly was William Thorndike, a rich merchant.[37] And so it was throughout the commonwealth. The supporters of education wrote the legislation, invested the money, and ran the enterprises that brought about the economic and social transformation of Massachusetts.

To note the business connections of education promoters is to highlight a key feature of the reform process. Educational reform at this time was essentially a *lay* (or amateur) achievement. On the state level the men who did the most to arouse the reform spirit, like Horace Mann, came to education from other fields; on the local level it was influential laymen who, for the most part, supervised and administered educational innovation. As we shall see, these lay reformers were often short-sighted and insensitive; however, despite its shortcomings, their style of educational reform had one great virtue: it represented a degree of participation in public education by lay communal leadership perhaps never again equalled in the history of American society. Whatever our opinion of their motives or their results may be, we must recognize that for about two decades at mid-century the men in communities busiest with their own complicated affairs expended immense amounts of time and effort in their commitment to improve and extend public education.

Wealthy groups had interests other than developing communal resources and promoting limited mobility when they advocated high schools. As changes in the nature of commercial life made a prolonged apprenticeship unnecessary, some merchants wondered what to do with their adolescent boys. On the night of June 9, 1834, a group of men, "chiefly engaged in commerce," gathered to discuss the education of their sons. Among those present was Nathan Appleton, and the secretary of the meeting was the eminent William Ellery Channing. The merchants agreed that the present system of apprenticeship had become inefficient and wasteful of their sons' time. The men also agreed that "gentlemen, who decline to send their sons to college as being an institution not suited to their preparation for active life, are bound to give them a better education than they now receive." The men had definite educational objectives for their sons, and these objectives suggest a portrait of the ideal New England merchant: astutely making a fortune, conscious of a deep sense of responsibility to society, and desirous of continually improving his mind. To the merchants the ideal school would be anything but a place of leisure since it was to provide an arduous preparation for a life in the counting room. A new type of institution was clearly needed, and the merchants thought they saw one at hand; "the present English high school (a very valuable institution) might be so extended as to give all the advantages which are needed." [38]

Certainly, many school committees, desiring to establish a high school, must have concentrated on convincing those with a stake in the economic progress of their towns. The Dalton school committee, for one, wrote in 1860 that a high school would offer "greater inducements . . . to capitalists from abroad to come and occupy your unoccupied building sites and unimproved water power." [39] Likewise, the Athol committee in 1855 contended that a high school would attract people "who have large scholars to educate . . . thereby increasing the population and business of the place." Aside from attracting capital and population, the committee continued, a high school "would greatly enhance the value of property in town, to a percentage, it is believed, which would of itself more than pay the expenses of the school." The committee concluded that "the town could not make a better pecuniary investment." [40]

If the promoters were correct, then towns which established high schools should have had a far higher per capita valuation than ones which did not. There should have been a significant and positive correlation between valuation and high school establishment. In a large sample of towns studied (see Appendix B) in both 1840 (before almost any of them had established a high school) and in 1865, those with high schools had a slightly higher per capita valuation than those which did not.* But there was no significant correlation between high school establishment and valuation for either year. Towns which established high schools were, and continued to be, more prosperous than ones which did

* Throughout Part I, I shall refer to the statistical study of the state. This study employed a variety of statistical techniques and was performed by computer. In the body of this study I present only the relevant conclusions of the statistical analysis. Interested readers will find a full discussion of method as well as tables in Appendix B.

not. Apparently, in spite of promoters' predictions, the high school had no effect on communal wealth.

From the analysis of the vote in Beverly we would predict that the more wealthy members of the community, as well as middle-class parents particularly concerned about their children's mobility, would not only support the high school but would also send the most students to it. This prediction is strengthened by the general tenor of the pro–high school arguments so far. The high school was billed as the harbinger of communal wealth, individual prosperity, continued industrialization, and social mobility. From the reaction of the Beverly working class we would expect but few of their children in the high schools. We should expect that high school students would comprise a minority of the eligible children in the town. We should expect, further, that the proportion of eligible children attending was inversely related to the size and rate of growth of the town: it was mainly immigrants and other laborers arriving to man new mills and factories who swelled the population of towns; thus, as towns grew, the working-class elements, who we are supposing did not use the high schools very much, would become disproportionately larger.

This expectation may seem contrary to current sociological theory, which stresses that an increase in the size of the middle class, or in the number of non-manual workers, often accompanies population growth. Current theory, however, is based on contemporary conditions. In the nineteenth century the structure of communities may well have been quite different. Although urbanization probably brought an increase in the number of white-collar jobs, the technological state of industry undoubtedly required a much lower proportion of white-collar to manual workers than in the twentieth century. (The whole topic of the historical relationship between urban population growth and social structure is one that requires much investigation.) As figures cited by Lipset and Bendix clearly imply, the transition from a rural, farming community to a non-farming community, the particular type of shift with which we are here concerned, is usually accompanied by a large increase in the proportion of manual workers. Moreover, in the nineteenth century it was immigrants who swelled the population, and such people usually congregated in the lowest status occupations.[41]

From a random sample of 10 percent of towns and cities that had high schools in 1860 both predictions are definitely confirmed: In the sample as a whole under 20 percent of the estimated eligible children went to high school. In the smallest and most static towns (1,000–3,000), about 28 percent of the eligible attended. In the medium-sized ones (6,000–8,000), about 15 percent, and in the large, expanding cities (over 14,000), approximately 8 percent.

The analysis of high school enrollment in individual communities (see Appendix C) supports the general finding that high schools were minority institutions probably attended mainly by middle-class children. One hundred and eighty-one students entered Somerville High School between 1856 and 1861; information about the parents of 135 of these has been gathered. These 135 children represent 111 families. In these 111 families, 44 fathers were owners of businesses (stores or manufacturing concerns), self-employed as merchants or brokers, or masters employing artisans. An additional 8 fathers were employed in businesses, mostly as clerks. Five were professionals and 6 public employees; 1 was a master mariner and 1 a shipwright. If we lump these people together as "upper middle class" they comprise 57 percent of the fathers of high school children. If we consider as slightly lower on the occupational scale, but still middle class, artisans and farmers, there were 26 fathers in the former and 9 in the latter category. There was 1 father who was a farm laborer and for 10 parents no occupation was listed. (Some of the latter were obviously widows.) No child of a factory operative or of an ordinary laborer entered Somerville High School in these years. Although there were over 1,500 Irish immigrants in Somerville, none of their children entered, and only 3 of the fathers were foreign born: 1 each in England, Nova Scotia, and Bavaria. Only 25 of the 111 families had children who graduated, but there was little difference in their social background. How typical was Somerville? An analysis of the graduates of Chelsea High School between 1858 and 1864 produces similar conclusions. In our "upper middle class" category were 29 out of the 43 parents. Eleven were artisans, 3 had no occupation listed. Again, no operatives, no laborers, no Irish sent children to the high school. In both Chelsea and Somerville it is reasonable to estimate that the lowest occupational categories included at least 40 to 50 percent of the population.[42] The high school was indeed a strictly middle-class institution.

So far there is a certain consistency between ideology and action on the part of high school supporters. These well-to-do individuals and these more middle-class supporters argued that high schools were desirable because they would foster communal and individual prosperity and promote social mobility. They assumed that industrialization was good and that it should be fostered; they felt high schools would serve this purpose, and they sent their children to the institutions that they established. However, high school supporters were often complex individuals, and another aspect of their reaction to social development is less consistent than the one already discussed. Educational promoters were ambivalent about the very industrial society that the high schools they supported were supposed to help develop. They felt that industrial and urban life produced the most frightening kinds of social and moral decay. Horace Mann, for one, maintained that a "cardinal object" of the state was the "physical well-being of all the people, — the sufficiency, comfort, competence, of every individual in regard to food, raiment, and shelter." But the "industrial condition . . . and business operations" of Massachusetts were producing "fatal extremes of overgrown wealth and desperate poverty."[43] Class divisions, moreover, were being intensified by the growth of cities, for "density of population has always been one of the proximate causes of social inequality." There was a danger, he warned, that America would follow the course of England, where agricultural feudalism had receded before a new industrial serfdom accompanied by novel forms of degradation and vice. Mann complained to J. A. Shaw of "the new exposure to error, with new temptations to dishonesty, which grow out of a more dense population." The problem became acute because of the shift from a farm to an industrial society: "If the spontaneous productions of the earth were sufficient for all," Mann claimed, "men might be honest in practice, without any principle of rectitude because of the absence of temptation." But the growth of cities and the introduction of machinery were the serpent in Mann's Eden: "as population increases, and especially as artificial wants multiply, the temptations increase, and the guards and securities must increase also, or society will deteriorate." Of all the "guards and securities," none, it will become clearer presently, was of more worth to Mann and his contemporaries than education.[44]

Another problem posed by the growth of cities and factories was the hostility of manual laborers to the cultivation of refined manners and taste as well as to benevolence and kindness. To Mann poverty bred barbarity. In cities, "poverty casts its victims into heaps, and stows them away in cellars and garrets"; and in cellars and garrets family life and morality degenerated into a mere mockery of their proper form. For Mann the results of urbanization were poverty, crime, and vice. Civilization itself was threatened by the rapid and uncontrollable growth of cities, and there was a consequently urgent duty to save "a considerable portion of the rising generation from falling back into the conditions of half-barbarous or of savage life." [45]

The second and third secretaries of the Board of Education, Barnas Sears and George Boutwell, also feared for the destruction of individual morality, the family, and society.[46] To Sears immigrants and cosmopolitanism were particularly pernicious. Cities, he claimed, "furnish peculiar facilities for the diffusion of corrupt principles and morals." Migrants to the cities found "in their new places of abode, pleasures set before them appealing to every sense, and in gradations adapted to every intellect." So strong was the "current of sensuality," warned a shocked and fearful Sears, "that it too often sweeps almost everything before it . . . This life of congregated human beings, where money, leisure, shows, and a succession of excitements are the objects of pursuit, is now, with inconceivable power, educating myriads of children." [47]

Boutwell shared this view of the city. Both were intensely aware that at least as much education took place outside the school as within it. Whereas Sears stressed, especially, the prevalence of sensuous temptation in the city, Boutwell emphasized the collapse of the family. In one report he listed the "facts to be considered when we estimate the power of the public school to resist evil and to promote good"; these were "the activity of business, by which fathers have been diverted from the custody and training of their children; the claims of fashion and society which have led to some neglect of family government on the part of mothers; the aggregation of large populations in cities and towns, always unfavorable to the physical and moral welfare of children; the comparative neglect of agriculture and the consequent loss of moral strength in the people." Elsewhere he was equally direct. "As in some languages there is no word which expresses the true idea of home," he proclaimed, "so in our manufacturing towns there are many persons who know nothing of the reality." Among this group were "multitudes of children and youth." In agricultural areas "such cases are rare: and I cannot doubt that much of the moral and intellectual health enjoyed by the agricultural population is due to this circumstance." [48] And this was the man who, practically simultaneously, delivered rapturous descriptions of the artist-laborer made possible by the machine.

To Massachusetts schoolmen the young, unknowingly, were caught in a Faustian dilemma, and Mephistopheles lurked in the cities. The reports of Sears were particularly gloomy. With all of society conspiring against them, what could the schools do? The question Sears and indeed everyone else refused to ask was: If the public schools aided and sustained the growth of urban-industrial civilization, and if, in turn, they were powerless to check its pernicious effects, then was not the extension of public education really the pursuit of social self-destruction?

Faced with the decline of the family and the disintegration of society, Massachusetts schoolmen proclaimed that the state must assert itself and emphasize its character as a parent who should guard its family of children. Mann stressed the natural right of the child to education and the duty of society, acting as a trustee and the final arbiter of property, to assure the fulfillment of the child's rights. The infant, he said, needed "sustenance, and shelter, and care." If its "natural parents" were removed, or "parental ability" failed, it was the clear duty of "society at large . . . the government . . . to step in and fill the parent's place." Massachusetts, to Mann, was a particularly good state since it was "parental . . . in government." To Sears, too, the state was kindly, a "nourishing mother, as wise as she is beneficient." [49] But the softness of the mother turned into the sternness of the patriarch as problems increased. In the writings of Boutwell and the fourth secretary, Joseph White, the state through its school system became an engine for instilling social discipline. To Boutwell the school "inculcates habits of regularity, punctuality, constancy and industry in the pursuits of business; through literature and the sciences in their elements, and, under some circumstances, by an advanced course of study, it leads the pupil towards the fountain of life and wisdom; and by moral and religious instruction daily given, some preparation is made for the duties and temptations of the world." [50] The school became the means of instilling in the population the qualities necessary for success in industrial society. Boutwell's successor, White, also stressed the formative qualities of education. "How great and good a thing," White wrote, "is the legislation which wisely seeks to train the intellect and form the character of a people." [51] The state, through the schools, should transform the tyranny of the majority into an organized and effective mechanism for social discipline.*

Local high school promoters shared the secretaries' analyses of the disastrous course of society and argued that the high school would solve at least three outstanding community problems. In the first place, the high school in theory catered to the poor as well as the rich and was a vital antidote to the stratification, strife, and social disintegration that educators thought they saw around them. The Winchendon school committee claimed that the influence of the high school "in binding the population together, and promoting good feeling and harmony, must be obvious to everyone." [52] To many Massachusetts educators an ideal society, one which represented the aims of the founding fathers, was free of rigid stratification, harmonious and without acrimony. To achieve this harmony, to recreate the alleged social unity of pre-industrial civilization, high schools were a necessity. Joseph White wrote of high schools:

> The children of the rich and the poor, of the honored and the unknown, meet together on common ground. Their pursuits, their aims and aspirations are one. No distinctions find place, but such as talent and industry and good conduct create. In the competitions, the defeats, and the successes of the schoolroom, they meet each other as they are to meet in the broader fields

* With Joseph White the tradition of eminent secretaries of the Board ended. White, unlike his predecessors, came from a well-to-do family of merchants in Worcester County. He attended Williams College and started to prepare for a legal career. Deciding against the law as a career, he instead took a position in Lowell as an agent for one of the largest cotton mills in the state. An ardent Presbyterian and a devoted Whig, White entered politics as a state senator. His term as secretary to the Board lasted seventeen years, and after his retirement he evidently devoted himself to the local affairs of the Berkshires, to the business of his church and of Williams College, and to the promotion of local historiography. One memorialist claimed that his term at the Board represented "much the most successful work of his life."

of life before them; they are taught to distinguish between the essential and true, and the fractious and false, in character and condition . . . Thus a vast and mutual benefit is the result. Thus, and only thus, can the rising generation be best prepared for the duties and responsibilities of citizenship in a free commonwealth. No foundation will be laid in our social life for the brazen walls of caste; and our political life, which is but the outgrowth of the social, will pulsate in harmony with it, and so be kept true to the grand ideals of the fathers and founders of the republic.[53]

When we understand the longing for unity of high school promoters and their essential ambivalence to the society they were helping to create, then we can appreciate better the attitude of Robert Rantoul and high school promoters in Beverly. Both Rantoul and Boyden stressed the desirability of a more organic, closely knit social order. Surely, they must have been aware that throughout the state people were arguing that a high school would promote this goal. The high school would provide a counterbalance to the same divisive economic forces that it was to help unleash. Thus, support for a high school was a complex reaction related in part to an essentially ambivalent perception of society. The high school was an ideal innovation because it would allegedly serve the frequently conflicting values and interests of educational reformers.

The high school was supposed to solve still other community problems. Promoters claimed that the school would serve as an agent of community civilization. The tone of the community would be raised; cultural as well as social unity would prevail and upwardly mobile youths could be socially as well as intellectually prepared for their new status. For example, the Lincoln school committee stressed that the effect of a well conducted high school was "to elevate the sentiments, the taste, the manners of the pupils." In the high school there would be "no room for the awkwardness, vulgarity and rudeness in behavior and speech, that are too generally tolerated and sometimes encouraged even, in common district schools." The high school inducted pupils into "a higher civilization and refinement, and does what otherwise might not be done, to prepare them for occupying exalted positions in social life, and for doing much for the welfare of their fellow men." Perhaps best of all, the benefits of the high school extended to the whole community: "the spirit of improvement here imbibed, goes home" with the students, "and the whole family feels its inspiration. The intellectual light that is kept burning here, sends its rays abroad through the community. The refining process here commenced, is carried into the social circle." [54]

Another problem was the attitude of parents, continually lamented by school committees. "The great defect in our day," observed the Barnstable school committee, "is the absence of governing or controlling power on the part of parents, and the consequent insubordination of children." As for the children, "self-will is their law; hence flows conceit, and a monstrous precocity . . . What the parent makes them, the teacher finds them." Concluded the committee, "Our schools are rendered inefficient by the apathy of parents." Parents failed to appreciate the values of education, spoiled their children, and frustrated the efforts of the school. The failure of parents to provide moral discipline and their general lack of interest in the schools was a persistent theme in every school report consulted. To school committees the problem was extremely serious because parental apathy and hostility were not only thwarting educational advance but promoting those very social tendencies that educators were trying to check. [55]

The high schools, Barnas Sears argued in 1854, were a means of overcoming the problem of parental apathy. The establishment of high schools, he wrote, "gives the schools themselves a place in the estimation of the people, which they never held before." Sears continued, "We need not go back many years to find a prejudice against the public schools," but the high schools had dispelled antipathy and apathy to public education. "There are no better schools in the Commonwealth than some of our public high schools, and to these families of the highest character now prefer to send their children." [56] But that parents of the "highest character," meaning probably the socially and financially prominent, used the high schools is no proof that the antipathy of the working class was overcome. In fact, the undisguised harangues of school committees made one aspect of educational reform particularly clear. The committees saw themselves arrayed against the mass of parents, whom they considered uncomprehending and indifferent. School committees were unashamedly trying to impose educational reform and innovation on this reluctant citizenry. The communal leaders were not answering the demands of a clamorous working class: they were imposing the demands; they were telling the majority, your children shall be educated, and as we see fit.

Promoters represented educational reform, especially the high school, as an innovation directly aimed at urbanizing, industrializing communities. The high school was simultaneously to foster mobility, promote economic growth, contribute to communal wealth, and save towns from disintegrating into an immoral and degenerate chaos. If these contentions were heeded, then it should have been in the communities undergoing the most rapid and severe transformation, the most urban and industrial areas, that high schools were established. It should have been in these places that schoolmen were contending most vigorously for innovation, most actively trying to overcome the apathy of the mass. In these areas the concern for education should have been most marked by both innovation and high expenditures on schooling.

An extensive statistical study of the state has demonstrated that these suppositions are, for the most part, valid. The establishment of high schools was related to all the dominant patterns of urbanism and industrialism; and it was in the more urban and industrial areas that greater numbers of children over fifteen attended school. High school establishment was, however, relatively more associated with urban than with manufacturing characteristics. This is not surprising, for it was more specifically the urban phenomena that were singled out by promoters as susceptible to correction by a high school. The harangues against the new society that have been presented stressed the problems of urban poverty, squalor, and social disorganization. Moreover, high schools were especially associated with large numbers of people employed in commerce. This is an expected conclusion, since it was to solve the problem of an anachronistic apprenticeship for adolescents headed toward a commercial career that the Boston merchants advocated a high school. The association of high school establishment with urban and industrial characteristics does not contradict the finding, already noted, that the lowest percentage of children attended high school in the most urban areas. High school establishment and high school attendance were very different phenomena. It was in the rapidly urbanizing places that communal leaders and middle-class parents most readily saw a need for a high school; it was also these places that had the most children from social groups least attracted by the high school and least able economically to make use of it.

As for measures of school spending, both high per-pupil expenditure and a high school tax rate were usually associated with the establishment of a high school. But this general relation obscures subtle differences. Spending on education was by no means as clearly related to social measures as was high school establishment. Usually, the higher the per-capita valuation of a town, the lower was its tax rate. The converse was true for per-pupil expenditure. These relations are predictable. The more money a town had the smaller the proportion needed to sustain a high per-pupil expenditure. In one situation, however, both measures of school spending were high. This was in wealthy suburban towns. This finding supports the contention that educational concern was primarily a characteristic of the middle and upper social groups, for in these towns, where manufacturing was not extensive, there would be fewer of the kinds of people who stood in the way of the improvement of schools. Similarly, in towns where agriculture became of increasing importance the school tax rate was particularly low. In these areas the townspeople would see but little relation between their own welfare and the furtherance of industrial growth, and they would be affected little by social disorder at their doorstep. Yet somewhat surprisingly, per-pupil expenditure was depressed by the rapid and sharp development of manufacturing. In this situation the lower expense was undoubtedly as much the result of an influx of immigrants with large families and few taxable resources as of parsimony. How the problem of population increase was in fact met is a topic that will be discussed presently.

To sum up the argument thus far: the vote on the abolition of Beverly High School and other data imply that the people of most wealth and prestige in communities, often joined by those of more middle-level social position, supported educational innovations, especially the establishment of high schools. These people shared an ambivalent perception of the growing urbanism and industrialism that marked the commonwealth. Cities and factories were necessary, good, and should be promoted; cities and factories brought social and familial disintegration and chaos. Related to their ambivalent perception of society were their contentions concerning the virtues of educational reform in general and the high school in particular. The high school would foster urbanism and industrialism by creating communal wealth, by training skilled workmen, by assuming the functions of outmoded apprenticeships, by providing necessary channels for mobility. The high school would curb the evils of urbanism and industrialism by unifying and civilizing the community and the family, by overcoming the hostility and apathy of parents to education. Essentially, the reformers looked to a parental state to sponsor education that would help build modern industrial cities permeated by the values and features of an idealized rural life. The relation between expenditures on education, high school establishment, and the nature of communities reveals the depth of commitment to this ideology, for it was in the more urban and industrial communities, those most in need of educational innovation according to the ideology, that educational change was most apparent. Educational change, however, was not a gentle process: educational promoters, convinced of the value of their wares, harangued and badgered the mass of reluctant citizens; the style of reform was imposition. Already, then, disturbing problems arise: the high school was not usually attended by the working class whom it was allegedly intended to benefit; it was not welcomed by the people for whom it was supposedly established. What, then, were the real functions of the high school? What was the relation between the ideology and motivation of promoters? These concerns will be returned to. Now it is important to look more closely at certain mechanisms through which high schools were supposed to accomplish their goals.

3. LOCAL OPPOSITION TO REFORM

Academies and Districts

The mechanisms through which high schools were supposed to accomplish their goals become clearer from an examination of another series of contentions advanced by their supporters. These arguments focused on the alleged deficiencies of academies. To build a truly effective system of public education, many schoolmen argued, it was necessary to eliminate the pernicious influence of private schools. The whole academy–private school issue is very complex. The word academy covered a multitude of institutions varying in character from small privately run schools to the famous endowed academies. The effect of an academy, of any type, upon a community and related issues are by no means as clear as is desirable. However, the anti-academy arguments are clear; and they are especially significant because they contain many of the same themes employed in another series of arguments, those criticizing the district schools. A comparison of arguments against academies and district schools highlights areas of concern to high school promoters.

Academies, it was frequently maintained, injured the public schools by dampening public interest in "those means of education which are common to the whole people." [57] At the same time, they withdrew many able children from public schools, and their existence, so critics said, provided a safety valve for disaffected children who, unhappy for some reason in the public schools, could always transfer. The committee claimed that in Hadley, one town where the latter problem had been especially serious, the replacement of the academy by a high school had increased the effectiveness of the whole school system.[58] Academies were also pernicious because they took children away from home. School committees repeatedly contended that, for some reason, children at academies were in moral danger. The academies were places of "temptation and vice." [59] Why this fear of academies? What was going on within their halls? The emphasis on the immoral tendencies of academies, the desire of Boston merchants to provide strong discipline for their children, school committee complaints of parental inability to control children: all suggest that adults had serious reservations about the inner strength of the younger generation, especially about adolescents. In fact, the high school was a major social innovation for handling adolescents. Besides cost, the key difference between a high school and an academy was that in the former children lived at home. This was critical because adolescents, it was widely held, got into trouble way from home. Thus, the way to control adolescents was to keep them at home, to prolong their dependency, to delay the time at which they sallied forth, independent, into the world. We can better understand just why the prolongation of dependency was so important after we examine pedagogical theory and compare the problems of academy, high school, and reform school, and this issue will be returned to in Part III.

There was, it must be added, more to the anti-academy argument than concern over adolescent behavior. Academies involved considerable expense; besides tuition there was the cost of board and spending money. "To send children to other places," pointed out one school committee, requires "a greater outlay of money, than would be needful to sustain a school at home." There were "the expense of traveling; the increased expense of living away from home; and the item of spending money, which will always be larger, and often necessarily so, than when the pupils remain under the parental roof." [60] The high school offered an economical means of solving a social problem.

In his reports George Boutwell sustained an effective harangue pointing out other failings of academies. Academies, Boutwell asserted, were generally in a more difficult financial position than public schools and, through lack of funds, could not offer an equivalent education. If academies were provided with ample money then parents were incurring an unnecessary expense. They were paying taxes to support the public schools and tuition at academies. The two sources of money, combined, could furnish one extremely effective system.[61] Besides, in academies the numbers were often too small to apply the latest pedagogical theory, which involved dividing the schools into grades (discussed below), an excellent innovation offered by a public school system that included a high school. Boutwell contended, moreover, that the academy offered too sheltered a life and did not prepare children for the realities of society: "In this age, the world is neither reformed, improved nor governed by the education of the cloister." [62] Boutwell, here and in other arguments, was asserting just the opposite of the contention that academies exposed children to debilitating temptations. Whatever interpretation one took of the morality of academies, it is clear they came out a poor second to public high schools. Finally, it was said, the high school, unlike the academy, was a thoroughly democratic institution since it fostered the principle of equality of opportunity. In the absence of high schools the relation between mobility and education meant that opportunity had become the prerogative of the wealthy. Comparing the virtues of academies and high schools, Joseph White argued that the latter "brings home the benefits of a superior education to all classes of the people, and thus beautifully illustrates and makes practical the theory of equal rights, on which our institutions are founded." Similarly, the Watertown school committee, criticizing academies, asked, "Shall not the field be left open for a fair intellectual competition? Shall the poverty of the parent be visited upon the mind of its offspring?" [63]

But the establishment of public high schools, as we have seen, did little to promote the mobility of the lowest social groups. Surely, high school promoters could not really have expected that the children of factory operatives and laborers would attend. They knew only too well the apathy of these people toward education. In this situation their ideology served partly as a rationalization. By stressing that high schools were democratic, that they fostered equality of opportunity, educational promoters could cover personal motives with the noblest of sentiments. What they were doing was spreading throughout the whole community the burden of educating a small minority of its children.

Interestingly, the terms of the academy–high school controversy were also largely the terms of the district–high school debate. Under the prevailing administrative system towns were divided into school districts, each of which maintained and managed its own school with the aid of funds from the town school committees and the state. For years educators vociferously and nearly unanimously condemned this practice. The "prudential committeemen" in charge of separate districts doled out teaching jobs to friends and relatives, often regardless of their qualifications, and the selection of teachers frequently became a source of intradistrict rivalry and animosity. The town committees, concerned with the whole town as opposed to single districts, distributed the money to the districts, and real or alleged inequities were frequently the cause of inter-district rivalries. School committee reports give the impression, both implicitly and explicitly, that districts often acted like separate towns. Another source of hostility within districts was the location of the school, an issue which frequently produced heated conflict.[64]

The first four secretaries of the Board of Education were all hostile to the district system, but none expressed their contentions with more detail and clarity than George Boutwell. To the preceding arguments Boutwell added the contention that the scanty population and financial resources of many districts made it hard to persuade residents to pay adequate taxes, and, thus, appropriations were not made according to what was desirable but according to the amount of money that could be raised. To convince knowledgeable and able men to serve as prudential committeemen was difficult, Boutwell lamented, and consequently district schools were usually administered in ignorance of the latest pedagogical theory. District policy was made by men "assembled by concert, in the shades of evening, in a dimly lighted house." There the policy makers hurriedly consummated "their schemes" and built an educational system suited to their own material or personal requirements, not to the needs of the children.[65]

Both the law and practical considerations required the high school to be a town school, administered by the town school committee, and drawing its students from all the districts. The high school was in one sense an administrative device for modifying the district system. Many districts resented the surrender of autonomy and power that the high school represented, and the district system proved an obstacle to high school development.[66] Many people argued, moreover, that large numbers of children would live too far away from the high school to be able to attend and that parents would therefore be paying taxes to support schools from which they could derive no benefit. The issue of school location, a source of intense controversy within the small districts themselves, became a major obstacle to the development of high schools when raised on the town scale.[67] Population density was an issue related to school location and inter-district rivalry, and towns which reported the greatest difficulties in overcoming the autonomy of districts were generally the ones which conceived of themselves as the most thinly populated. Nearly every set of school reports read, as well as other sources, considered relatively high population density a prerequisite for the founding of a high school.[68]

The district system also fostered a pedagogical practice that most educators felt was unsound. In most district schools children of all ages were taught in one room by one teacher. Throughout the pre–Civil War period educators argued that this was an inefficient method of instruction and that children would acquire a better education in graded schools. In Beverly the school committee reminded the town that there was no longer an academy and called attention to the pedagogical problems of district school teachers who tried to introduce high school subjects. Both younger and older children suffered, and the harried teacher was unable to do anything effectively.[69] Graded schools, in which students of the same age worked together and stimulated each other, were a more effective and efficient pedagogical device, and the high school was to form the apex of a reorganized, graded school system which would include, ideally, a number of district schools, and, at the top of the system, a high school.[70]

George Emerson, a member of the Board of Education and the first high school teacher in America, stressed another virtue of graded schools. Class rather than individual promotion, he maintained, would offer a "healthful stimulus to exertion." The prevailing practice of school organization, like the monitorial system, fostered intense competition. Children were often seated in rows according to their rank in class, and when a child failed

in recitation, he moved to the end of the row. Most educators
agreed that some type of competition was necessary as a stimulus,
but intra-personal competition, competition with oneself, would
produce an equal amount of effort without harmful social implications, without reinforcing the enervating and disastrous competition characteristic of a materialistic society. Intra-personal was
the type of competition encouraged in graded schools, where ad-
vancement was by class, so that all who attained a prescribed
level would be promoted. "Strive not," Emerson told the students
of Boston English High School, "to surpass each other, — strive
rather to surpass yourselves." Similarly, at the state normal school
in Lexington, Cyrus Peirce had his first class of students discuss
the question " 'whether the pupils in school should change seats,'
and all were found to agree in the negative." Mr. Peirce's reasons
were: "1st that it would tend to foster bad passions as pride,
emulation. — 2nd it turns the attention from the chief thing and
induces a desire to excel others. 3rd it lays the foundation for
competition and strife and emulation." [71]

Graded school systems had still more benefits. First of all, a
high school would raise the inadequate educational attainment of
the children through inspiring a whole school system to greater
effort as well as through its own curriculum. Pupils would strive for
the prestige of success in the entrance examinations, and teachers
would strive for the prestige of having successful pupils. This would
be a beneficial competition, for the high school, open to all who
qualified, offered the supreme advantage of a reward attainable by
all through hard work. The high school was the embodiment of
equality of opportunity. Second, educators maintained that sepa-
rating the older from the younger pupils would eliminate many
discipline problems and would allow a correct sex distribution of
teachers. [72]

Pedagogical theory held that female teachers were preferable
for younger children and male for older. [73] "Among teachers of
equal literary qualifications," wrote the Braintree school com-

mittee, "there may be a great diversity in their capability of governing and disciplining a school. Females, generally, are best adapted to govern and instruct the Primary schools." Experience taught that with children "of that variety of age usually found in large districts" the best results came from "placing the older and the younger in separate schools, with a female teacher for the latter, and a male teacher for the former." [74] A streamlined school system would require, in addition, no increase in the number of schools, and if all the older children were gathered into one school, only one male teacher need be hired. Thus, a number of the more expensive masters in district schools could be replaced by females paid a third to a half as much. George Boutwell implied that the feminization of the teaching force was more than desirable; it was a necessity, since men were leaving teaching for more lucrative opportunities.[75]

Evidence to support Boutwell's statement is hard to find. From one small sample, however, comes data for his case. Biographical data exist for thirteen male teachers at Holliston Academy between 1836 and 1844. Of these thirteen, four were ministers. Of the nine who were not ministers, seven eventually left teaching for a full time business career and two for medicine. One of the ministers also left both religious and pedagogical callings for the textile business. Except for one of the physicians, none of the nine future businessmen was in college when he was teaching at the academy. Thus, they do not fit the stereotype of the ante-bellum male teacher as a vacationing college student. All seven of the future businessmen also taught at schools other than the academy, in different communities. Their tenure varied; two stayed in teaching for five years, one for four, one for two, one for twelve, one for eighteen and one for "several" years. Apparently none ever did attend college. These men did not, however, lose all contact with educational affairs; at least four of the seven businessmen were active on local and state education committees. Some probably had intended to make teaching a career, only to be lured away by developing commercial opportunities. Others may well have looked on teaching as a way both to stay alive and to establish a local reputation while waiting for the right business opportunity to appear. This small sample, then, suggests that one variety of male teacher was the young man on the make. Whatever their reasons for leaving, the teachers at Holliston Academy do support Boutwell's assertion that young men were quitting the pedagogical business for more lucrative opportunities.[76]

Thus, female teachers could be argued for on various grounds: they were more appropriate for young children; they were cheaper; they were, amidst the increasing scarcity of men, a necessity. In fact, between 1840 and 1860 the percentage of males teaching school dropped from about sixty to fourteen (see Appendix A). Which was the real reason: economy or propriety? If all went according to the theory, we should find that feminization was associated with graded school systems, which would be marked by a high school. We should find, too, that feminization was not associated with a low level of expenditure. For it was presented not as a means of achieving a reduction in expense but as a way of getting more for the same money. These expectations are not confirmed by the statistical analysis. There was no significant relation between feminization and high schools. There was a significant association between feminization and a low level of expenditure on public education. For the most part, female teachers were introduced because they were cheap. As Charles William Eliot observed some years after the feminization of primary school teaching was largely completed: "It is true that sentimental reasons are often given for the almost exclusive employment of women in the common schools; but the effective reason is economy . . . If women had not been cheaper than men, they would not have replaced nine tenths of the men in American public schools." [77]

Of course, there were excellent reasons for a mild parsimony. The number of children was increasing rapidly, and the additions to the population were mainly the children of poor immigrants who could contribute little to school taxes. To run the educational system economically and efficiently was not stingy but realistic. Essentially the same group of people as before had to pay for the education of many more children. This is what made feminization so important. Here, too, the arguments against the economic drain caused by academies and for the economy of high schools become particularly relevant. Feminization and high schools, however, were sincerely believed to be desirable for their own sake. Deeply pervading educational thought was the belief that both economy and improvement were possible. This was a key assumption of nineteenth century educational thought. Actually, throughout this period per-pupil expense increased markedly, but the school tax rate did not. Rising property valuations enabled towns to increase the amount of expenditure on schools while spending the same proportion of their income. All this points to a conclusion that taxpayers were unwilling to spend more than a fairly fixed amount of their income on schools and that one important dynamic of educational reform in this period was the effort, under the impact of a growing population, to extend and improve education within this limit.

The parallels between the methods of educational and industrial reorganization in this period are striking. Women made up an increasing proportion of the industrial as well as the educational labor force. In industry the growth of larger units of production was part of a process of rationalization: the subdivision of processes in the manufacture of goods and the gathering of all the workers engaged in making a product under one roof. Workers, moreover, were given training to increase their efficiency. Educational reorganization reflected the same trends. The teaching process was to be subdivided; each teacher, ideally, would be responsible for but a part of a student's education, and the teachers would be trained in the new normal schools. Overlap between schools, where possible, was to be eliminated and larger, more efficient units created through regrouping. Rationalization, the division of labor, training, and feminization all marked both industry and education. To account for these innovations in industry and to explain their comparatively more pronounced features in America than in England, H. J. Habakkuk has argued persuasively that the dominant cause was a shortage of labor. Spurred on by the scarcity and high cost of labor, manufacturers had

> a greater inducement to organise their labour efficiently. The dearness of American labour gave manufacturers an inducement to increase its marginal productivity in all possible ways . . . the shortage of labour led generally to longer hours of work, to a general emphasis on the saving of time and a sense of urgency about getting the job done . . . In the U.S.A. the proportion of employed females to males was higher than in England . . . The most conspicuous example of the efficient use of labour is the training that the American manufacturers gave their workers so that each was able to handle more looms . . . It is not an accident that scientific systems of labour management originated in America.[78]

Habakkuk's argument can be extended from industry to education. School committees were faced with a rapid increase in numbers of children because of immigration, a scarcity of men because of industrial and commercial opportunities, and a consequent probable enormous rise in school costs. In this situation schoolmen, like industrialists, sought to increase the "marginal productivity" of labor through training, feminization, innovation, and reorganization.

At this point it is important to note the similarities, already referred to, in criticisms leveled at both academies and district schools. Boutwell, it will be recalled, argued that both academies and district schools had financial resources too limited to allow the institution of grading and effective pedagogy. Both, moreover, involved the duplication of facilities and the consequent doubling of expenditures. In the long run, public, town-administered schools would be more effective and less expensive. Academies and district schools alike contributed to the maintenance of community strife and prevented the attainment of the social harmony necessary, more than ever, in an industrializing society. Both were essentially undemocratic. Parents could not control private schools and cliques controlled districts while both hindered equality of opportunity. The poor child could not receive the benefits of an academy education, and children suffered in districts too poor to have adequate schools. Finally, the existence of both academies and district schools allegedly hindered the institution of high schools. In attacking private and district schools high school promoters were fighting the same battle.

But did academies really hinder the development of high schools? Was educational improvement the real motive behind the dual fight of high school promoters? The answer to the first question must be considered in two parts, for unincorporated and incorporated academies. The statistical study shows that the sort of town that had the most unincorporated academies in 1840 had a public high school by 1865. These were the urban towns with large numbers of merchants. In light of the merchants' favorable attitude toward high schools, it is not surprising that this shift occurred. As a rule then unincorporated academies did not hinder the establishment of public high schools. For incorporated academies the evidence is not so clear. Apparently, in communities with large numbers of professional people in 1840 there was often an incorporated academy, and this academy usually continued its existence through the next two and one-half decades. In some instances such an institution hindered the development of public high schools. Such an instance was Groton. Like Beverly, Groton was not a town of great significance, and developments there had little, if any, impact upon the rest of the state. However, again like Beverly, Groton suggests answers to important questions concerning education throughout the state. The state set and loosely enforced only general guidelines for reform; the actual process of change was enacted primarily within individual communities, and it is only by taking a detailed look at local history that we can begin to explain adequately how and why reform took place and what it meant. By looking at Groton we can watch the development of the twofold battle of a school committee against a district system and an academy. We can also suggest an answer to one troublesome question, the real motives of the beleaguered committees, and we can connect their two-pronged attack more clearly with the battle to establish high schools.

Groton: A Case in Point

"In 1835," according to George Boutwell, "the town of Groton was a place of much importance relatively. It was the residence of several men of more than local fame." In the late thirties Groton was primarily an agricultural community with very few manufacturing establishments. Twelve men and 6 women made boots, probably at home. Two tanneries employed 4 people; 6 men and 5 women made hats in 1 factory and 2 establishments for the manufacture of chairs and cabinet wares employed 6 individuals. Two hundred and forty-five women made clothing, probably at home, and an unspecified number of individuals made palm leaf hats, also at home. During 1837 somewhere in the town 130 soapstone pumps, 64 axletrees, and $300 worth of mathematical instruments were manufactured.[79]

By 1865, the amount of manufacturing had increased considerably. Two establishments for the manufacture of ploughs and other agricultural implements employed 125 persons. Two "paper manufactories" gave work to 23 men and 20 women; 1 tannery was staffed by 75 "hands," and there was a variety of small establishments: 2 bakeries, 3 saw mills, 1 tinware manufactory, 4 blacksmith shops, 4 master builders, 1 clothing factory, and 1 establishment for making soap. Domestic, home-centered industry had virtually disappeared. Although Groton remained more agricultural and less industrial than most towns that established high schools, the degree of change in the town between 1840 and 1865 was relatively more marked (see Table 1). In fact change was

Table 1. Growth of Groton, 1840–1865[a]

Variable	1840	1865	Percent change
Population	2139 (2023)	3176 (3059)	45 (51)
Total employed in manufacturing	113 (259)	281 (616)	148 (137)
Agricultural employees	799 (273)	300 (229)	−63 (−17)
Number foreign born	—	506 (498)	

[a] Numbers in parentheses are average figures for all towns studied that, like Groton, established a high school by 1865.

felt especially strongly in Groton because manufacturing was concentrated in one part of the town, Groton Junction. Virtually uncultivated in 1830, the Junction became a thriving commercial and industrial center when it was made the place of meeting for a number of different railroad lines.

The town newspaper, the *Groton Mercury,* chronicled and welcomed the growth of Groton Junction. In December 1851, the *Mercury* greeted the erection of an agricultural tool factory: "The facilities for transportation at the Junction are probably better than at any other place in New England, the Railroads there diverging in all directions. We prophesy that sometimes, this celebrated Station . . . will be a considerable . . . town." Two years later the paper welcomed another agricultural works factory that was moving to the Junction from Rhode Island and bringing with it all its employees ("some 60 or 70") and their families. The company was building "two large boarding houses" as temporary accommodation and erecting an "immense factory" and a "large Foundry." Others at the Junction were also prospering. A soap manufacturer had "lately put up a building for the manufacture of this article in all its varieties"; a number of homes and stores were slated for erection in the spring, "and a site had been selected for a spacious Hotel." Within a few years Groton Junction was "destined . . . to be a large and flourishing town." The growth of the Junction, of course, would "diminish what little business there is now doing in the village." But, stressing the difference between the sections of the town, the editor wrote, "it will leave dear old Groton as ever, a most beautiful and desirable place of residence — none the less so, that the noise and bustle of business is far from it." But the *Mercury* was not always so charitable to the "village." The "old fogies" who lived in the village but owned property in the Junction, it chided, retarded the latter's growth by refusing to sell land to all the manufacturers who wanted to build factories.[80] The tensions between the sections of the town were reflected in the development of public education; eventually they became so severe that in 1871 Groton Junction severed its ties with the village and became the town of Ayer.

In 1830 the school committee in a letter to the short-lived *Groton Herald* complained of the low state of the town's schools. "So far as we have had the means of judging, we are convinced there has not been that improvement made in our schools generally for years past, which we think might reasonably be expected." The problem centered in the lack of care with which teachers were chosen. Sometimes they were allowed to begin teaching before being examined; sometimes they were not examined at all; and the standard of the examinations was much too low. The town erred by insisting on cheap teachers and the schools suffered.[81] By 1842, however, the school committee was reasonably optimistic. Over the past year, they noted, there had been a general improvement in the schools, and the committee was particularly happy about the number of parents who had attended the closing exercises. Nevertheless, a few problems remained. A number of children had been overheard using profanity; some of the districts had to be combined; and the wealthier children in the town were receiving some unfair advantages. They could attend academies, Sunday Schools, and "social libraries." In spite of these difficulties the committee was rather pleased with the state of the town's schools, but six years later in 1848 the committee was once again complaining that the educational situation had deteriorated. Their report for that year initiated a mounting crescendo of criticism that would abate but slightly over the next seventeen years.[82]

Better discipline among both students and teachers was imperative, for the manners and grammar of the latter were faulty. Better financing was also necessary, and the committee buttressed their appeal with the familiar contention that there was an inverse relation between education, pauperization, and crime and a high positive correlation between education and the economic and political greatness of Massachusetts.[83] The heart of the 1848 report, however, was a lengthy demonstration of the superiority of public to private education. This argument was really the slightly veiled start of a decade-long harangue against the town's academy and its supporters.

Groton Academy was founded in 1792. In "the early part of the year," wrote Dr. Samual Abbott Green, the town historian, "a voluntary association was formed . . . by certain people of the town and neighborhood, in order to establish an academy where a higher education could be obtained than was given at the district schools of that period." Subscriptions were collected and shares of stock in the academy sold. The association organized itself and chose trustees and other officers on April 27, 1792. The academy was maintained continuously thereafter.[84] But in the early 1840's financial difficulties made its continued existence uncertain. One of the trustees, Dr. Joshua Green, wrote Amos Lawrence, perhaps the most eminent alumnus of the academy, and told him of its difficulties, including a falling enrollment.[85] Lawrence responded with munificence. In 1846 he and his brothers endowed the academy with between eighteen and twenty thousand dollars, providing, consequently, enough financial security to enable expansion.[86] The school, not surprisingly, was renamed Lawrence Academy. With ample finances its situation improved; between 1845 and 1850 its enrollment increased by more than one hundred students, and Groton children accounted for nearly a fifth of the increase. The coeducational academy offered both a classical and an English course, which indicates that it prepared students for both college and business.[87] It is significant, therefore, that the first sustained attack on the academy by the town school committee occurred in 1848.

The proprietors of the academy emphasized the moral as well as the intellectual aspects of the education they provided. "The discipline of the school," they wrote in 1845, "commends itself to parents and guardians, securing the greatest intellectual progress in connection with a desirable moral influence . . . The settled policy of the Principal" was to "allow no incorrigibly idle or vicious pupil retained in school." The "constant object and desire of effort," claimed the catalogue, was "a pure and peaceful community." In 1849 another passage was inserted in the catalogue emphasizing that the teachers and proprietors of the academy would keep a more than watchful eye on the morals of the children entrusted to their care: "None are allowed to frequent the stores, or taverns, or other places, where they may become contaminated." And in 1850 they added, "There is no attempt to secure popularity made at the expense either of thoroughness of instruction or strictness of discipline." [88] If one believed the official statements, no one would be able to accuse Lawrence Academy of immoral influence.

Nevertheless, the *Mercury* presented a slightly different picture when it reported the following conversation: " 'Dick,' said a student of Lawrence Academy, the other day in the Post Office, 'Bill wishes you would write to him.' 'I'll see him damned first,' replied his mate." The paper asserted that such language was not uncommon among academy students.[89] The Groton school committee also attacked the academy's claims of moral superiority, arguing that because public education was based on a philosophy of exposure rather than seclusion, it was a better preparation for life. In the public schools one did not see life "in an artificial state," and the carefully nurtured children of the rich would be thrown into a "world of children, all classes surround them — poor boys and rich — those of good — those of bad habits." In short, they would see "the world as it is." The wealthy children educated in public schools would have, in later years, the practical advantage of "being able to resist the temptations of life — while, perhaps, those whose education has been more carefully watched, discover themselves exposed to temptations, the existence of which, they have been notified — alas! too late." Public education also offered other advantages: in a public school children learned the great American principles, especially the fact that "all men are born equal," and in public schools no notions of aristocracy could be fostered or tolerated.[90] The Groton school committee employed strong language, but then it had a formidable foe.

In 1850 the committee noted with pleasure a growing parental interest in the schools but complained that the town's parsimony kept school appropriations low by comparison with other, similar towns. Tardiness, absenteeism, and in some cases "insubordination" were hindering the work of the teachers.[91] These considerations, nevertheless, received relatively brief attention since the committee delivered its principal lecture for the year on the need for a high school. Unite a few districts and decrease the number of lower level schools, the committee proposed, and a high school will involve no increase in taxation. The separation of the older from the younger children would permit the more efficient instruction of both, and the desire for success in high school entrance examinations would stimulate the common schools to "increased exertion." Perhaps most important, a high school would "break down the popular prejudices" that, the committee now openly proclaimed, received "no little support from the existence of an Academy . . . It would be much better for the town if no such institution . . . existed." The committee reinforced this contention with a discussion of the relation between the high school and equality of opportunity and the importance of the latter for the preservation of democracy.[92]

A look at the Lawrence Academy catalogue for 1851 reveals the source of the school committee's anxiety and their reasons for pressing for the establishment of a public high school at that time. Referring to Groton, the catalogue stated, "The population is highly intelligent and refined, which end the common schools of the town have mainly contributed to effect." This was indeed unobjectionable, but the catalogue continued, "The youth of the place, obtaining the rudiments of a good education in our excellent public schools, pass into the academy, which occupies the relative place of a high school." The academy was consciously in competition with the desires of the school committee. The description of the academy was, in fact, much like that of a high school. In the academy, the catalogue explained, the students "are further instructed in such branches as fit·them for various departments of business or professional life." The catalogue proudly and truly announced that "youth from abroad also largely participate in these inestimable blessings." [93] Lawrence Academy must have been well known. In 1851, for example, its enrollment included seven students from New York, two from Missouri, two from Michigan, one from Maryland, one from Louisiana, two from Kentucky, one from Washington, D.C., and one from Canada. In 1852 the student body included five South American pupils, one Cuban, and one Canadian. In 1853 a student from Spain was added; and, rather startlingly, one Leonida D. Rodocanachi from Smyrna, Asia Minor, made his appearance in the same year, followed in 1858 by a boy from India.[94] With such an institution as a competitor the fight for a high school would not be easy.

Throughout 1851 and 1852 tension mounted between the school committee and the town. Appropriations improved but poor discipline remained. The great issue of these years, however, was the battle between the school committee and District Fourteen.

District Fourteen had been troublesome before. In 1839 and 1840 the town and district argued over who was to pay for the moving of a school house to a new location. The town won. In 1847 the town meeting permitted a group of people to transfer a portion of the school money from District Fourteen to District Three, a move hardly calculated to improve relations between the town and district.[95] These struggles between District Fourteen and the town represent the tensions between the old and new parts of Groton. District Fourteen was a commercial part of the town. Tables 2 and 3 list the occupations and property valuation of the fathers of children at school in District Fourteen in 1852, the first year in which registers could be obtained. The tables imply that District Fourteen was non-agricultural, commercial, and peopled largely by artisans of little wealth. This conclusion is reinforced by the probable location of District Fourteen. The only map with school district boundaries that could be located was drawn in 1830. On this map there were only thirteen districts. But Districts Twelve and Thirteen were near the side of the town that eventually became

Table 2. Occupation of parents of children at school
in Groton, District Fourteen, 1852[a]

Occupation	Number	Percent
Professional	0	0
Business[b]	2	8.3
Artisan	15	62.5
Laborer	3	12.5
Farmer	1	4.2
None listed (no father)	3	12.5
Total	24	100

Source: 1850 manuscript census.
   [a] Table represents 31 out of 49 children attending, or 63.3 percent, and 24 out of an estimated 37 families, or 64.9 percent.
   [b] The two fathers listed under business were an innholder and a teamster.

Table 3. Distribution of value of real estate among parents of children at school in Groton, District Fourteen, 1852[a]

Value	Number	Percent
$0–999	15	62.5
$1,000–4,999	9	37.5
$5,000 or more	0	0
Total	24	100

Source: 1850 manuscript census.
[a] See note a, Table 2.

Groton Junction. The one large chunk of unpopulated land was the portion of the town that within a decade became the Junction, and this makes it reasonable to suppose that the next district created, District Fourteen, was located in the newly developing section of the town.[96]

The controversy in the 1850–51 school year arose when District Fourteen took it upon itself to hire a teacher without consulting the town school comimttee. The Revised Statutes of the Commonwealth of Massachusetts unambiguously stated that teachers first selected by the prudential committee in charge of a district had to be approved by the town school committee. "In direct and palpable violation of these plain enactments, the gentleman acting as a prudential committee for District No. 14, employed a person and put her in charge of one of its schools, without the knowledge or approval of the superintending committee." When the school committee learned of this act, they assumed the prudential committeeman intended to establish a private school, but they "learned from his own lips that he had established it as a public school, and that its expenses would be defrayed by public money." In the "most friendly manner" the town committee informed him of the illegality of his actions and urged him to discontinue the school. He refused, and the town informed him that they would themselves establish a public school. The committee also sent "a respectful note to the person whom he had employed as an instructor, desiring her to relinquish her charge without delay, but it was treated with silent contempt." The town committee then hired a teacher and prepared to open a school in the district.[97]

But the prudential committeeman did not accept defeat. "The key of the door opening into the school-room was withheld," and another "school was opened in close proximity to the school-house, purporting to be a free school, and the same person who had illegally assumed to instruct the public school, officiated as the teacher." "Vigorous efforts were made to draw away the children from the public school and prejudice the minds of parents against it." The legitimate teacher received insulting "anonymous letters" that threatened legal action. But she carried on and "accomplished as great an amount of good as could reasonably be expected under such disadvantageous circumstances." The town committee's difficulty was compounded by the town treasurer, who refused to pay the teacher they had appointed in spite of the fact that "she was justly and legally entitled" to her salary. Consequently, the town committee's teacher started prosecution against the town, and the town was faced with an expensive, clearly losing, legal battle. The school committee in no uncertain terms censured the treasurer, doubting that he possessed the authority "to determine what number of duly qualified teachers ought to be compensated for their services, and what number ought not to be." [98]

During the winter term the situation in District Fourteen did not improve. The town school committee assumed the job of the prudential committee since the person supposed to act in the latter capacity "gave . . . no intimation that he regarded himself as sustaining any official relation whatever, to the District." The town hired two "competent instructors," and one committeeman called on Mr. Shattuck, the prudential committeeman, to obtain the keys to the school and the wood-house. But Mr. Shattuck refused to hand over the keys, and the town committee had to "force the locks in order to gain admittance." This was done and the school made ready. "But on arriving at the school-house on Monday morning with our teachers, we found the doors locked against us, and a company of men standing around the door of the wood-house, for the purpose, apparently of preventing us by force from entering that building." Rather than use force the town committee temporarily obtained fuel from another source. "Ultimately, however," they "were compelled to use force in entering the wood-house, that the District might avail itself of the wood which had been provided for its use." Still "repeated assaults were made on the wood-house by fastening the door, until the District called a meeting, and appointed a committee to prevent if possible a repetition of similar acts." The overtly hostile acts ended, but Mr. Shattuck sent the town committee's instructors letters "implicitly forbidding them to enter the school-house, if they would avoid the penalties threatened by law for housebreaking." The instructors ignored the letters and carried on as best they could.[99]

The school committee claimed they had had "no private ends to answer nor private piques to gratify. Contention and strife are not congenial to our taste," and they proffered to their antagonists "the hand of kindness and affection." [100] But in spite of the proffered hand strains remained between District Fourteen and the town. For instance, in 1853 the town meeting appointed a committee to determine why District Fourteen had received more money than had been voted it. The report of the committee the next year was accepted and put on file.[101] The earlier struggle with District Fourteen was important because the success of the district would set a precedent whose consequences would destroy public education. If prudential committees could "employ instructors, and place them in charge of our public schools without their being examined and approved by the superintending committee, then the best system of public instruction existing in our country will be prostrated in the dust." [102] In spite of its humorous qualities, the struggle between District Fourteen and the town was significant. It illustrated, first, the tensions between the newly developing industrial and the old agricultural section of the town. Second, it revealed the magnitude of the resistance to the establishment of a town high school, which would eventually eliminate the power and autonomy of the districts.

Surely, however, prudential committeeman Shattuck must have known that the town committee would oppose his flagrant flouting of state law, and hence he must have desired to make a deliberate test of the committee's strength. His reasons can more easily be understood after a consideration of the movement to establish a high school.

The politics of high school establishment were extremely complicated in Groton. Between 1851 and 1859 town meetings passed and tabled a number of contradictory motions. In 1851 the meeting "passed over" a motion to establish a high school; in 1854 it accepted a committee's report that it was not expedient to establish a high school at present; later the same year it referred another motion to establish a high school to a different committee and the next year accepted and printed its favorable report. Backed by the report of the committee, the town voted to appoint another committee to select a site for the high school but not to spend any money before gaining the approval of the town at its next meeting.[103] But the encouragement was short-lived; in 1855 two motions were indefinitely postponed: to send all children to Lawrence Academy and pay the tuition of the poor and, second, to establish schools equivalent to high schools in the districts.[104] In November the town voted to postpone any further consideration of a high school for one year, but early in 1857 it voted to reconsider that motion and appointed a committee to begin establishing a high school. Shortly after appointing the committee to go ahead with the high school another town meeting indefinitely postponed all motions regarding a high school, and at its next meeting the town voted to postpone the proposed high school at Groton Center for one year.[105] Finally, in 1859 the town voted to begin a high school in a brick building to be built as a combination school and town hall. This time the high school supporters managed to defeat a reconsideration vote.[106]

High school supporters were led by the school committee, which kept up its appeals throughout the years of changing votes. In the school committee's view the villain holding up educational progress in Groton was, aside from District Fourteen, Lawrence Academy. In 1854 the school committee report launched another withering attack at the academy, which, they maintained, divided "the interest of parents" and withdrew "many of the advanced pupils from the common schools." The influence of the academy was, therefore, "prejudicial" to the interests of the public school system and, by implication, to the establishment of a high school.[107] The 1855 report also included a lengthy harangue aimed at the academy. This denunciation ended, interestingly, with a revelation of the allegedly egalitarian sentiments of the committee. "Once," the report contended, "a collegiate education was almost essential to social distinction in Massachusetts." Happily that time had passed and now "the highest honors" were open to graduates of the common school. "The trader, the farmer, the mechanic, at present crowd our halls of legislation," the committee noted with satisfaction, perhaps thinking of their ex-member, now governor, George Boutwell, and soon the day would arrive when "the day-laborer, so-called, will put in his reasonable claim for greater social consideration." The report claimed with ill-concealed pleasure that "professional men . . . must not unfrequently stand back. Men of deeds rather than professions, will often take precedence of them." [108] The sheltered and privileged students at the academy were thus served notice and if they knew their own best interest, would quickly transfer to a common school.

The school committee was indeed trying to find a way of striking effectively at the academy. A passage added to the academy catalogue in 1855 indicates some of the bases of competition between the two, for the academy described the comprehensiveness and quality of its education in terms that made a high school seem superfluous. "The Classical Department includes the studies required for admission to college, and instruction in French, Spanish, and other modern languages. The English Department comprehends, in its two courses of study, the common branches taught in the elementary schools, and all the higher branches of a complete English education. In this department special pains will be taken to prepare teachers of common schools for their work, and to furnish young men with what they need in business and commercial pursuits." [109]

The 1855 school committee report also contained a discussion of the relation of education to economic development, for the committee believed that settlers of the "best character" would be attracted to a town largely by its schools. If Groton wanted to grow in wealth and population, the implication was clear. A third major argument in the 1855 report was the necessity of indoctrinating the young with Christian morality.[110] This point was also the subject of a lengthy lecture in 1857, because by that date the Groton school committee, undoubtedly shocked by the transformation of Groton Junction, had become thoroughly alarmed at the social alterations they saw rapidly transforming their town and state. In their eyes Massachusetts was rather like the Wild West. Men were relying "upon the knife and the revolver rather than upon law, for their personal safety. Lawlessness [was] rife everywhere." The effects of social chaos on the schools were compounded by the fact that "family government" was "more and more declining." If the family failed to enforce rules within the home and to cooperate with the school, the latter would be left helpless. A moral renaissance was required to avoid the destruction of society and the dissolution of a civilized community.[111] Unfortunately, the committee noted in their next report, parental cooperation had not increased, and when a community "feels more interest in the training of their colts than their children, the character of their schools may be easily inferred." To the committee the failure of the family was not, then, the sole responsibility of the poor Irish.

In 1859, the year in which the high school proponents were finally permanently victorious, the committee renewed their case for public secondary education. The committee admitted the difficulties created by a widely scattered population, but they felt that a high school was, nevertheless, feasible. The report repeated the former contention that the high school combined with consolidation was an economic innovation and that the high school would democratically spread to all the advantages presently available to the wealthy. The committee countered in advance a possible rebuttal that "prejudices between different districts . . . will interfere with such arrangements." If this were true, "the sooner they are done away with the better." The school committee, representing the parental state, would engineer social harmony in the most efficient way: namely, by bringing "the scholars of the different districts, as much as possible together." [112]

The thesis that district jealousies were hampering the creation of the high school was supported by the *Mercury*. An early proponent of the high school, the *Mercury* based an 1855 argument on the need for intelligent citizens and the difficulty of paying both tuition at the academy and school taxes. After the initial vote in favor of the high school in 1857 the *Mercury* tried to convince townspeople not to reconsider the motion. As in other battles within the town, the opposition was coming from Groton Junction. People from the Junction "with some others in remote parts of the town, have caused a warrant to be posted for another meeting . . . to see if the town will not reconsider the vote." The reconsideration move stemmed from the fact that "some of the people of this village cherish a bitter feeling towards everybody in town" and were consequently objecting to what the newspaper claimed was a very small tax.[113] A large part of the objection, unmentioned by the *Mercury,* was probably the decision to build the high school in Groton Center, a far distance from Groton Junction, which was becoming the center of the industrial and commercial activity and population of the town. In other towns reports implied and stated that outlying districts opposed high schools because children could not reach them. Groton was unusual in that its outlying district was populous and dense enough to sponsor a cohesive and, for eight years, successful movement against the Center.

Significantly, the District Fourteen battle occurred in the same year as a serious plea by the town school committee for the establishment of a high school. This coincidence of date implies that the Junction's opposition to both the high school and the town supervision of district hiring practices were part of the resistance of the district to a loss of autonomy. Probably the resistance sprang from Junction residents' resentment of the older section of the town. After all, as the quotation cited earlier from the *Mercury* indicates, the reluctance of the old residents to sell land to Junction manufacturers retarded the growth of that part of the town, and the populous and prosperous Junction was undoubtedly supplying a disproportionate share of town taxes. Residents probably felt that their contribution to the town treasury coupled with their economic distinctiveness entitled them to both an increased share in the management of their own affairs and a chance to benefit equally from any new town educational facilities.

Yet the alignment of forces in the district-town fight was odd. Surely, the rhetoric of educational reform and the correlates of high school establishment suggest that it should have been the industrial, urban Junction, not the agricultural Village, that urged the establishment of a public secondary school. The town committee did use arguments stressing the relation between the high school and economic growth, but perhaps these were contentions thrown out to convert the stubborn residents of the Junction. At stake really was the control of the town. If the Junction could flout the school committee and prevent the centralization of power represented by a high school in the Village, too far away for them to use, then they could effectively control their own educational system. And this might be only the harbinger of future issues. This assumption of power by the district, this loss of accustomed control over the town, is probably what the Village and school committee worked so energetically to prevent. Thus, the battle of District Fourteen and part of the fight for a high school represented a major power struggle within the community.

To point out the elements of a power struggle in the district-town controversies is to raise a major question concerning the use of ideology by the committee. They phrased their goals not in terms of power but in terms of the accepted and respectable ideology, even though in this case it bore little relation to their own economic interests. Ideology was a kind of cloak with which they could cover their less idealistic motives, an unanswerable set of arguments to hurl at their opponents, who, in turn, had nothing with which to reply. Ideology became the rationalization of interest; and it served well, for the committee won.

The extent to which ideology masked a power struggle little concerned with educational issues is revealed by the early history of the town of Ayer. When Groton Junction became Ayer in 1871, opposition to a high school seemed to vanish, and the new town started its school system with no districts and with a high school. Indeed, in their first report the Ayer school committee listed improvement of the high school as their first priority.[114]

The *Mercury* agreed with the school committee that district jealousy was hampering the establishment of a high school. Yet it rejected the argument that the academy was a hindrance. "The story concocted that those interested in the Academy are averse to the High School is all moonshine," wrote the editor. "So far from it," he continued, "they encouraged it — voted for it, and one of its benefactors, Mr. A. A. Lawrence, wrote a letter advising the Groton people to push ahead and establish it." [115]

Still, the presence of an academy offering an equivalent education was a major hurdle to high school promoters. Like most of the other school committee appeals for a high school, the 1859 plea appeared in the same year that the academy posed a new challenge to public education. The catalogue for 1859 contained an announcement implying some exaggeration in the school committee's assertion that the benefits of the academy were open only to the wealthy. In an announcement entitled "Aid to young men fitting for college," the catalogue declared:

> Provision is made by funds of the Academy, given for this purpose, to aid those who need assistance in obtaining a liberal education. Those who receive the benefit have their tuition remitted for the first term of their preparatory studies. Afterwards, they receive a sum not exceeding one dollar per week, including their tuition. The conditions are, good moral character, talents, and scholarship, and the *avowed purpose to obtain* a liberal education. No preference is given to any one of the learned professions; and by the will of the donor, the late William Lawrence, no discrimination is made in favor of any denomination.[116]

Thus, the Groton boy whose parents could not afford the thirty-five to forty-five cents a week tuition could still be prepared for college.

Groton High School, which opened on March 11, 1860, surrendered in one respect to the academy. It offered only an "English" or non-collegiate course,[117] and the school committee diatribes against the academy ended. The academy, however, did not give up its English curriculum and therefore still competed with the high school, for both offered the same sort of training. In Groton the struggle for a high school masked a struggle for control of the town. Much of the rhetoric of the anti-academy and anti-district fight throughout the state probably served the same purpose. In Groton as in Beverly the fight for a high school reflected a deep communal division. But in Groton the greatest tension was not between social classes but between sections of the town. Nevertheless, even in Groton educational reform and innovation was essentially an imposition by one group upon another, an imposition only partly prompted by altruistic and humanitarian concerns.

Except in the case of Groton Junction it is not yet clear why reform and innovation had to be impositions. There is evidence that citizens seemed reluctant to take the largess offered them by reformers, that they did not share reformers' faith in the advantages of education, but we still cannot account for the phenomena that we can identify. To make the nature of opposition clearer it is necessary to return to Beverly.

The Working Class against Reform

Recall that in Beverly the citizens of least wealth and least occupational prestige successfully opposed the high school. Recall, too, that the high school was strongly supported by those at the other end of the social and economic scale. The supporters used arguments similar to those expounded by high school promoters around the state. The opponents were, to understate the case, less vocal, at least in print. The least affluent citizens of Beverly recorded their opposition to the high school in votes, not in words. No record of their reasons for opposing the persuasive rhetoric of promoters exists. Yet good reasons for opposition can be inferred from a consideration of their social and economic situation. The abolition of Beverly high school occurred amidst the greatest social crisis in the history of the town. In the same week that they voted four to one to abolish the high school, the shoemakers of Beverly, the dominant occupational group in the town, went on strike, and so did thousands of other shoemakers in Essex County. The walkout by Essex County shoemakers in 1860 was the largest strike in the United States before the Civil War.[118]

Beverly had been a small and homogeneous community until the advent of the railroad in 1840. From the 1840's through the mid-1850's a number of manufacturing enterprises started in the town.. The industries were of various types, and it seemed as though Beverly would turn into a small but diversified manufacturing center. During the depression of 1857, however, many of the new, small industries with little capital failed, never to revive. Equally good harbors and better facilities for manufacturing, such as water power for mills, existed elsewhere in Massachusetts. Only for the shoe industry, which it could supply with many skilled workers, did Beverly provide an attractive outlet for capital. (See Appendix D for economic and social statistics on Beverly.)

As Beverly developed into a one-industry town it experienced the grave social consequences that accompanied the transformation of shoemaking. It was in the 1850's and 1860's that shoemaking became mechanized. Factory production replaced the skilled craftsman. Technological change hit shoemakers with the impact of modern day automation. With the introduction of machines the number of shoes manufactured per shoemaker rose rapidly, and the increased output soon exceeded the demands of the market. As apprenticeship ceased to be necessary, manufacturers hired unskilled, untrained workers who swelled the ranks of shoemakers to overflowing. Overproduction and a plethora of workmen produced a crisis in the industry, and the price of shoes declined drastically. In this situation, manufacturers introduced a sizable pay cut, and the shoemakers struck.[119]

The shoemakers of Beverly left no written records, and the timid town newspaper tried to pretend that the strike did not exist. To find the attitude of the strikers one must turn to Lynn newspapers. In both places shoemaking dominated the economy, and it is reasonable to assume that within the same county technological developments were closely paralleled from town to town. Moreover, within the area that serviced the Boston market prices would be similar. One can assume that the attitude of the Lynn shoemakers was shared by the hundreds of their colleagues who struck in Beverly, and it is the attitude of the strikers that is important, because this reveals the social gulf that widened with industrialization and contributed to the abolition of Beverly high school.[120]

Articles in pro-strike papers stressed other than strictly economic grievances. One writer proclaimed to the mechanics of Lynn that "those occupying a position in society different from yours . . . have wantonly and ill-advisedly insulted all that is manly in your breasts"; [121] and in a very real sense the strike was about manliness, about the preservation of honor. Another writer delineated the grievances of the strikers: the tensions and opinions engendered by the strike were "the unerring indications of a social wrong, felt to be such by the whole community, yet so interwoven with our social condition that its reform has become the most perplexing problem of the age." The "wrong" was the increase in both the inequality of the distribution of wealth and the loss of independence by the artisans. "Great fortunes" were being concentrated "under the control of a few manufacturers" in Lynn while "hundreds of workmen" were "gradually crowded from the independent positions they formerly occupied." Shoemakers, noted the writer, were "men of more or less means." In fact, as a group they probably owned more property than the manufacturers; clearly this was no strike of a proletariat. But shoemakers were being compelled to relinquish "the luxuries, next the conveniences, and finally the necessaries of life." [122]

Two consequences stemmed from the deterioration in their position: while the country became richer, the shoemakers became poorer; and they were progressively unable to take advantage of the new educational and communal facilities being introduced. "We have better streets, better schools, and more wholesome sanitary regulations," one article declared, "but we do not get an education commensurate with the increase of our facilities." Children were being "removed from school two or three years too early," and an alarming "number of young men and women" were sinking "into early graves." Why? The writer rejected the thesis that shoemakers removed children from school through cupidity:

For every parent who took a boy of thirteen from school for selfish reasons, a hundred did so from necessity. "The parent finds the expenses of his household constantly increasing, while the wages of his labor are steadily diminishing," and he has no choice but to submit to that which he considers a wrong to his family. But in the wonderful, inventive nineteenth century, "to say that such a thing is either right or necessary, is a libel upon the age." The promise of industrialization was being betrayed; "the benefits resulting from a proper division of labor and the application of machinery [were] monopolized by the few, instead of being diffused in just proportions." The author stressed, in his conclusion, not the drop in wages, but the tendency "plainly to break down the independence of the laborer, and to abridge the various sources of his social enjoyment." [123]

The protest of the shoemakers was an agonized remonstrance against the loss of personal and financial independence, and indeed, of a whole way of life. One old shoemaker, according to the editor of the pro-strike paper, perfectly summed up the issue of the strike in a single phrase: "Once it was *honorable* to labor, now it is a disgrace." [124] The great Essex County shoe strike was a last protest against the modern world of the machine and factory. To a certain extent the shoemakers shared the ambivalence of educational promoters. They saw the promise of a better life in the machine and in the process of social change occurring around them. Yet they, especially, felt the hard consequences of mechanization, and it is likely that they swiftly became less ambivalent, that in their minds the machine became tarnished to an extent never shared by promoters like the Rantouls and Boydens.

Thus, the shoemakers who voted against Beverly High School had a rather different orientation from the Rantouls and Boydens. For the core of opposition to Beverly High School the future was not promising. The shoemakers were the propertied, once moderately comfortable and independent group whose life was being altered by technological development. For the shoemaker the past, certainly, was better than the ominous future. And it was an urban-industrial future, precisely, that the high school was supposed to promote. In Beverly, Rufus Putnam among others had spread the doctrine, prevalent also throughout the state, that the high school would promote economic development. If this were true, if the shoemaker accepted the logic of the educational promoter, then the last institution he would want to establish would be a public high school. Moreover, to property owners whose incomes had been reduced, as many shoemakers' were, any proposal that would raise taxes would hardly be appealing. Besides, to what avail was the democratic argument advanced by Boyden? The high school might be there, but, as the shoemaker in Lynn pointed out, modern economic conditions were so hard that children were forced to begin work precisely at the age when they could benefit from a high school.

Farmers, too, probably would be moved by some of these arguments. For them the advance of industrial society offered little but a lure to their children. As Rantoul observed, more and more boys were leaving the parental farm for the city. The decided weighting of high school opponents' property toward real estate rather than personal estate symbolized their roots in a community being torn apart by the forces backed by the supporters. The high school issue brought into focus the different orientations toward social development within a nineteenth century New England town.

At the time of the high school vote the shoemakers in particular were hostile to the representatives of the manufacturing and commercial interests, who had lowered wages. Yet the tradition of machine breaking and direct physical assault, prominent in other countries, did not spread to America in this period. In voting to abolish the high school, a favorite innovation of their antagonists, the shoemakers had an opportunity to vent their anger in a perfectly legal way. The shoemakers, it has been argued, and most likely other groups of little wealth as well, were hardly enthusiastic about the social and economic alteration taking place around them.

But industrialism is a diffuse antagonist; it is hard to assault directly. The high school, explicitly billed as the harbinger of manufacturing and urban growth, was a convenient issue to attack.[125]

For three reasons, then, the Beverly citizens voted to abolish the high school: first, people, those without children especially, protested the raising of taxes; second, the least affluent citizens felt that the high school would not benefit their children; third, they were hostile both to the wealthy leaders of the town and to the onset of industrialism. The educational promoters, who were by and large the wealthy and prominent citizens, failed to preserve the high school because they advanced arguments unacceptable to the less prosperous citizens and because they overestimated their own powers of leadership. The supporters based their pro–high school arguments on mobility and economic growth; what they failed to see was that their own values were not shared by the entire community. The promoters who stressed mobility and wealth as products of education appealed to exactly the wrong values in terms of an outlook skeptical of progress. A strike was some evidence of social division. More subtle, but more devastating, was the community leaders' failure to perceive the weakness in their own rhetoric and the limits of their prestige and power. Their probable assumption that the rest of the town would docilely follow their advice was rudely disproven. In the first week of May 1860, the shoemakers of Beverly staged a dual revolt against these communal leaders. They struck, literally, at the source of their income, and they rejected their favorite educational innovation.

The underlying cause of both the establishment and abolition of Beverly High School was the shifting economic base and the consequent social division in both the town and the state. It was to keep pace with these changes that promoters urged an extended educational system; it was to assure opportunity for the individual within an altered economy that the high school was argued; it was to reunite a splintering community that a high school was necessary. The unraveling of the social fabric that accompanied the growth of a manufacturing economy heightened the distance between the members of the community; it produced the decaying economic position of craftsmen and became the source of the antagonisms that finally erupted in the great shoe strike and the abolition of the high school.

How typical was the Beverly experience? Can we generalize from it about educational controversy throughout the state of Massachusetts? The geographic location of Beverly on the coast and its dependence upon one industry are factors that make it somewhat distinctive. Nevertheless, the underlying causes of communal dissension, the impact of the introduction of manufacturing upon society, occurred throughout the state, often with more swiftness than in Beverly. Attitudes toward social change were shared by educational reformers throughout Massachusetts. Everywhere the high school was urged for the same reasons. The problems raised by industrialism, too, were similar. Not only the large body of shoemakers but the hand-loom weavers and other craftsmen were affected adversely by the coming of the factory and machine. The tensions that erupted in Beverly were inherent throughout most of the towns in the commonwealth. Because of a conjunction of circumstances they became particularly visible in Beverly in March 1860. The events in Beverly formed one of those moments that illuminate for the historian widespread smoldering controversies. The nature of the controversy in Beverly, moreover, suggests that the identification of antagonists by older historians was essentially correct. In spite of the predictable and continuing parsimony of childless taxpayers and the mixed reaction of certain middling social groups, two distinct clusters of antagonists emerge: prominent, prestigious leaders and a working class. But the antagonists' attitudes defined by older historians must be reversed: the Beverly experience reveals that one dynamic of educational controversy was the attempt of social leaders to impose innovation upon a reluctant working class.

Predictably, the high schools forced upon reluctant towns met

many problems. During the first few years after the founding of
a high school committees usually reported euphorically on the
achievements of the new institution,[126] but after a time difficulties
generally arose. By itself, separation from younger children failed
to make the older ones more obedient, and discipline was frequently a serious problem within the high school.[127] Attendance
and tardiness were two issues related to the problem of discipline.
Indeed, irregular attendance and truancy were the most persistent
and common complaints of school committees, and, in some towns,
the worst offenders were high school students.[128]

School committees were virtually obsessed with the problems of
punctual and regular attendance.[129] It is not unreasonable to assume
that these concerns were based on real problems. However, the
concern with time and reliability implies that schools were to serve
the new society in part by producing those habits particularly
needed in the work force and in an urban population. A writer in
the *Massachusetts Teacher* asserted:

> That the habit of prompt action in the performance of the duty
> required of the boy, by the teacher at school, becomes in the
> man of business confirmed; thus system and order characterize
> the employment of the day laborer. He must begin each half day
> with as much promptness as he drops his tools at the close of
> it; and he must meet every appointment and order during the
> hours of the day with no less precision. It is in this way that
> regularity and economy of time have become characteristic of
> our community, as appears in the running 'on time' of long
> trains on our great network of railways; the strict regulations
> of all large manufacturing establishments; as well as the daily
> arrangements of our school duties . . . Thus, what has been
> instilled in the mind of the pupil, as a principle, becomes
> thoroughly recognized by the man as of the first importance in
> the transaction of business.[130]

Indeed, the problem of transforming agrarian habits in which precision and promptness are less emphasized into the traits necessary to conduct city life and large scale manufacturing is characteristic of urbanizing and industrializing societies.[131] Without regular and prompt attention neither the city and factory nor the school can function adequately. Industrialists explicitly recognized that the school served as a means of disciplining the work force. This was patently, sometimes even crudely, clear in the responses that Mann and Boutwell received in 1841 and 1859 to circulars questioning manufacturers on the value they saw in educated labor. Two examples make this evident. From Lowell in 1841 H. Bartlett, who had "been engaged, for nearly ten years, in manufacturing, and . . . had the constant charge of from 400 to 900 persons," replied in part: "I have never considered mere knowledge . . . as the only advantage derived from a good Common School education." Workers with more education possessed "a higher and better state of morals, [were] more orderly and respectful in their deportment, and more ready to comply with the wholesome and necessary regulations of an establishment." Perhaps most important, "in times of agitation, on account of some change in regulations or wages, I have always looked to the most intelligent, best educated and the most moral for support." On the other hand, "the ignorant and uneducated I have generally found the most turbulent and troublesome, acting under the impulse of excited passion and jealousy." Similarly, in 1859 William B. Whiting, who had entered a cotton mill at the age of eleven and had, over a thirty-year period, worked his way upward, wrote that the educated always try, "by diligence and a willing acquiescence in necessary regulations, to merit the good opinion of their employers and the community"; they "secure . . . by the same means, the respect and confidence of their fellows," and "oftentimes exert a conservative influence in periods of excitement of great value pecuniarily and morally." [132] The educated, in short, were seen as company men.

Some school committees also had a problem rather different from irregular attendance. Many parents applied steady pressure to the committees to lower the entrance requirements for high schools, thus threatening the standards of the new schools.[133] Parents mobilized personal influence and pressure against the committees; in sociological terms they were emphasizing ascribed rather than achieved qualities, and it was precisely this emphasis that schoolmen were trying to eliminate from the educational system. Likewise, complaints about the unfair advantages academies offered children of the wealthy and complaints about the hiring of unqualified friends and relatives as teachers were protests against rewards based on ascription rather than achievement. The ideal school system was graded, promotions were equally open to all solely on the basis of merit, teachers were hired for their professional qualifications; this ideal school system reflected a belief that status based on achievement should pervade society. In a rural, agricultural society labor is divided within the family; for the most part jobs require little special skill and formal training; responsibility is based largely on age; the social hierarchy rests mainly on custom; and few pressures force an alteration of traditional attitudes. In such a society ascription forms a relatively powerful criterion for the assignment of status. Industrialization, on the other hand, dissolves the traditional social fabric; many tasks become highly specialized and technical competence becomes of paramount importance. To cope adequately with its business an industrial, urban society must award relative priority to achieved rather than ascribed qualities. Achievement is of course a fundamental criterion for reward in democratic theory, but the stress on achievement in this period is particularly significant. The transition of the state from an agricultural-commercial to an industrial economy required a corresponding shift in the basis of social valuation. By trying to institutionalize achieved status through public education and to indoctrinate parents with its virtues, schoolmen again were facilitating economic change through the transformation of social attitudes.*

The virtues that education promoters attached to schooling apparently did not appeal to the people as much as they had hoped. In the mid-sixties school committees were still complaining of a parental apathy that resisted the efforts and achievements of educational reformers. The Groton school committee, for one, virtually confessed failure. Public interest in education had not increased, and how the school could be maintained without this enthusiasm and support was uncertain.[134]

In fact, the high school was failing to serve the community in the ways its advocates had predicted. Promoters had emphasized that the high school would promote social mobility, unify and civilize communities, awaken and sustain a community-wide interest in education, and raise the value of real estate. In reality, the high school did none of these things: the statistical analysis, the facts of high school attendance, the developments in Beverly and Groton, and the complaints of schoolmen all make this clear. Only a minority of the children in a community, and those mainly from the more well-to-do sectors, attended the high school. The

---

* David McClelland started an extensive cross-cultural examination of children's readers with the hypothesis that achieved status would be more prominent in rapidly developing countries. This notion, he states, is agreed upon by all sociological theorists. His findings, however, do not confirm the hypothesis. Nevertheless, there is a hypothesis that he does not investigate. McClelland considers countries in 1925 and 1950. Lumped together impartially are countries at very different *stages* of economic development. What he does not consider, and what this study suggests, is that a stress on achieved status may be a characteristic of societies *in the process* of transition from an agricultural to an industrial economy. The process of industrialization itself, bringing with it major changes in all the relationships of men, may necessitate a shift in social attitudes during the period that Rostow calls the "take off." Later, as industrialism becomes firmly established and self-perpetuating, as re-orientation of the population becomes no longer necessary, new bases of status may emerge, new distinctions become hardened, and the stress on achievement less emphasized. David C. McClelland, *The Achieving Society* (New York, 1961), pp. 183–186.

high school could not serve as a means of boosting many poor children up the economic ladder.

The high school was, however, relevant to the mobility of middle-class children. For middle-class boys the high school probably served as both a means of status maintenance and an entree into the business world. Information in school registers has been found concerning thirteen boys who left Somerville High School between 1856 and 1860. Of these, eight became clerks, two entered business, and three became apprentices. For all but one of the apprentices the jobs represented an occupation different from that of their fathers, who with the exception of three businessmen were artisans and farmers. These seven, sons of artisans and farmers, very likely saw the high school as a way of helping to retain a middle-class status at a time when mechanization and other economic alterations made the future of their fathers' occupations less secure. They may have hoped, as well, that through business they could rise above the social level of their parents.

The high school also had obvious uses for middle-class girls, and substantially more girls than boys attended. The high schools usually offered preparation for teaching; and teaching was undoubtedly the most attractive vocational goal for the middle-class girl who wanted to earn some money because all the other occupations populated by large numbers of females were manual, arduous, and decidedly lower-class. According to the state census of 1865, the largest number of employed females, 27,393, were domestics; next came operatives (meaning factory workers), 20,152; third came teachers, 6,050. Other groups of more than one thousand females were, in order of size, seamstresses, shoe workers, tailoresses, dressmakers, straw and palm leaf workers, milliners, laundresses, nurses, and clerks. The middle-class girl who wanted to work at something respectable had little choice; teaching it almost had to be. For girls who had no intention of becoming gainfully employed the high school must have offered a relatively painless way of passing the time until they came of marrying age.[135]

Thus, the fable that the high school served the entire community was naturally attractive to middle-class parents because it justified having the entire community support an institution most useful to the middle-class. Through the high school they could spread among the population at large the burden of educating their children. The ideology of communal benefit served wealthy groups well too. Prosperous parents, owners of successful businesses for instance, may have been moved by the same concerns as the Boston merchants. For them the high school would provide a fine way of occupying their sons during the years of adolescence when an extended apprenticeship was no longer necessary. Moreover, the most articulate spokesmen for high schools, often also economic promoters, were deeply ambivalent toward the society for which they were responsible; and they sought innovations that would simultaneously promote economic growth and prevent the consequences that industrialism had brought in other societies, especially England. The high school was an ideal innovation because it would allegedly serve both these ends. Promoters' attachment to this ideology gave them a good psychic reason for avoiding a confrontation with the actual facts of high school attendance and with the impact of a drive for educational innovation upon a community. To have admitted the disparity between theory and actuality would have raised too many haunting questions, too many doubts about the real nature of the promoters' own impact upon society.

To recognize that the high school did not meet its goals, to suggest the functions that it did in fact serve is not to explain *why* it failed or where reform went wrong. Obviously, the ideology of reform was confused, since it simultaneously advocated and damned urban, industrial society. The two sides of the ideology offered a set of highly incompatible goals. Nevertheless, reformers might have argued that it was the obstacles within old towns rather than the incompatibility of their goals that had frustrated their efforts. If only they could have a chance to build a system from scratch, then they might produce the small city on a hill of which American communal leaders had dreamed since the seventeenth century. The opportunity of constructing a school system in a new town would provide a test case for the viability of reform theory. In Lawrence reformers were given their chance.

4. LAWRENCE: FROM MODEL TOWN
TO PRIMARY SCHOOL OF VICE

The early history of Lawrence is the story of the fading of a utopian vision before the realities of urban-industrial life. In 1830, even in 1846, Lawrence was a strip of land beside the Merrimack River. In 1865 Lawrence was a booming factory city. The onslaught of urban problems is predictable in the rapid creation of a large city from a river bank, and this fact alone would make Lawrence an interesting study; but Lawrence is particularly fascinating because, as much as Brook Farm or a twentieth century English New Town, it was the conscious and deliberate creation of men who had a utopian vision. Pecuniary gain was certainly a motive, but the founders of Lawrence were also inspired with a vision of a new type of community: a modern, industrial city in which would prevail the harmony and morality of the Lawrence brothers' boyhood memories of Groton. In Lawrence the contradiction at the heart of the social thought of Massachusetts educators was clearly exposed. Education failed to create the country in the city: with the best educational system that could be devised Lawrence still developed the universal diseases of urban life. The early history of Lawrence also suggests that education was not the driving force in industrial development. The labor power that built and manned the great mills and factories was not the loving hand of the artist-laborer but, for the most part, the untutored efforts of uneducated Irish immigrants and their children. Contrary to Mann and Boutwell's arguments and surveys stressing the productivity of educated labor, Lawrence combined industrial greatness with mass ignorance.

The first American industrialists were keenly aware of the misery and degradation characteristic of the great European manufacturing centers, and they had no intention of recapitulating the experience of the old world in the new. On a visit to England Nathan Appleton, a leader in early textile manufacture, asked whether the "degradation" of the operatives "was the result of the peculiar occupation, or of other and distinct causes." He concluded there was no reason "why this peculiar description of labour should vary in its effects upon character from all other occupations." Part of the problem in Europe stemmed from a lack of concern for the morality and welfare of the operatives, and American manufacturers determined to prevent the development of social misery through a paternalistic supervision of their workers. In the first place, they assumed that their labor force would come not from the lowest levels of society but from New England farms. They planned to create a work force of farm girls who would spend a few years in a mill accumulating money for a dowry. In the second place, they determined to oversee the girls carefully and, consequently, erected the now famous boarding houses in which the conduct of the girls was to be strictly supervised.[136] For the first few years at least the system seemed to work, and Appleton felt that America had avoided copying the British experience. "The contrast in the character of our manufacturing population compared with that of Europe," he wrote, "has been the admiration of the most intelligent strangers who have visited us." [137]

Appleton referred mainly to Waltham and Lowell, but the ideology he represented characterized Lawrence too. According to the most recent historian of the city, it was to be a "model town." "Conceived, built and directed by Boston Brahmins, it was designed to produce cottons and woolens, but to do it in an environment that was physically and morally sound. To Lawrence would come sturdy mechanics to do the city's work and be uplifted in the process." [138] In creating a model town the early years were particularly important. The formative period offered "a golden opportunity . . . of laying a broad and deep foundation for a virtuous and thriving population." A strong and vigilant city government was a necessity: "Let the idea once become prevalent abroad that in Lawrence the reins of government will be holden with a lax, a feeble hand," wrote the editor of the *Lawrence Courier,* "and the better portion of our country will be deterred from coming here." [139] As important as firm government was a good system of schools.

On February 8, 1848, Charles Storrow, a civil engineer, one of the founders and first mayor of Lawrence, wrote Horace Mann a letter outlining both the central role that education was to play in the new city and some of the key assumptions of the founders. Lawrence was to be a controlled environment in which industrial overlords paternally shaped the morals and intellect of a city. Storrow remarked to Mann that since their last meeting, three months previously, the population of Lawrence had doubled and was, at present, six thousand. The population had "come here mostly from New England homes, and therefore" had "New England wants among which schools are first." One of the educational needs of the people with New England wants was a high school; and Storrow told Mann, "Before commencing operations . . . I must see you again and have your advice."

Storrow had decided that Lawrence would be the ideal location for the state's fourth normal school. The area around Lawrence needed a normal school, and Lawrence provided an ideal location since "six railroad lines" would "shortly meet here, by means of which we shall communicate directly with Boston, Salem, Newburyport, Portland, Manchester, N.H., and Lowell." But Storrow also argued his case on grounds higher than geographic accessibility. He asked Mann to "think also for a moment of the influence which such an establishment would exert upon a community like this." In a revealing question Storrow asked: "Where else can you find as here the elements of a society ready to be moulded into a good or an evil shape; nothing to pull down, all to build up; a whole town composed of young people to influence and train as you would a school?" Lawrence was to be a huge school whose mind would be formed by Storrow and his associates. The echoes of the theory of the paternal state are clear. Clear too is a curious mixture of benevolence and hunger for power. Storrow reminded Mann that he himself had commented on the "influence [exerted] in a remote and uncultivated district by the presence and effort of a single well educated teacher of agreeable manners and elevated moral character." Storrow continued, "Let then the crowd of young women soon to assemble here see before their eyes such examples." Through the power of example young women would turn willingly to the schools of Lawrence.[140] Thus would Storrow insure the preservation of female virtue, Home and Mother in industrial society.

Table 4 reveals the rapid growth of Lawrence and the predominance of the textile industry. Nearly half of the population, including women and children, were employed in a manufacturing

Table 4. Population and industrial employees, Lawrence, 1855–1865

Category	1855	1865
Population[a]	16,114	21,698
Foreign born	9,383	9,217
Hands employed in		
Cotton industry, male	712	1,012
female	1,873	1,715
Woolen industry, male	1,310	758
female	1,000	1,290
Other industries	2,007	4,216
Total	6,902	8,991

Source: State census of 1850 and 1855; Censuses of Industry, 1855 and 1865.
[a] The population was 8,358 in 1850 and 17,639 in 1860.

industry. Of these employees, over half worked in cotton or woolen mills. The people from "New England homes," however, soon lost their dominance in the population. Seven years after its founding Lawrence was roughly half immigrant, and most of the newcomers were Irish.

The thought and care represented by the creation of the school system reflected the importance Storrow placed on education. In their report for the school year 1848–49 the Lawrence school committee set forth their conception of an ideal school system. Interestingly, one of the members of the first school committee was J. D. Herrick, whose career was a commentary on the assumptions of the leading citizens, who saw little distinction between agencies of social control. Herrick eventually served as superintendent of schools and head of the police force.[141] In the school committee's blueprint for an ideal school system the high school was the apex of a four-stage system of schools. Each stage was of importance to the committee, who claimed, "We would not dispense with one of the series." The report's detailed discussion of school furniture and architecture further emphasized the committee's desire for the most modern and efficient school system possible.[142]

Yet even the best possible school system failed to maintain prosperity, social harmony, and morality. In 1856 the editor of the *Courier* claimed, "It is no use to deny that Lawrence is a very fluctuating and uncertain place of business — today flooding and overflowing every branch of business — tomorrow, withdrawing almost the means of subsistence, from the most cautious enterprises and the most assiduous industry and perseverance."[143] Indeed, the newspapers are studded with reports of depressions and booms, the most disastrous being the depression of 1857 when banks were suspended and, at one time or another, every mill was closed.[144]

Newspapers also reported that immorality and poverty accompanied the failure to maintain a steady prosperity. In 1855 the editor of the *Courier* lamented the low reputation of the city: "As the abode of swindlers, as a stopping place for thieves, as a resort for gamblers, this city is not entirely an unknown quarter of the globe." [145] But the problem had not taken a decade to develop. Even in 1846, during the construction of the city, the *Merrimac Courier* noticed with dismay, "Drunken men stagger and reel through our streets — night is made hideous by their yells, and honest men fear their personal safety." Nor did the problem disappear with time. In 1864 the *Lawrence Sentinel,* for instance, complained of the "immorality and blackguardism exhibited upon our public streets and commons." [146]

Poverty, too, was a serious problem. During the depression of 1857 the president of the Provident Relief Association told of "nine different families, *wholly without food or fire* — the children huddled in bed or perhaps trying to keep warm by the fragments of their scanty stock of furniture, while the thermometer was near or below zero." In 1859 the *Courier* reported another example, supposedly far from atypical. Except for a few odd jobs the father of a family of respectable church members with four children had been unemployed since the depression of 1857, and the family lived on the earnings of two boys, aged eight and twelve. "Their chief articles of food had been potatoes and cabbages, and the woman said no one knew how much she had suffered nights from the cold." [147] With poverty came serious housing problems. Boarding houses for single workers may have been satisfactory, but benevolence did not extend to the tenements for families. In a complaint echoed throughout this period one correspondent to the *Courier* claimed that "the poor whatsoever may be their character, must be crowded into ill-constructed and inconvenient houses, several families under one roof." [148]

The general lament of the newspapers was echoed by schoolmen, who looked with horror at the fate of children in Lawrence. When Lawrence officially became a city in 1853, the pattern of school administration changed, and reports were written henceforth by a paid superintendent elected from the members of the committee. With dismay the first superintendent admitted that the schools had failed to reach large numbers of children. "There are now in the city upwards of *two hundred* boys and girls between five and fifteen years old who keep aloof from school and have no regular employment." The superintendent described the occupation of these children who spent their "time in prowling about shops, alleys and backyards, pilfering swill, fuel, old-iron, and such more valuable articles as happen to be unprotected." Yet, the committee noted, these children were educated. The superintendent had a broad definition of education that included all formative influences; and of these there were plenty in Lawrence: "These two hundred little marauders rarely if ever enter a school of literature and science, of wisdom and virtue; but through each live-long day they are taught by example, and their knowledge fixed by practice, in the school of the street, where the violation of every moral precept and duty form the morning and the evening lesson." [149]

The superintendent declared that in its "minor bearings" this was a situation of considerable importance. "The losses from theft, the malicious mischief done to public and private property, the occasional disturbance of schools and religious meetings, and the frequent and increasing insults to women and children" were unfortunate. But more serious was the influence of the two hundred vagabonds on the respectable children who, brought into contact with them, were "introduced to the Primary School of Vice." Even worse, perhaps, was the fact that these urchins would soon be parents, "training up a new generation after their own ideas and exerting an equal power to the most exemplary in determining the character of our institutions." [150] In five years Lawrence had changed from a model town of New Englanders hungry for schools to a Primary School of Vice.

To schoolmen the apathy of parents had a critical influence on the moral degradation of the children. George Packard, the superintendent in 1855, claimed that the school committee's failure to create public interest in education was attributable to both native and Irish parents: "We have a large foreign population, many of whom are almost wholly untaught themselves, and are strangely indifferent to the education of their children. Too many instances of the like sad indifference occur among American born parents. All efforts to awaken . . . the class . . . have thus far signally failed." [151] With similar motivation the superintendent for 1858, Henry K. Oliver, addressed five requests to parents: he urged them to allow their children to complete the entire school course, to enforce regular attendance, to insure punctuality, to visit the schools, and to keep informed of the progress of their children. He addressed himself especially to the parents of high school students:

> The pupils of High Schools are more prone to fail in these points and to be absent for less pressing causes than the general run of scholars of other schools. Their near approach to that period of life when they are to become lawfully independent of paren- tal sway and the common custom among parents of holding older children under diminished restraint, cause them to feel less responsible to the checks that ordinarily control, and more disposed to act for themselves and under the impulse of their own inclinations. They begin to feel themselves to be more than incipient men and women, and that in "putting away childish things" they may fairly put away that very childish thing . . . reverenced . . . heretofore, called parental authority.[152]

According to the superintendent's report for 1859 morality was indeed on the wane. Many children were being brought up to an "inheritance of vice . . . educated to skill in practical crime, and to skill in adroit concealment of crime and escape from its con- sequences." The whole pernicious tendency was reflected in the growing stratification of society, "an increasing separation and enlargment of distance between the several classes . . . from increase of wealth . . . civilization . . . high intellectual development." Sometimes high intellectual development dampened a person's social sympathies, and this was extremely unfortunate at a time when the lower classes required the ministrations of the intelligent. To halt the decay of society which, the superintendent admitted, was "invariably resultant from high civilization" was the duty of the government, which should "step in to protect, to defend, to reform, and to punish." If compulsory education was evaded, compulsory reform school should follow.[153]

The nature of the population of Lawrence posed a number of specific problems for the schools. One problem was the fluctuation in enrollment. Again and again schoolmen reported that a drifting but increasing population made enrollment impossible to predict, and hence planning was extremely difficult.[154] During the depression of 1857 children lost their jobs and, unemployed, turned in droves to the schools. Schoolmen welcomed them, claiming that some good might result from the evils of the depression, but overcrowding became acute. The fluctuating and growing enrollment, however, was not spread evenly throughout the four kinds of schools. In 1858, for instance, 2,016 children attended the primary and middle schools and only 1,044 the grammar and high schools. On the one hand, argued the superintendent in 1860, primary school enrollment was high since mothers who needed to work placed their children in school at the earliest possible time; on the other hand, industrial and commercial employment opportunities militated against children staying a long time in school and, indeed, going to the grammar school at all.[155] Within the high school the enrollment was continually low, a cause of "notoriety," according to one superintendent. In fact, most of the students who remained in high school until graduation were girls. The low enrollment of the high school and the high proportion of drop-outs (generally around two-thirds of those who entered) were constant complaints throughout reports, problems that schoolmen remained unable to solve.[156]

Schoolmen also failed to find a satisfactory way of coping with truancy, a problem related to enrollment. As early as 1848 the school committee complained of irregular attendance. In 1850 they urged the passing of by-laws to deal with truants because the problem was increasing.[157] By 1854 the school committee, increasingly disturbed, was unsuccessfully urging the establishment of a special school for truants. The city did establish a truant committee that was supposed to review cases and decide how to deal with offenders, but in 1860 the superintendent complained that the committee was ineffective and urged the appointment of a regular truant officer.[158] One concrete action had been taken; in the school year 1859–60 the sub-master of the Oliver grammar school started a class to which the most recalcitrant truants were sent. Those who failed to reform or to appear were usually sent to the state reform school at Westborough.[159] During 1861 a school janitor, probably with encouragement from the superintendent, began seeking out truants and urging them to attend school, and soon he was officially appointed truant officer. The magnitude of the problem of truancy in Lawrence is indicated by the fact that in his first year of regular service the truant officer handled over five hundred different cases.[160] At first the superintendent reported glowingly on the results of the truant officer's work; but his satisfaction lasted only a short time, for mass truancy failed to disappear. Finally, after much urging, the city council passed a more rigorous set of by-laws including a provision that truants be sent to the city almshouse. The almshouse was to be partly remodelled and turned into a truant school. But the vote of the council did not solve the problem, for the next year the superintendent reported that the new by-laws had remained inoperative and that the almshouse had not been made ready for the reception of truants.[161]

The problems of enrollment and truancy were compounded by the confusion caused by the establishment of Catholic schools early in the history of the city. The school committee frequently made hostile comments about parochial schools, and their bitterness culminated in 1854, a year of intense and widespread Know-Nothing activity in Lawrence. During 1854 a number of incidents underlined the native-Irish hostility in the town. Irish and Americans rioted in the streets;[162] in June an Irish girl who lived with an American family was walking to public school when her sisters grabbed her and tried to force her to come away with them. Native bystanders intervened, and a serious brawl nearly started. The town marshal arrived quickly and took the girl to the courthouse where she tearfully admitted that she wished to go with her sisters. This the marshal permitted, and the girl was hustled out through a back door to avoid the angry crowd waiting in front. Later the same month a similar case occurred, but this time the girl elected to stay with the American family and became a target for epithets hurled at her by the Irish.[163]

In their report for 1854 the school committee, complained that the parochial schools (they termed them "Romanist") had undermined educational planning. Catholic children were leaving and re-entering school at such an erratic pace that no enrollment predictions could be made. Even more serious, the very children "emanating from a class of our population so destitute of domestic advantages, as to make them special candidates for all the benefits of our school system" had been removed from the influence of excellent teachers and facilities and placed in decidedly inferior institutions. In criticizing the Catholic schools the superintendent realized the gravity of the charges he was making, but he felt that he had obtained sufficient evidence. Large numbers of children who were allegedly attending Catholic schools were in reality roaming the streets, and the task of determining who was a truant had become impossible. Children returning to the public schools brought shocking stories; and the returning students, teachers charged, had declined mentally during their term at the Catholic school. What could be done? The superintendent realized that Catholics had every legal and constitutional right to establish their own schools, but he urged the state legislature to pass a law establishing qualifications that would apply to the teachers and conduct of both private and public schools.[164]

In spite of the urging of the state representative from Lawrence, the legislature did not pass the law, and the problem became more acute. State law required children employed in manufacturing to obtain a certificate signed by a teacher stating that they had attended school for a stipulated number of weeks. At times superintendents of mills overlooked the regulation; at other times they accepted certificates signed by the teachers of parochial schools. The school committee avoided challenging the latter practice until after the great fire in the Pemberton Mills in 1860 when a factory superintendent, inundated with new certificates (the old had been burned) asked the committee if he could legally accept those from the Catholic teachers. The committee's lawyer maintained that it was necessary for the certificates to be signed by a teacher approved by the town school committee. The committee thought this implied that only public school certificates henceforth would be accepted.[165]

To the consternation of the committee the teacher of the largest Catholic school appeared with his staff and requested an examination. After some hesitation the committee agreed to examine the Catholic teachers. The committee claimed that they had asked their usual questions and had found that all but the principal were grossly incompetent and could not be judged suitable persons to certify the education of the children employed in manfacturing.[166] The outcome of the examination is, however, unclear since it is not certain that factory superintendents heeded the finding of the school committee. Many children continued to be enrolled annually in the Catholic schools, and if they had been unable to obtain employment with the certificates from their Catholic teachers, their parents very likely would have sent them to public schools. Thus, in spite of the examination the problem of the alleged inferiority of the Catholic schools remained unsolved. One issue was resolved, however; Catholic teachers cooperated with the town truant officer, and it became possible to separate truants from students enrolled in parochial schools.[167]

Schools became a partisan political issue for the first time during the Know-Nothing agitation. Since the founding of the city each political party had offered a separate slate of candidates for the school committee, but the party press did not criticize the committee that was elected, even when it was dominated by the opposition. In 1855, however, when the Know-Nothings captured the committee, both the Whig and Democratic papers were hostile, the latter most virulently. Attacks centered on the alleged incompetence of the superintendent. His report was criticized as semi-literate; his custodial care of school property was attacked, and his conduct of the annual examination of teachers was mercilessly lampooned. According to the Democratic *Sentinel* the superintendent asked ridiculously easy questions until the end of the examination, when he introduced a spelling word that none of the teachers had ever heard before. When asked to define the word, the superintendent suddenly became flustered and changed the subject. The charge was expressed vividly by a poet in the *Sentinel:*

> Rusher's Examination of Teachers,
> An Accurate Account of What Actually Happened in Ye Town of Laurentium, in Ye 19th century, compiled from ye Best Authorities.

A teacher is wanted — the order has gone forth,
Young ladies from far — and young ladies more near,
In response to the summons quite promptly appear,
And assuming their places are ready to show forth
How well they're prepared for the pedagogue's sphere.

So there sat the ladies, demure in a row
While the learned Sandhedrin for judgment prepare,

With their stock of strange questions selected with care;
And the chief, girding on now, his buckler and bow
Gazes round on his victims with terrible stare.

Addition, subtraction, Division, and all that,
And twice ten are twenty, and twice two are four,
And a thousand's a *lot;* if it isn't some more,
Were examined in turn, til the Rusher's block hat,*
Crowded off with the pressure, and fell to the floor.

Then next came the spelling — a full, thorough trial
With words of one syllable, sometimes of two,
One h-a-t hat, r-a-t rat, and c-a-t cat,
Were all passed in review.
All thought, but the Rusher, the spelling was royal,**
But without the *great* question, *he* could not be through.

So here he brings forward the charm talismanic,
The touchstone of learning and talent and wit —
FEOFEE — that's the word, and who cannot spell it,
Tho' possessed of all knowledge, and virtue's angelic
For a primary teacher, oh sure she's not fit.

.   .   .   .

But alas! and alack! from one to another
The fatal word passed to the end of the row,
And no one could spell it, — They e'en did not know
Its existence before — and so in a bother
Requested the Rusher its meaning to show.

He scratched up his scull cap — he rubbed up his eye.
And he twitched at his collar — still nothing would do —
Then he thumbed his old nose til they say it was blue;

---

* It is said yt ye Rusher is much given to wearing of ye hat in meetings.
** Ye term Rusher, it hath been said, was first applied to ye individual in question from ye fact yt he is one of ye unfortunates, who *will* rush in where angels fear to tread.

Til at last in despair, he confessed with a sigh
That he "hadn't *examined from that point of view.*"***

*** Ye reports say yt Rusher appeared at this juncture terribly obfusti-
cated and he seemed desirous of changing ye subject.[168]

The *Sentinel* charged Superintendent Williams ("Rusher's" real
name) and the committee with being so incompetent that the
old school committee had to conduct the examination of high
school students, which they did free of charge. The nativist paper,
of course, tried to refute the charges of the *Sentinel* by claiming
that Williams had held responsible posts in educational administration before coming to Lawrence and had conducted the teacher
examinations well. In his annual report Williams himself answered charges of mishandling school maintenance. Actually,
Williams' report is far from semi-literate and compares favorably
with most others. In fact, the Know-Nothing city administration
must have cared considerably for the schools. In 1855–56 both
the per-pupil expenditure and the school tax rate were the highest
in the history of Lawrence in this period. These observations
suggest that the motives of the *Sentinel* were not altruistic. In fact,
Williams' literacy and the high spending imply that the charges of
the *Sentinel* were founded primarily on a combination of political
animosity and hostility to an increase in taxes. A similar event
occurred during the same year. Mr. Fairfield, a teacher in the
South grammar school, was fired. The Democratic *Sentinel* attributed the firing to Fairfield's refusal to join the Know-Nothing movement. The nativist *American* claimed he was incompetent and
personally disagreeable. In this case a group of the most distinguished citizens of the city signed a memorial testifying to Fairfield's high qualifications, a fact which implied that the *Sentinel*'s
charges may have been justified.[169]

Private schools other than Catholic also posed a problem
for the city. From the founding of Lawrence, newspapers had advertised private schools offering both primary and high school education. The most successful and respected was Mr. Blaisdale's

school, which was operated from the earliest years of the city until Blaisdale's death in 1861. One newspaper correspondent charged that the school committee members themselves sent their children to Blaisdale's and to other private schools and academies.[170] The school committee maintained that some of the parental apathy toward education stemmed from the private schools. In particular, private schools, they held, cut down the attendance at the high school. In 1865 the superintendent asserted that the high school offered an education both excellent and practical, but he was severely disappointed at the response of the citizens. He asked: "Do the citizens of Lawrence realize that their high school furnishes better facilities for the education of their sons and daughters than many, not to say any, of the academies of the land? If they did, would there not be many more of their sons availing themselves of the rich privileges it offers at their doors?" [171]

The "rich privileges" of the education offered in Lawrence schools were intended to be more moral than intellectual. It is "obvious," superintendent Henry K. Oliver said, "that heart-culture should be paramount to brain-culture, moral culture to intellectual culture." [172] Oliver warned of dire consequences "unless the heart be so influenced in the tenderness of its young growth, that goodness becomes part of its nature, unless the mind be so trained in the pliancy of its formation, that habits of right are ingrained into its very constitution, so that . . . the evil that abounds in the world and that gloats with triumphant riot over the ruined hearth-stones of millions, will be resisted by the novices that are successively assailed as they enter upon life's duties." Schools were the "most effectual means of guarding the young against the many evils that surround them in childhood and will environ them in all of subsequent life." [173] Heart culture was especially necessary in Lawrence, which required influences "counteracting the growth" of the "stupendous evils" surrounding students. Without education of the heart, society itself might crumble: "as surely as darkness succeeds to the absence of sun, so surely doth the misery of the individual and of society — so surely does the insecurity of society in every matter — follow from the absence of a right education of the individual." [174]

Because of the special importance of heart culture in the urban environment of Lawrence, schoolmen felt that primary schools required more attention than they were usually given. The first influences upon a child were crucial; thus, "Primary Schools have an influence over the future education of the children, that should cause them to stand very high in the estimation of the public." In Lawrence, unlike other cities, there was a "fuller recognition of the greatness of the work to be done in them," and consequently "we pay their teachers the same salary as the teachers in the Middle and Grammar Schools." [175]

Purely intellectual education, warned Superintendent Oliver, could be positively harmful if carried too far, and he was especially worried about the girls of Lawrence. He complained that their "mental education" was carried to such an extreme it became debilitating, and their education for motherhood was neglected. "We have no romping girls, no capering 'tomboys,' with straight limbs, active frames, and plump with robust health . . . but a dwindling race of pale-faced, sallow-skinned, wasp-waisted damsels." Moreover, girls were neglecting the "trying matters of housewifery." In addition to the skills of literacy and arithmetic, girls should receive a thorough education in the "elementary" branches of advanced subjects such as moral, intellectual, and natural philosophy, physiology ("by all means"), chemistry, geology, astronomy, history and algebra. But when girls left school at eighteen, their studies should be completed by "Home and Mother," something "much and transcendently important." [176]

Although Lawrence schoolmen emphasized the importance of moral education, they did not neglect the intellectual, as their frequent and careful revisions of the high school curriculum revealed. In 1853 the committee extended the classical course to four years, and in the late 1850's they revised the whole curriculum.

Throughout the state, argued the superintendent, more subjects than could be covered adequately were being added to the curriculum, which grew by a process of accretion; the result was "superficiality" and "ostentation." Instead the correct way of altering the curriculum, and the one adopted in Lawrence, was rigorously to prune from the course all subjects not essential and all advanced topics more suitable for college. The result was a carefully structured curriculum including, in the three-year English course, mathematics, natural sciences, modern languages, Latin, English language and literature, and history.[177] The four-year classical course included Greek as well. The committee also considered the grammar school curriculum carefully. They tried to make the grammar school course complete in itself, a thorough and good education for the many students who would not go on to high school. The superintendent argued that bookkeeping and drawing were essential. These subjects were so important for business that if they were not included in the public school curriculum, students would have to go to private school in Lawrence or Boston to learn them.[178] The committee and superintendents urged other innovations as well. They stressed the importance of music and at times hired a special music teacher.[179] In the late 1850's and early 1860's they began to emphasize physical education and object teaching and, in a few years, reported with satisfaction that these subjects had entered the curricula of most of their schools.[180]

Voluntary associations attempted to meet particular educational needs not satisfied by the public schools. In 1861 a joint committee of all the religious denominations except the Catholics established a free evening school to be conducted by the City Missionary. The school taught the rudiments of literacy, arithmetic and some bookkeeping, and all the students were over fifteen years old. The extremely large enrollment of the school, often well over three hundred, testified both to its popularity and to the educational level of a significant portion of the population. Like the public institutions, the evening school was intended to have a moral as well as an intellectual function: "Many persons have . . . been stimulated and aided in acquiring the elements of reading and writing, or of other fundamental branches of education, and at the same time have been secured from the manifold temptations spread broadcast around them, during the long evenings of the Winter months." According to the school committee and the City Missionary, the free evening school was a complete success. The adult students who came voluntarily were eager to learn and gratifying to teach. Yet, noted one newspaper, Lawrence lacked provision for the factory operative who wanted to acquire a secondary education after working hours, for the instruction in the free evening school was strictly elementary.[181] But the newspaper's complaint apparently met with little response, and the gap in the city's educational facilities remained.

In 1853 the Essex Company donated ten choice acres of land on a hill overlooking the city as a public park. In rapturous terms the *Courier* responded: "In the rapid development of our young community, in the midst of the material and moral changes taking place yearly and daily around us, it will surely hereafter be interesting to find one spot at least retaining most of its original features; one wooded summit, which while all around its base is undergoing transformation, shall remain sacred from the intrusion of the spade and shovel, and whose trees so lately waving over neglected farms, shall grow to adorn with their shade the abode of civilization and the arts." [182] These words symbolized the goal of the founders of Lawrence: the preservation of the best features of an idealized rural life in the midst of a manufacturing community. The primary mechanism for effecting this delicate balance was education. In education they invested heavily, and the leading citizens of Lawrence were proud of their school system. Indeed, they argued more than once that it was among the very finest in the state.[183] And they had cause to be proud: their school system represented the most advanced system of grading; teachers were hired with great care; curricular and pedagogical innovations were adopted. Yet in spite of the excellence of their schools and the intensity of their efforts Lawrence schoolmen watched with dismay the development of typical urban problems as the city grew. Despite the best educational system a group of informed Massachusetts citizens could devise, Lawrence was a city characterized by discord, immorality, and poverty. Lawrence had offered Massachusetts educators a chance to play their trump card; instead it called their bluff.

The failure of the schools of Lawrence to reach their goals represents the failure of urban school reform, a failure echoed around the state. The schools failed to reach their ends, first, because those ends were impossible to fulfill. They failed, second, because of the style of educational development. Educational reform and innovation represented the imposition by social leaders of schooling upon a reluctant, uncomprehending, skeptical, and sometimes, as in Beverly, hostile citizenry. Social and cultural antagonisms that delayed and made difficult the achievement of innovation could not be simply erased after new schools had been built. From on high the school committees, representing the social and financial leadership of towns and cities, excoriated the working-class parents. They founded schools with a sense of superiority, not compassion. They forced education, and they forced it fast and hard; no time was allowed for the community to accustom itself to novel institutions or ideas about the length of school life. School committees hoped to serve their own ends and the ends of the status-seeking parents that supported them; one of those ends involved the unification of urban society. Ironically, their ideology and style could not have been better designed to alienate the very people whom they strove to accommodate in a more closely knit social order.[184] In making the urban school, educational promoters of the mid-nineteenth century fostered an estrangement between the school and the working-class community that has persisted to become one of the greatest challenges to reformers of our own time.

Every period of purely mechanical organization is sure in those at the head of affairs to result in a condition of intense self-satisfaction and contentment . . . Accordingly the self-sufficiency of the Eastern educationists, as a class, — their satisfaction and thorough contentment, both with themselves and with the situation, — was up to a quite recent period, most discouraging.

Charles Francis Adams, Jr., 1880

Part II.   The Uses of Pedagogy:
Teachers and the Educational Process

I. THE HERESY OF CYRUS PEIRCE

Cyrus Peirce was one of the most respected educators in the state. Horace Mann had been so impressed by a visit to Nantucket High School that he had chosen its principal, Peirce, to head the first public normal school in America, founded in 1839. Peirce's struggles in the early days of the normal school had been truly valiant, but overwork had ruined his health. When he had to retire, praise was heard on all sides. By 1839 Cyrus Peirce was an elder statesman of the educational revival. Therefore, when in 1853 that august body of reformers, The American Institute of Instruction, long champions of normal schools, viciously attacked as heresy a mildly censorsious speech by Peirce, something was very wrong.[1]

By 1853 educators had developed an emotional commitment to an ideology that awarded them the critical role in the salvation of mankind. Throughout Massachusetts the development of a theory of administrative and institutional reform was accompanied by the growth of a theory of the educational process. Joined to the making of urban schools was the making of an urban pedagogy. In this urban pedagogy educators acquired a tremendous personal stake. And it was precisely because they felt such a stake in the dominant ideology that educators viciously attacked Peirce. What the ideology of pedagogical reform was, why and how it became dominant, and why it so bound schoolmen are questions that lead to the origins of critical deficiencies in contemporary urban education.

Schoolmen, as we have seen, agreed that Massachusetts should continue to strive for a prosperity based on large-scale industrial development. They also agreed that the growth of cities and factories fostered familial and social decay, and they argued that education should both promote and counteract urbanism and manufacturing. High schools, one feature of a system of administrative and institutional reorganization, were to accomplish both goals. Another means of reaching the schoolmen's goals was to try to transform the educational process. Schoolmen agreed that economic transformation produced social decay through its pernicious effects on personality. To counteract these effects they proposed that the inculcation of restraint as a trait of character become the goal of the educational process. Assumptions concerning the effects of society on personality and the goal of the educational process were widely shared, as were assumptions concerning the nature of that process itself. But a debate emerged over the methods through which shared assumptions and goals should be translated into practice. Both sides in the debate argued that the techniques of the other would not produce the restraint necessary to counteract society's harmful influence on personality. In a sense, both sides were right, for there was an unresolved contradiction in the arguments of each. And the side that clearly won, the side whose arguments became elevated to the status of a dominant ideology, diffused a theory that reflected the ambivalence of schoolmen toward society. The victorious schoolmen advocated a pedagogical theory designed to counteract social ills, but they failed to recognize that in reality their innovations would produce personality qualities that would augment the worst of these ills. Intimately related to the development of an ideology of the educational process, moreover, were the status problems of teachers, the real issue, as we shall see, behind the ordeal of Cyrus Peirce.

2. SOCIETY'S HOT STIMULUS OF ACTION
AND THE NECESSITY OF RESTRAINT

The shared assumptions of schoolmen concerning the pernicious effects of society upon personality relate to their observation that urbanism promoted a reliance upon external stimuli rather than upon the dictates of an inner sense of purpose and a personal set of ethical standards. America, according to an article in the *Massachusetts Teacher,* had a universal reputation for "activity, practicality and material prosperity." The distinguishing features of this prosperity were "a flourishing agriculture, and a commerce of unrivalled growth" combined with remarkably rapid urbanization; cities "were springing into life on every side." The steamboat, the railroad and the telegraph revolutionized communications and other inventions made industry "every day more speedy and profitable." In surveying the scene, the article claimed, "the national heart leaps and well nigh bursts with exultation."

But the national heart also had cause for concern. The triumph of the material aspects of civilization was accompanied by the frantic pursuit of wealth and the ostentatious and wasteful extravagance of the newly rich. American society, the article proclaimed, revealed "a baneful love of *display.*" [2] This love of display had become "one of the greatest motive-powers of American society," and the criteria of merit had become "dress, equipage . . . style of living," and "real or feigned possessions." In an increasingly affluent society ostentation had become the mark of the American. "The spirit of the people is almost *wholly* directed to that which is outward. Here lies the essence of the materialism of the age." Another writer echoed the same point: the admirable material progress of Massachusetts had fostered "energy, activity and enterprise," but, unfortunately, it had also promoted "the noisy, the showy, and superficial, to the neglect of what we most need — the broad-based and deep-rooted in mind and morals." [3] As the point of reference for their actions Americans were taking not the promptings of conscience or internal standards, but the possessions and opinions of others, of a venal and shallow society.

Materialism and shallowness were inherently dangerous because they bred the temptation to more serious sin. Massachusetts, according to an article in the *Common School Journal,* was in particular danger: "What we call civilization and progress, have increased temptation a thousand fold; — in this country, ten thousand fold. The race for wealth, luxury, ambition and pride, is open to all. With our multiplied privileges, have come not only multiplied obligations, which we may condemn, but multiplied dangers into which we may fall . . . In this country, all that is base and depraved in the human heart has such full liberty and wide compass, and hot stimulus of action, as has never been known before." [4] The problem was that everything was easy. Sin was to be had without difficulty; so too, unfortunately, were money and luxury. In the softness of affluence one point was forgotten, and schoolmen waged a continual battle for its re-entry into the public mind; that was, simply, "that nothing worth possessing can be had without labor." [5] Schoolmen applied their dictum to education: "Nothing is truly valuable in education that does not cost real, steady, energetic effort to secure." [6] One commentator thought country boys succeeded better in adult life than city youths because of their tough education. "Too much direct help, too much pampering" had begun "in the metropolitan schools" and was "permeating all the institutions for instruction." Pampering was pernicious because it sapped the strength of the individual and injured him in his adult life, where there would be "no friendly arm to lean upon, no cultivated determination to brace up, but a faltering incompetency that ends in vain wishes and empty resolutions." And how would "faltering incompetency" and "empty resolutions" fare when confronted with the city's "hot stimulus of action"? Students needed "a strong and resolute well-balanced character," a character obtainable only through "severe discipline." [7]

Any term referring to an easy or soft quality was pejorative, and such terms were used repeatedly to describe parents' attitude toward their children. Society as a whole was soft; so too were metropolitan educational methods; so too was the family. For instance, educators' exhortations regarding the necessity of regular and punctual attendance of children at school were almost always accompanied by terms referring to parental management as indulgent and permissive. "Let 'Need I go to school today?' be a question to be settled every morning, between a boy six years old, and his indulgent, yielding mother" and pernicious effects will follow, thundered a writer in the *Massachusetts Teacher*.[8] The "indulgent," "yielding" character of family life implied a clear duty for the schools. If society was characterized by temptations to softness, and if suspectibility to these temptations was reinforced by the home, and, finally, if these attractions were dangerous snares, then clearly an institution had to intervene. The role of the school became to break dependency, to wean the child from the parent to the real world: to perform aspects of the socialization process that parents had become unable to carry out.

"Children," one author analyzed, "are the center of observation, care and attendance of the whole family" as long as they are in the "nursery or the sitting room." There, they learned "to feel themselves as individuals." "Adults," however, were "treated by society in an entirely different way." The world of the adult was one of fixed laws and customs, wholly impersonal, often "one-sided and . . . unjust, annihilating individual liberty and dignity in a high degree." The child, in this situation, had to make a difficult transition: "The child stands between the two extremes and a transition from the one to the other, sudden or gradual, methodical or planless, will make a vast difference in the formation of the child's character." To effect this transition, to induct the child into the adult world, was the duty of the school: "The important duty to act as a medium falls upon the school in general, and upon the Primary school in particular." [9]

A contributor to the *Common School Journal* claimed that the schools' assumption of socialization, including induction, resulted from the increased complexity of society. Moral and vocational education, he said, had previously been the duty of the parent; but, he continued, "in the present state of society, a vast majority of parents are unable, either on account of their own deficient education, or from want of time, to attend, in person, to the discharge of this duty." Schools were a result of this situation; schools, that is, represented "an arrangement" entered into by all the residents of a given area to "associate themselves together, and in their joint capacity, employ a teacher, to perform for them in the education of their children, a duty which they cannot attend to, or can only discharge imperfectly." The hiring of a teacher to educate children should not be a cause for concern because the employment of a teacher was an example of the division of labor characteristic of the times. "In the present complicated relations of society and of business," claimed the author, "most men undertake to do more than they can personally accomplish." [10]

The Boston school committee, describing their task, made it clear that the school's expanded responsibility included acculturation: "taking children at random from a great city, undisciplined, uninstructed, often with inveterate forwardness and obstinacy, and with the inherited stupidity of centuries of ignorant ancestors; forming them from animals into intellectual beings, and . . . from intellectual beings into spiritual beings; giving to many their first appreciation of what is wise, what is true, what is lovely and what is pure." [11] Education, then, was partly a breaking away from the home, an eradication of pernicious or infantile qualities; but it was also a substitution; and schoolmen agreed quite precisely on what was to be replaced and on its replacement.

Schoolmen assumed that the unfavorable influence of society upon personality was to be countered by the inculcation of a restraint based upon sublimation, a substitution of "higher" for "lower" pleasures.[12] In 1858 the Boston school committee reminded parents that "every pure and refined pleasure for which a child acquires a relish, is to that extent, a safeguard against a low and debasing one." [13] To assist the child in substituting higher pleasures for lower was a key function of the school. Students were to learn to check firmly the passionate and to avoid the sensual; this, moreover, was a realistic goal for education: "Those, whose minds and whose hearts have been properly trained and disciplined by education, have control over their passions. Having cultivated a taste for simple and innocent pleasures, rather than a love for vicious excitement, their desires are awakened by objects higher than any gratification merely animal." [14] In Beverly the same argument was used to urge the establishment of a public library. It would afford "a profitable source of recreation, and thereby" lessen "the temptation to amusements of an unworthy character." "Nothing can be more true, than that the best means for destroying a taste for a lower pleasure, is by cultivating a taste for a higher." [15]

The control of the passions coincided with another goal, especially necessary for social mobility but usually expressed in rather different terms: the ability to plan for the future. "Forming plans for a distant future," individuals "rise nearer and nearer to a spiritual existence." [16] Ideally the parents and, if not, the school had to teach this lesson: substitute future for immediate gratification. The key words became control, self-discipline, and restraint. No quality was more useful and necessary to both society and the individual than self-restraint. Restraint it was that separated the child from the adult. Men, claimed one writer, "act from principle . . . The restraints of society are felt. They can see remote consequences. But children act from the impulses of their natures quickened by the objects around them." [17] Thus, restraint was the personality characteristic central to education; on restraint focused the work of the schools, and educators repeatedly stressed the associated virtues of "concentration" or "fixing the attention," "earnestness," "control," and "self-discipline."

On the surface a contradiction existed in educational thought. Many schoolmen emphasized the importance of the natural, of educational methods that accorded with nature. But restraint was designed to control natural impulse. The conflict is only surface deep, however, because of schoolmen's conception of the natural. "Every living thing below man, except those designed to share in his toils," claimed a writer in the *Common School Journal,* "may be said to be perfectly educated by Nature, or in accordance with the will of God"; and man was no exception; the realization of God's will was also the end of the education of man. But God's will was embodied in nature, and thus, "nature is as truly the standard for him, as for the nightingale or the honey-bee." Herein was a problem. Would not the work of the teacher represent artificial tampering with the work of God? Was not the man closest to the standard of nature the uncivilized, the uneducated? Schoolmen repudiated this implication. The "state of nature" was "very different from . . . a state of brutal simplicity, without brutal innocence, a state that would paralyze every power possessed by man, except the lower agents of sensuality."

The hero, the model of the natural man, was not the primitive, as the same writer's description of the Indian made clear: "In our western forest is the rude child of Nature, and the least caressed of any of her children; he is so low, that even the dog, his constant companion, deteriorates in his society; he has rarely sufficient to make himself comfortable for a single week; he has no means of increasing his knowledge, but his senses and the council-fires of his fathers; when civilization touches him, it is with so rude a shock that he retreats or dies." Rude nature, then, needed man; the ideal was not the wild but the cultivated. Man improved nature; and the divinity of man was represented by his latent but inherent capacity for the mastery of the untamed both within himself and in the external world. Thus, concluded the author, the "natural state of man is a higher state of civilization than he has ever yet known, a state that would require the use of all his powers, in their most perfect condition." [18] The stress on the "higher state of civilization" and on control reflect an often explicit fear of the passionate and sensual. One writer exclaimed typically: Without counter-checks upon passions "what would our race be!" [19]

The combined emphasis on the substitution of pleasures and the inculcation of restraint coupled with the prevailing conception of nature reveals a deep fear of the passionate and the sensual; this fear reveals a conscious attempt to sublimate, to rechannel energies away from activities leading to social and individual failure and into those fostering industrial productivity, social cohesion, and individual mobility. If citizens needed an example of the failure of sublimation, they had only to look at the Irish: "Did wealth consist in children, it is well known, that the Irish would be a rich people; and if the old Roman law prevailed here, which granted special privileges to every man who had more than three, this people would be elevated into an aristocracy." [20] As anyone could see, the Irish were not an aristocracy, and wealth did not consist in children. Was the opposite true? Certainly the regular appearance of advertisements for alleged birth-control and abortion-producing pills in most newspapers of the period implies an effort to reduce the size of families. But birth control through artificial means was not a generally accepted notion, even if the pills did work. Thus, if it were necessary to limit family size in order to maintain an adequate standard of living and to provide for one's children, then what remained, except restraint? Historians have pointed out the status anxieties of people conscious of the fluid uncertainties of life in the mid-nineteenth century, the fear of falling on the social scale. Here this anxiety is evident at the heart of the new urban pedagogy, in the central goal of the educational process. [21]

When they asserted the virtues of self-restraint and the pernicious effects of the easy life, schoolmen visualized themselves counter-acting the dominant tendencies of their time. In 1848, for instance, the editor of the *Common School Journal* warned that "nothing has yet been done to counteract what must inevitably lead to the ruin of our free institutions," and called for an increased attention to morality and virtue in the schools. [22] Authors frequently juxtaposed the characteristics of Massachusetts, the domination of the workshop and factory or "insane competition for gain," "base iniquity and fraud," and the qualities and social characteristics that schools should produce — qualities such as respect for learning *per se,* or "equity and virtue." [23] The goal of education became the reformation of society through the formation of personality.

In sum, then, the educators' immense task was to supply individuals with a set of inner restraints: "Those external restraints of blind reverence for authority, and superstitious dread of religious guides and fiery penal codes, which once repressed the passions of men and paralyzed all energy are now lifted off. If internal and moral restraints be not substituted for the external and arbitrary ones that are removed, the people, instead of being conquerors and sovereigns over their passions, will be their victims and their slaves." [24] The emphasis on "internal" is crucial. Educators were to change the point of reference for human action from the external opinions and possessions of others to an intrinsic regulator. The child, with the help of the school, was to exchange both the indulgence of his parents and the gratifications proffered by a vain, materialistic society for a set of intrinsic controls. One schoolman exhorted, "Instil the desire to *be* rather than to seem." [25]

3. THE TRUE IDEA OF EDUCATION

The assumptions of schoolmen concerning the methods of instilling restraint rested on a tripartite definition of the educational process. "A teacher once asked a boy, 'What do you intend to be?' " reported the *Massachusetts Teacher;* the boy replied, " 'I shall strive to be a *man.*' This answer embodies the true idea of education — moral, physical, and intellectual." [26] Massachusetts schoolmen generally would have agreed with this conclusion; three kinds of education, they claimed, existed, and each, in the proper balance, was essential to the well being of both the individual and society. In fact, the omission of any one kind could spell disaster. For instance, purely physical education would produce men "of godly appearance . . . only superior to the untamed hero of the brutes in its erect posture." The pure intellectual would have "the power to grasp the universe . . . but his rule would be the despotism of evil," and the merely moral would be a pathetic figure, "a beautiful but humiliating negation of itself." The physical and intellectual alone "would place the soul of a fallen angel in the body of a giant; while that of the moral and physical . . . might prolong the life of virtue, but only to keep it timidly in known and beaten paths." Finally, the last combination, "the moral and intellectual . . . would soon wear itself out in the intensity of its effort to work wonders without the proper mechanism." [27]

The task of the educator was clear, if immense. The assumption that the school has responsibility for the "whole man" was not a product of late nineteenth century social reform invading the school. It grew, instead, in the first flush of urbanization and industrialization in the mid-nineteenth century, because even then schoolmen asserted explicitly that the role of the family and church had altered and weakened, and they argued that the maintenance of social cohesion, even of civilized social life, rested upon the school's assumption of the process of socialization.

Prescriptions for intellectual education derived from a particular conception of mind. "The mind is a storehouse as well as a garden," wrote an author in the *Common School Journal*. This distinction was the epistemological basis of educational theory. The mind was both active and passive, and education had to serve both aspects. One object of education was to "quicken" the mind's perceptions; to enable it "to see effects in causes." Its other object was "to store the mind with useful information." [28] This distinction between the aspects of the mind provided a way of combining both the older Lockean epistemology and the newer Romantic theories, which stressed the inborn, native powers of the individual. Perhaps more important, the distinction had definite implications for teaching.

The "garden" aspect of the mind referred to its innate potentialities; till the soil carefully, implied the theory, and powers of
thought, invention, reflection, in short, the faculties, would grow
to maturity. These required a careful husbanding; they grew strong
through practice and activity, not through passive reception. Mem-
orizing facts did not aid their growth; instead, "principles must
be investigated." [29] Through the investigation of principles the
power of mind would grow to its ultimate goal: the pupil would
learn *"to think* and *to think for himself."* [30] The emphasis was
clearly on penetration and mastery. Education was to "prepare the
mind to grapple with the difficulties of life, just as we sharpen tools
in the mechanic arts," [31] and education had to insure that the boy
could digest knowledge and proceed from "fact to principle," that
he could "generalize and deduce." The active mind was the prerequisite for the active world of Massachusetts, whose citizens'
"habitual mental state" was one "of tension." In such an atmosphere
the rote learner would lose in the "struggles of" the "arena, for
these require not 'words, words, words,' but ideas, which are the
realities of things, and mental energy, that is, activity and perseverance in the use of them." [32] The cultivation of the powers of
perseverance, mastery and penetration of appearance, were necessary for more than the business world; they were necessary also
for the spiritual. Because God communicated with man through
natural laws embodied in all the manifold objects and processes of
the universe, it was not external reality itself that mattered most
but the divinity or law it represented. The power to penetrate,
principle over fact, again became the object of education. And
since God's universe was immense and its lessons countless, schoolmen argued for a conception of education as a continuous process,
one in which schooling prepared the mind to acquire its continuing
education for life: "To have finished education in any part of this
life, is the boast and complacency only of fools." The "process of
education is as enduring as immortality." [33]

Tilling mental soil was only one part of intellectual education.

"The organs of sense," according to an article in the *Massachusetts Teacher,* "are mere vehicles of ideas, and the mind is a blank, upon which the records of knowledge are to be inscribed." The Lockean side of educational theory clearly implied an important, if subordinate, place for the inculcation of useful knowledge. Indeed, the Boston English High School, which prided itself on its enlightened pedagogy, required all students to memorize, precisely, the entire United States Constitution.

The educators' Lockean view of the infant mind as, "in a great measure, passive, subject to just such influences as others may choose to impress upon it" led to a concern with environment as an educational force. The early passivity of the child, the time at which the mastering and penetrating faculties would be but seeds, left the child almost cruelly exposed to environment. The first social conditions with which the child was associated would have a tremendous impact upon his character as an adult; and when the "primitive impressions upon the infant mind" were "of an adverse nature," the teacher's work increased "tenfold." "The work of eradicating noxious weeds is often vastly greater than that of rearing an abundant and life-giving harvest." [34]

Perhaps most educative within the environment were individual human models. The child learned by imitating adults, and a glance at the adult models in Massachusetts made some educators shudder. One writer referred to the growth of cities, luxury, drinking, and other vices and answered complaints about the growth of "juvenile depravity" with the rejoinder, "Compare these things together, and then say whether *men* can any longer talk of *juvenile* depravity, without blushing to blistering." [35] Another way in which pernicious models were set before children was exemplified by the habit "among the higher and wealthier classes of society" of placing children, "particularly during the earliest portion of their existence," under the care of "domestics who, not infrequently, are ignorant, superstitious, and depraved." For the teacher, the stress on the importance of models meant the necessity of placing "*an elevated standard* . . . before the mind of the pupil." [36] The teacher had to create a model environment in which he himself exemplified the behavior of the paragon as well as the skills of the pedagogue.

The tension between the active and the passive qualities of mind, the innate and the blank, is not a contradiction. What were innate were capabilities and dispositions: the ability to think, for instance, and the capacity to be moral. Not innate were facts, concrete conceptions. The ideal became to develop the innate and supply the facts. Although the conception of gardening was widely used to express the former, this metaphor was not employed consistently. Another common conception, one sometimes used by the same people who also spoke of gardening, was shaping or molding: the teacher molded the plastic mind of the child. As the Lawrence school committee wrote, "How pliable are the young minds of the little ones who attend these schools in the hands of a kind and faithful teacher; truly they are 'as clay in the hands of the potter,' they can be formed and moulded at the pleasure of the affectionate teacher." [37] The conceptions behind molding and gardening certainly differ, but the literature of pedagogy leaves the impression that they were not used to convey different ideas of mind, but, rather, quite loosely employed to convey the idea of innate potential at the mercy of a powerful teacher.

The mind, we must remember, was only one of the three main responsibilities of the teacher. "Moral education," wrote a prize-winning essayist in the *Massachusetts Teacher* in 1856, "is the great want of the age." This complaint was foreshadowed in the early forties and echoed in the sixties. Schoolmen felt themselves far more successful in reaching the intellect than in touching the heart. The education of children in morality was especially difficult since the times conspired against the schools: "The close application to business, the incessant intellectual activity which mark [sic] the times, have a tendency to check the flow of affect and harden the heart, while the arts and commerce, the fashion and etiquette, the trade and politics of a refined civilization, foster a voluptuous materialism that would revel in ostentation and luxury." The assignment of final influence among home, school, and church was not entirely clear in this period, but there was widespread agreement that the school would have to undertake the bulk of moral education since this task was beyond the competence of the two other institutions. But how? Here again, the emphasis was on learning through models and grasping the truth underlying appearances. The student would not learn morality through "lecturing on ethics, but by an upright example . . . and by improving favorable opportunities for the practical inculcation of moral truth." [38]

If upright examples and favorable opportunities failed, however, there was no hesitation about using more forcible methods to insure desirable behavior. Take, for instance, the case of *Commonwealth* v. *S. M. Cook*. The teacher, Cook, had beaten an insolent and disobedient boy, one Lewis Winchell, whose father entered charges of assault. The judge emphasized that the teacher, standing *in loco parentis,* had every power of correction in the school that the parent did in the home. The duty of both was to "maintain good government . . . and secure proper subordination in all . . . members." Besides, pointed out the magistrate, the law explicitly sanctioned resort to corporal punishment when physical force became necessary to maintain the teacher's authority and preserve the order of the school.

In fact, continued the judge, not only was corporal punishment permitted, it was an *"imperative duty."* The schoolmaster was liable only if he had acted from "vindictive feelings, or under violence of passion or malevolence," but this, clearly, had not been the case. In language that might have been applied to a crime against the state as well as to an act against a teacher, the judge noted that the boy "assumed at the outset an attitude of defiance; and through the whole manifested a spirit of rebellion against the authority of the master, by open and violent acts of resistance, and the most insolent and profane language." One duty of the school was to insure civil and social order at a time when both were increasingly in jeopardy. Schoolmen preferred inner controls; but when indulgent parents and a pernicious environment bred unquenchable defiance, then the real fear of social chaos and the determination to insure order behind pedagogical theory came forth in an unflinching assertion of the combined power of the state and teacher over the individual child and his parent.[39]

Moral education was, in fact, a kind of intellectual totalitarianism. Relativism was inconceivable. The schools were to transmit, if possible by example and experience, if not by force, a pre-defined set of ideas, behaviors, and standards. Moral education was based on the assumption of the rationality of man and the universe. If children could only see the natural law, the divinity behind appearance, they would understand and consent to the regulations of adult society. Nineteenth century Massachusetts schoolmen drew a sharp line between individualism and deviance. Individualism in the pursuit of the "good," in terms of both method and goal, was laudable; deviance in either respect was suspect and socially dangerous.

The final ingredient in education should not be neglected. Horace Mann's many reports on improved methods of school construction stemmed from an enlightened appreciation of the importance of the physical. Interestingly, the arguments for the introduction of formal physical education into schools in this period became associated with schoolmen's perception of the consequences of urbanization. "Under the present conditions of city life at home and at school," wrote the Boston superintendent of schools in 1860, "a child stands a poor chance to enter upon the career of life having a good physical system, a body healthy, strong, well formed, and of good size"; and he noted that the relatively uneducated country boy fared better in the "race of life" than his highly educated city-bred competitor.[40]

When schoolmen wrote of the unending nature of education and the intrinsic pleasures of learning, they came close to defining the goals of education in terms of the joy and delight it brought to the individual. But they always stopped short of this point and turned to extrinsic goals. In the last analysis, their own perception of social need shaped the schoolmen's objectives. Here, then, we see that education was an imposition in three senses. In the first place, as the previous part of this study has shown, educational reform was imposed by the prominent upon the community. Second, the goals of that reform represented the imposition of upper- and middle-class fears and perceptions of social deficiencies. Third, the content of a reformed education represented an imposition of the values of communal leaders upon the rest of society. There was little of the humanitarian in educational reform; it was principally indoctrination, an attempt by promoters to re-make the rest of mankind in their own image. It would be wrong, however, to criticize reformers for not accepting now current notions of cultural relativity, for this is a modern concept. Reformers did not share our own haunting doubts about forcing middle-class values on the working class; they were confident that their own values were right.

4. A NEW MOTIVE TO MORAL EXCELLENCE VS. EMULATION

Schoolmen agreed on the overall nature of the educational process; they even agreed on the ends of schooling. The sordid materialism of society bred personalities that took as their standards for action, their cues for behavior, the vain and often dangerously immoral code of those around them. The duty of the school was to supply that inner set of restraints upon passion, that bloodless adherence to a personal sense of right, which would counteract and so reform the dominant tone of society. This goal was to be attained through nicely balancing intellectual, moral, and physical education; and the forms of education were to stress hard work and the provision of the models that, more than any lecturing, would form the personality of the child. On the matter of the means of education, however, there was disagreement. No one dissented from the glorification of hard work and the repudiation of softness; but a debate emerged on methodology and curriculum. Ranged on one side were schoolmen who advocated educational innovations termed soft and debilitating by their opponents. The soft-line educators, as the innovators will be termed, accused the proponents of the hard-line, as their antagonists will be called, of catering to the very motives that had hastened the decay of society. In both cases charges were levelled at the social implications of motivational techniques; in both cases those implications were thought to hasten the further disintegration of public and private morality.

Rote recitation based on the diligent adherence to a textbook, claimed one writer, gives "the scholar a distaste for the study." Instead, "the child should be interested in what he studies." [41] Likewise, in answer to the all-important question, "How shall the teacher form in his scholars, habits of industry and perseverance?" another commentator replied, *"by exciting their curiosity."* [42] Here was the essence of the ideology of the soft-line educators; they would reform instruction to accord with the interests of pupils; they would develop in students the necessary intrinsic self-controls through leading them to internalize a love for knowledge. Thus, according to one description, the model teacher "should connect with his instructions, as far as possible, what is interesting and attractive; so that the associations, formed in the minds of his pupils, will leave them in love with the subject of investigation, and, in proper time, bring them back to the pursuit with readiness and alacrity.[43]

But interest was not to be equated with ease; there was here a fine distinction, and the teacher "should be careful, that awakened curiosity be not gratified too soon, by unnecessary and superabundant aid, leaving no motive and no opportunity for effort, on the part of his pupils." On the other hand, interest should not be allowed to suffocate beneath a cloak of "appalling difficulties." Ideal teaching should strike a balance. The teacher "should intermingle with text-book instruction a due proportion of familiar lecturing; enough of the one with the other to guard against the pernicious effects of excess in either." "The pupil must be made to work; but he must work voluntarily, cheerfully, with hope." [44]

"The matter of object teaching," reported a pleased writer in 1860, "is rapidly growing in favor with leading educators." Object teaching, which originated in Europe, meant different things to different people; in general, however, the term refers to a type of pedagogy stressing the structuring of individual lessons, especially in science, around students' observations of natural objects presented by the teacher. Object teaching was a favorite innovation among the soft-line educators. In childhood, they claimed, knowledge is acquired "through the senses"; to disregard the senses, therefore, "is to violate the first principles of correct teaching." With both children and adults, moreover, comprehension and appeal are usually correlated, and "the study of objects under a skillful teacher, is sure to secure the attention and interest of the child." [45] Object teaching was a desirable innovation because it met the new criterion of appealing to children.

Schooling, some soft-line writers advanced, should be concerned with the real world; and proponents of this point of view were definitely in the camp of the soft-line educators. Their arguments for curriculum reform were concerned with two issues; one was the introduction of drawing and bookkeeping, the other was a lessened emphasis upon the classics and a correspondingly greater stress on the sciences. The soft-line educator's attempts to introduce drawing into the schools were dismissed typically by one hard-line critic as "pretty generally . . . condemned, as the idle and unprofitable resort of those who are prone to make caricatures of visible objects, rather than puzzle their heads with close application and hard study." [46]

The advocate of drawing, however, rejected the implication that he was equating interest and ease, thereby violating the dogma of the virtues of effort. Instead, he attempted to demonstrate the practical utility of drawing to engineers, professionals, architects, machinists, and mechanics: "in a pecuniary point of view," he concluded, "skill in drawing must prove highly beneficial to almost every class of the community." No educator, of course, could justify a subject on merely utilitarian, especially fiscal, grounds, since the acceptance of the financial criterion as sole arbiter of the content of the curriculum would represent a capitulation to the worst qualities of the times, indeed, a reinforcement of the very tendencies that schools were to offset. Thus, the drawing advocate defended his subject on other grounds: "Independently of its utility as contributing to success in business, its refining and elevating effect is by no means unimportant. He who has learned to depict the beauties of nature and art, more highly appreciates, and more keenly relishes those beauties; and hence has within himself an additional source of innocent enjoyment, and a new motive to moral excellence." [47] In sum, drawing conveniently united sublimation and preparation for business success in one curriculum reform.

An even stronger statement was provided by an advocate of bookkeeping who contended "that much of our instruction is unpractical; it does not assimilate easily with the wants of future life." To "render education practical . . . to select practical studies; and not only that," but to give "them all a practical turn" was his goal. The failure of students to acquire an acquaintance with the practical branches of mathematics, he argued, caused considerable inconvenience; and it was "far better" for students to learn relatively simple, but practical, numerical operations in school than "amid the cares and necessities of business, when perhaps a 'firm' may be obliged to go into bankruptcy in consequence of a few luckless mistakes and omissions." Yet, even the extreme practicalist could not omit his obeisance to the sacred aspects of educational theory: "such things are not to be learned at the expense of a sound and thorough discipline; by no means. That is the great end of all intellectual training. For this we must ever rely mainly upon the severer branches." [48]

Some advocates of innovation, however, argued that subjects other than the traditional "severer branches" combined mental discipline with other desirable qualities. An instance of this sort of argument was a speech of Thomas Sherwin, principal of Boston English High School, in an 1856 debate concerning "The Relative Importance of Ancient Classical and of Scientific Studies in an American System of Education." Sherwin began by admitting that classical study had many benefits. His criterion, he somewhat disarmingly admitted, was usefulness, "in its largest and best sense." Usefulness was "one great end and object of life, and he regarded him as the greatest man who contributes most to the physical, intellectual, and moral good of humanity." Here, Sherwin felt, the sciences were clearly superior to the classics, and as evidence he cited social and industrial improvements made possible by advances in pure and applied science. Not content to rest his case on utilitarianism, Sherwin turned to the traditional defense of the classicists and asserted, "As a mental discipline, the study of science may boldly challenge comparison with that of the classics." And he meant the applied as well as the pure sciences.[49]

Finally, Sherwin revealed his real affinity with the soft-line educators. "The interest which it awakens," he claimed, "is another benefit of the study of the sciences." He knew many boys who, "disgusted with the dry details of Latin and Greek Grammar," had become disciplinary problems in school; but when these same boys were introduced to science, "they had no time for mischief." The interest aroused by science teaching was an intensified form of that aroused by object teaching, since "new truths" were "constantly presenting themselves and the pathway of the learner" was "strewn with objects, each of which invites and fixes his attention." The arousal of interest, admitted Sherwin, is not always a measure of worthiness; "yet when the highest degree of utility and the loftiest mental efforts present also a strong attraction to the learner, this attraction is a recommendation." Moreover, "except to a few peculiarly constituted minds," it is doubtful, Sherwin contended, if the appeal of the classics can ever equal the attraction of the sciences. In other words, the sciences, at the least, were not inferior to the classics in terms of either discipline or utility; thus, all things being equal, it was legitimate to employ interest as the criterion for judging between the relative merits of the. two. This criterion accepted, the sciences clearly won the dominant place in the curriculum.[50]

Advocates of pedagogical reform gradually succeeded in spreading their notions to the schools. School reports, especially in the sixties, reveal that innovations were entering the schools, that in some instances the process of education was changing. In Lawrence, as we have seen, object teaching, physical instruction, and music entered the curriculum. In Beverly the same three innovations were all initiated and sponsored by the school committee, and the high school curriculum was liberalized in a way that would have made Sherwin happy. Latin became optional and bookkeeping, botany, geology, and chemistry entered the curriculum as electives. The ideal of their schools, proclaimed the committee, was a sound mind in a sound body.[51]

Another important educational issue was reflected in Beverly. On March 26, 1827, the grammar school master in the Grammar District, Rufus Putnam, Jr., advised the school committee of his dissatisfaction with a system of school "government" that offered as inducements "to a proper . . . effort, and to close application" only "the hope of distinction in school, or the fear of censure and punishment." The attainment of eminence in the future hardly moved young scholars, who cared only for "some *immediate,* or not *very* distant reward." On the other hand, the problems with punishment were twofold: it had a tendency "to cramp the mental energies and prevent the faculties from exerting their whole strength in a proper manner"; and second, it could control only a few pupils at any one time. What was needed, said Putnam, was a system of school management avoiding corporal punishment and offering immediate rewards. To meet these criteria Putnam recommended the appropriation of a small sum of money to be divided weekly among students, according to a system of merits and demerits.[52]

Although no record exists, it is doubtful that Putnam's suggestion was adopted, because one of the leading school committeemen was William Thorndike, a wealthy merchant who advocated a theory of motivation very different and more in line with the contentions of soft-line educators throughout the state. Thorndike, too, looked to a system of school government avoiding physical punishment and providing immediate gratifications. But he argued that the praise and affection of the teacher were themselves rewards of the highest order, as were the internal pleasures that came from both learning and a job well done. In fact, according to one town historian, Thorndike's influence was instrumental in persuading the town schools to discard emulation, which previously had been used as the principle of motivation. In a report on discipline Thorndike stressed that his goal was:

> to secure the attention of the scholars to the duties required of them, by engaging their affections, and offering as a reward for faithfulness, not the record of their good deeds, or the tempting allurements of gifts, but the smiles of a kind and endeared instructer [sic], and the satisfaction of an approving conscience, — feeling anxious that purer motives should stimulate the mind and swell the heart, than those which proceed from the promise of pecuniary rewards, or the display of acquisitions, the only value of which is their secret influence, and the tone they give to character and principle.[53]

Thorndike was echoing the contentions of the soft-line educators who attacked currently practiced techniques of motivation. Like Thorndike, the soft-line educators directed part of their assault at the appeal to emulation as a motive for learning. An example is one educator's criticism of the practice of the Boston grammar schools, which awarded medals and premiums to the most successful scholars. Awarding premiums for achievement, wrote this school-man, was pernicious: students "with a premium before their eyes" were "tempted to study for . . . *effect* . . . rather than for a deep, thorough acquaintance with the subject; to *appear* well, rather than to *do* well." Premiums, he continued, provided an "artificial stimulus" that reinforced the very social tendencies schools existed to eradicate. His "chief objection" to premiums was that they fostered "emulation" and tended "powerfully to excite and foster a class of passions and feelings which are al-ready . . . too active, and are producing much unhappiness in the world." Emulation, in short, was "the commencement of that competition, — that perpetual scrambling for the loaves and fishes, — that feverish aspiration for office and place, — which we see in after-life going on all around us, and which makes the eye of en-lightened humanity weep." Emulation was, moreover, according to definition, "a desire to excel for the *sake of the gratification of being superior to others*." In this sense, emulation reinforced the shallow, materialistic, and ostentatious aspects of society; it pre-vented the schools from instilling within students an intrinsic set of controls and standards. At the same time, it appealed to the desire for gratification, and gratification is a passion. Thus, in reinforcing a passion, in catering to the sensual, emulation counter-acted the school's attempts to substitute non-sensual for physical pleasures; it defeated the work of sublimation, which schoolmen strove to foster. "Let us," concluded the writer, "at an early period, begin to treat children as intellectual and moral beings, susceptible of influence from considerations of a pure and noble nature." [54] If man could be touched only through emulation, then he was in reality no better than an animal. If man could be touched only through emulation, then the whole carefully constructed rationale for his own existence would tumble down about the teacher's head, and teachers, it will be pointed out shortly, had more than an intellectual stake in the ideology of educational reform.

Who, then, supported emulation? Who were the hard-line educators? The answer is not entirely clear, but various sources connect opposition to object teaching, curriculum reform, and other innovations with opposition, sectarian and secular, to the Board of Education and its secretaries. In 1844, opposition came to a head when thirty-one grammar school masters of Boston violently attacked the seventh annual report of Horace Mann. In this struggle, at least, the lines were clearly drawn; and the hard-soft dimension became the focus of the controversy. To the grammar school masters Horace Mann and his supporters were dangerous radicals, whose attempted innovations were directed, consciously or otherwise, at undermining social and familial stability as well as further unravelling the moral fibre of Massachusetts children.

"The object of the elementary instruction of our public schools . . . is, not alone to impart a certain amount of knowledge," declared the grammar school masters, "but to give training . . . to discipline and strengthen their minds, and prepare them, as far as is possible for that independent action, which will be required of them in the discharge of the duties of life." The grammar school masters also wanted an essentially strong citizenry guided by intrinsic standards. Their enemy in the attainment of their objective was, they asserted, Horace Mann and his innovating followers. The masters centered their attack on Mann's appeal to the interest of the learner as a motivational technique. One critique of reliance on this sort of motivation was connected with the masters' objections to object teaching. In his seventh report, Mann had stressed the virtues of object teaching as practiced in Prussian schools. The masters replied:

That the method pursued by the Prussian instructor, is calculated to interest the mind of the pupil, we would not deny; for the variety of information and illustration must, without fail, gratify his curiosity, and for the time arrest his attention; but it will in no degree induce that habit of patient and constant attention to a subject, to which we have before alluded. On the other hand, the variety of information presented, and the novelty of illustration, would tend rather to dissipate, than to strengthen the habit of calm and deliberate attention to a single subject. And the mind of the pupil, instead of forming the habit of independent and individual effort . . . would become accustomed to act only through the force of that excitement which is supplied by the teacher.

The essence of the masters' criticism was that the pupils became dependent upon an outside stimulus; they became "accustomed to depend, for their motive to mental effort, upon that excitement alone which is furnished by their teacher." Object teaching fostered an accentuation of child-like dependency and its corollary, the lack of internalized motivation. Both of these were conditions that both hard- and soft-line educators said the school was to overcome. The appeal to interest expressed in object teaching had disastrous social implications: "And we most earnestly pray that our country, — whose citizens are already, to a great extent, destitute of habits of independent thought and deliberate action, and too much accustomed to think and act through the forced excitement of motives that may be, and often are, supplied by wicked and designing men, — may be kept forever safe from a system of public instruction which we think calculated to augment so great an evil." The masters were indeed firm in their rejection of motivation based on the interest of the child. "Nothing," they declared, had yielded more "mischief," and had been more "subversive of real happiness, than mistaking what may afford the child present gratification, for that which secures him lasting good." This had been precisely the mistake of Horace Mann, who would "have the teacher first amuse the child, so as to gain his goodwill at any expense, and would, then, have him attend to duty as a secondary matter." Mann's course of assigning priority to the pleasure of the child threatened "the welfare, both of the individual and society, by sending forth a sickly race, palsied in every limb, through idleness," and determined "to gratify a morbid thirst for pleasure." [55]

The masters also attacked other educational innovations. Of Mann's attempt to encourage the teaching of reading through the method now known as "look-say," the masters, predictably enough, snorted that it was an instance of his "misguided effort to make that pleasant, which, to some extent at least, must be disagreeable; to make that easy, which, from the nature of the case, is beset with unavoidable difficulties." They also attacked other actual and proposed innovations: the normal schools, the criticism of corporal punishment, and the disparagement of emulation. In their attack on the denigrators of emulation the real concerns of the masters began to emerge. Emulation was an important point because it was related to the problem of authority, perhaps the issue at the heart of the masters' worries. The masters considered themselves realists, in contrast to the soft-line educators, and they urged the "great importance" of "taking human nature as it really exists." Their view of human nature was essentially Calvinistic. The Emersonian emphasis on the inherent goodness of man, which the masters rightly claimed was reflected in the theories of Mann and his followers, was to these experienced schoolmen a naive example of wishful thinking. Perhaps unfortunately, but nevertheless undeniably, emulation was a basic human instinct. Therefore, a judicious appeal to emulation was a necessary component of educational practice, since teachers had to take into account all of man's motives and instincts. "Since nature has admitted its [emulation's] existence," wrote Reverend Leonard Withington in a passage approvingly quoted by the masters, "we are to allow it . . . Within bounds . . . emulation may fire the genius . . . without inflaming the passions or corrupting the heart." [56] With few statements could the soft-line educators disagree more.

The errors of the soft-line educators, the masters claimed, led them not only to overlook a basic facet of human nature but also to neglect the very foundations of school discipline. "But upon what shall school discipline be based?" asked the masters. "We answer unhesitatingly, upon *authority* as a starting-point." [57] It is scarcely too much to say that nothing was more important for the masters than submission to authority, and their protestations concerning the necessity of authority indicate their sense of the fundamental alteration occurring within the power structure of society. The masters reminded their readers that even in a democracy authority was necessary: "He who would command even, must first learn to obey." Indeed, when authority was the issue, the masters were unequivocal that:

> implicit obedience to rightful authority must be inculcated and enforced upon children as the very germ of all good order in future society, no one, who thinks soundly and follows out principles to their necessary results, will presume to deny. Yet, it is quite offensive now-a-days to ears polite, to talk of authority, and command, and injunction. We must persuade, and invite, and win. Respect for law is hardly sufficient to insure the infliction of its severe penalties. Thus the restraining influence of fear is ineffectual where most needed. Penalties, being too much dreaded by the innocent, are, for that very reason, too little dreaded by the guilty; who soon learn to avail themselves of the protecting shield that overstrained mercy casts before them.

The age was soft; it was an age "remarkable for the ascendancy of sympathy over the sterner virtues. Kindness, powerful, overwhelming in its proper sphere, has assumed a false position." Nevertheless, reminded the masters sternly, kindness was secondary; "kindness cannot supply the place of authority, nor gratitude that of submission." [58] The masters, in fact, were caught in a contradiction. They called, on the one hand, for individuals with internalized standards; persons whose actions adhered to an inner sense of right, not the dictates of society. Yet, on the other hand, they emphasized and preached obedience to an external authority; it was, moreover, an unquestioning obedience for which they asked. From whatever portion of the "great chain" of authority emanated a command, the "bounden duty of all" was not to "demand to know the reason of the command, as a necessary condition of obedience, but simply" to ask "if it be really the voice of rightful authority that speaks." "True obedience is a hearty response to acknowledged authority. It does not voluntarily comply with a request, but implicitly yields to a command." [59] The ideal of the masters was not the society that was emerging, but an older, perhaps idealized order, in which roles and relationships were fixed, in which the "great chain" of authority was well-defined.

On the basis of their assumption of the importance of authority, the masters had due cause for worry. "Authority . . . is clearly the starting-point of all government; the corner-stone of all order. Remove it, and the reign of anarchy and chaos instantly succeeds." And its removal is precisely what Horace Mann and his associates were trying to accomplish. The person who permitted any deviation from "docility" or "obedience" was a "disorganizer . . . weakening and dissolving the primal bond of civil society; and sapping the foundations of social order." [60] And this is what the theories of Mann intended; these theories claimed to follow nature, but their romanticized view really meant capitulation to "mere inclination." Children were taught "to lean upon the experience of others, to notice merely the superficial relations of things, and to trust for knowledge to the easy process of cursory observation. Now this propensity to observe without analysis, nature provides for without any artificial aid. Indeed, it predominates in children and savages." [61] And is this where Massachusetts was heading? Toward a society of children and savages?

Part of Mann's problem, according to the masters, was that he was an inexperienced theorist. "Education," wrote the Reverend Leonard Withington, "has often been tampered with by vain theorists." Indeed, a strong, explicit dislike of theory permeates the masters' diatribes; in their elevation of tradition and common sense and in their opposition to rationality and theory the masters revealed their almost classic Burkean conservatism. Withington, for instance, asserted, "Our conviction is" that education has "much more to hope from the collected wisdom and common prudence of the community, than from the suggestions of the individual"; and he proceeded to attack Locke, Milton, and Rousseau.[62] Mann was, in fact, more than a theorist; to the masters and other hard-line educators, he and his followers were dangerous radicals. Radical was to them a pejorative term of the utmost power. Thus, in a discussion of Mann's advocacy of normal schools and of his theories in general, the masters asserted with condemnation, "It is hard to conceive of any thing more radical and less conservative than such views." [63] Horace Mann and his cohorts had broken with the past; and their break, felt the masters, threatened the future of society.

The advocates of educational reform, associated with the advocates of social reform in general, threatened more than the future of society. They threatened the grammar school masters themselves. Pleas for educational reform implied that the grammar school masters were using cruel and obsolete methods and were unfit for their jobs. At least this is how the masters perceived the appeals for innovation. George Emerson wrote to Mann that the masters "say you are not sufficiently acquainted with the Boston schools, and that you do them an injustice when you imply that that there are better schools in Prussia." [64] The grammar school masters were career, not itinerant, teachers; they were proud of their work and felt that they were the representatives of an honorable educational tradition within the city. Yet, "the public mind," complained the masters, "has been so far poisoned, that great distrust is felt in all teachers of the *old* school." [65] And to them the old school, which they represented, was the good school. Even worse, Mann's seventh report, to the schoolmasters the most objectionable of the generally pernicious educational tracts of the times, would be widely circulated both within America and in foreign countries. People living outside the state would assume that Mann's disparaging remarks concerning Massachusetts teachers applied specifically to Boston, since Mann had an office in Boston and since Boston and the state were often equated in the eyes of outsiders. "Who, at home or abroad," complained the aggrieved masters, "will not think of the metropolis, when they read the secretary's *reflections* upon the teachers and the schools of Massachusetts?" [66]

The attack of the masters was the culmination of three types of assaults on educational innovation. One was the assault on the motivational techniques of the reformers, already described. The second was the assault on the secular nature of Massachusetts education under its more recent legislation. The masters themselves referred to Mann as sacrilegious, but Withington made the explicit connection between the modern softness in teaching methods and a pernicious new softness in school religion. "Children," he complained, "were to be led along by the cords of love." A "general Christianity," was to be taught, one "so weakened and diluted that infidels might believe, and sensualists applaud it." Part of the authority that modern education was challenging was that of religion.[67] Withington's harangue provides a link with a third kind of attack on educational innovation: the attack on centralization. Four years earlier a committee of the Massachusetts legislature had reported in favor of abolishing the Board of Education and the normal schools. Withington referred glowingly to the committee and urged legislators to re-read its report.[68]

The Board of Education, according to the committee's report, was founded as an instrument of recommendation only but had become an organ of regulation. The Board made recommendations that were virtually rubber-stamped by the legislature. Even if the Board had been adhering to its statutory functions, the authors of the report would still have opposed it since they argued that, in any case, voluntary teachers' associations were the best sources of information and recommendation.[69] Unhampered, inter-association rivalry would most effectively produce and promote pedagogical advance. However, these associations, which had done an outstanding job before the creation of the Board, were declining. Who, for instance, could speak freely at a convention called by a governmental agency? [70]

At any rate, the progress achieved in professions not under governmental control demonstrated that it was wisest to leave innovation to "private industry and free competition." The regulation and dissemination of pedagogical ideas was not, however, the worst sin of the Board. Most dangerous of all, the Board was trying to remodel Massachusetts education on French and Prussian lines, and both were highly centralized systems. Centralization, according to the authors of the report, would destroy the distinctive virtues of Massachusetts. They cited Tocqueville as the source of their observation that New England had derived great strength from its system of local self-government and that the absence of public spirit was, in Europe, "the greatest obstacle in the way of public improvements." Our "system of public instruction," argued the committee, "has proceeded upon the idea, that the local administrators of affairs, that is to say, the school committees of the several towns and districts, are qualified to superintend their schools, and might best be trusted with that superintendence." This was the American way; local administration "is not confined to public schools, but extends to every other department of life." Besides, local administration, the committee noted with accuracy, "interests a vast number of people in their welfare, whose zeal and activity, if they find themselves likely to be overshadowed by the controlling power of a Central Board, will be apt to grow faint." Thus, to the committee the Board represented "the commencement of a system of centralization . . . contrary, in every respect, to the true spirit of our democratic institutions." To the authors of the report the demands for statistics, the normal schools, and the creation of school libraries were the Board's primary agents of tyranny. Without any doubt, the committee noted, "common schools may be used as a potent means of engrafting into the minds of children, political, religious and moral opinions." But, "in a country like this, where such diversity of sentiments exists, especially upon theological subjects, and where morality is considered a part of religion, and is, to some extent, modified by sectarian views, the difficulty and danger [of trying to] introduce these subjects into our schools, according to one fixed and settled plan, to be devised by a Central Board, must be obvious." [71]

The report, therefore, recommended the abolition of the Board of Education* and the normal schools, which departed from precedent by taking education out of the hands "to which our ancestors wisely entrusted it." The Board was attempting "to form all our schools and all our teachers on one model"; and such an attempt, the authors concluded, "would destroy all competition — all emulation, and even the spirit of improvement itself." [72]

In all three types of complaints — instructional innovation,

---

* In 1860 there was another proposal to abolish the Board of Education. This time the committee investigating the matter reported in favor of retention (*House Document 127,* 1860). In order to demonstrate the nature of the opposition to the Board, the committee printed a few of the petitions it had received. These spoke louder than any arguments, for, by 1860, opposition to the Board had sunk to a bumbling semi-literacy, as the following passage (mis-spellings and grammatical errors reproduced) makes clear. "All parties want to see education thrive in massachus what will become of those orphan such as our Honerable secretary pict up down to Salem without something bearing resemblance to what I have been saying, why not take care of these things by the school districts it is much cheaper . . . it seems to me this will raise the lower end & bring them all into a solid phalanks to march onword & upword to gether & not have them scattered from dan to basheba. it seems to me this will not only be the best way but the ceapest way, for I know something about the value of money as means to ends & this is another reason why I ask you to divide the Fund (and he further demanded) the abolition of the Board of Education, who are prodigating the people's money, & sticking their hands into the money up to their elbows. till their eyes stick out with fat; (he demanded it) in the name of the Great Jehova and the Continental Congress, (who for their blessed deeds) . . . have been judged worthy to enter their fathers house not made with hands and eternal in the heavens & that to day are ranging those bright elysium fields that sourround their father mansion" (pp. 4–5).

secularization, and centralization — the reformers were perceived as radicals, altering the tried and true, the source of stability, strength and virtue. The opponents of the Board, its secretaries, and its ideas wanted, in part, to turn back the direction of development and return to a simpler, static society, a society in which the sources of authority were clear, a society in which the schoolmaster and the clergyman were important and in which decisions could be made, as they had always been, by the townspeople mutually associated and free from the pressure of a state government presiding over and fostering the creation of an urban-industrial society.

These critiques of innovation underscore two extremely important points about education in this period. First, there was virtually no opposition to education *per se,* or to public education. Virtually everyone agreed, or if they did not they kept still, that it was a good idea for a child to get some schooling. It is sometimes implied in historical writing that attacks such as that of the legislative committee on the Board were attacks on education. This is simply not so. The committee wrote, "An attempt may be made to identify the interests of common schools with the existence of the Board of Education, and any objections to that Board, may, perhaps, be regarded by some, as a covert assault upon our long established system of public instruction." According to the committee, however, this would be wrong, for the public schools far antedated the Board; and criticism of the Board was thus basically irrelevant to attachment to common schools. "It is, indeed, the attachment of your Committee to that system," the legislators asserted, "which has induced them to investigate, with care and attention, the tendencies of the Board of Education." [73] The same could be said of the masters and, probably, of many sectarians. The controversies of the time were not between pro- and anti-education forces; they were, rather, between advocates of different types of educational administration, of different styles of educational development, of different techniques of pedagogy. This is not to say that the controversies were only skin deep; they were not. People felt passionately about the issues involved and they often had much at stake; but they did agree that some sort of public schooling was a good thing.

To realize that the opponents of Horace Mann and his followers were not opposing education but were arguing for a different sort of education is to see, also, the existence of an alternative to the kind of reform that prevailed. This is important. This study has been, and will continue to be, critical of the reformers. So far it has charged that the fast and hard imposition of educational innovation upon skeptical and reluctant citizens contributed to the estrangement of the school from the culture of the working-class community. However, if this were somehow inevitable, if the reformers of the time had no other choice, then the criticism might be excessively moralistic or simply irrelevant. But there was a choice, at least at the beginning of the movement. A vocal and articulate group argued, in effect, for more slowly paced educational development. The legislative committee advocated schools that would continue to be integral parts of the community, responsive to its values, sustained by its efforts. They wanted change to come through community action; they sought, in short, an indigenous rather than a "hot house" style of educational development. These critics of Mann and his supporters sensed that professionalization and centralization would, to a large extent, cut off the school from the community; and they were right.

In spite of their denigration of the altered social and economic characteristics of Massachusetts, the soft-line educators were more in tune with their society than were the proponents of the hard line. The former group's emphasis on teaching through an appeal to interest was, implicitly, an assertion of the importance of the individual. They recognized the irrelevance of old sources of authority in a society of altered roles and relations. What would be the point of teaching obedience to external authority, if external authority could not be located? Yet the innovators believed that the complete absence of any authority over actions would lead to chaos and only intensify the socially disintegrating tendencies, about which they worried quite as much as their antagonists. Thus, the soft-line educators sought to internalize the source of authority, to create individuals who could steer their own way in an industrializing, urbanizing society, but who would steer with propriety, decency, and compassion. The soft-line educators claimed they were concerned with the higher, spiritual aspects of life; ironically, they stressed the very qualities most necessary for social mobility and economic success. Their ideal product would be superbly equipped to enter the competitive arena of Massachusetts business life. He would possess all the qualifications necessary to continue the development of urbanism and industrialism, all the qualities necessary to foster those aspects of society that had a pernicious effect on personality, and through personality on the life of the commonwealth.

The significance of the hard line is threefold. In the first place, the battle was a manifestation in the educational arena of a conflict in other areas of reform, a conflict in other states as well as in Massachusetts. In the 1840's especially, prison reformers advocating an environmental theory of crime and a penal system based on kindness and an effort to rehabilitate fought against experienced wardens of prisons who, pessimistic about the possibilities of rehabilitation, argued for a harsh system of punishment and an effort to break a man's will and produce repentance.[74] As one historian put it, "We may summarize the debate over capital punishment as a struggle between reformers who emphasized the effect of environment on moral behavior, arguing that criminals should be cured instead of being punished, and traditionalists who finally abandoned the rationalistic theory of deterrence and fell back upon a doctrine of intrinsic and absolute justice."[75] Other reformers struggled against what they considered harsh and obsolete methods of treating the insane; and psychiatrists lamented general practitioners who rejected modern theories, continued to try to cure mental disease through physical means such as bloodletting, and who almost totally refused to testify that any criminals were insane.[76] The process of creating new institutions, or reforming old ones, to cope with mounting social problems was characteristic of the 1840's. Essentially, this process generated a fundamental debate on the nature of man. Arrayed on one side were theorists representing an environmentalist, optimistic viewpoint. On the other side were practitioners, reflecting a more Calvinistic, pessimistic, and conservative approach to problems such as crime, insanity, and education.

In the second place, the soft line clearly won in mid-nineteenth century Massachusetts — in the material consulted for this study no other significant outburst of the hard line appeared — and the victory of the soft line marked the ending of serious educational debate. Its virtues or failings aside, the vigorous articulation of the hard line had fostered a healthy situation. From the conflicting viewpoints might have arisen a genuine and constructive dialogue that would have forced educational promoters to face the contradictions in their own ideology and to examine, refine, and improve their theories. A continuing debate between socially respected opponents might have forced educators continually to confront their ideas critically; it might have prevented the onset of the complacency that helped make educational thought increasingly sterile, unreal, and routine. The victory of the soft line was a major defeat for the quality of American education.

But why did the soft line spread through school reports and teachers' journals and become elevated to the status of ideology? One reason was the political power that Mann and his supporters wielded during and after the controversy. It is the consequence of this almost brutal exercise of power that marks the third way in which the controversy between Mann and the masters was significant. One political tactic was for Mann's friends immediately to petition the legislature to establish a new normal school. The bill they sponsored was successful, and in this respect Mann and his followers proved their power to further their favorite innovation in spite of widespread public criticism. In the state legislature it was clear on whose side power lay.

The other ploy was the concerted attempt by Mann's friends, particularly Charles Sumner and Samuel Gridley Howe, to spearhead a takeover of the Boston school committee. "Once in office," writes one historian, "they would have the whip hand over the masters and could put through a 'purgation' of the personnel of one school, replacing them by progressives who could then run it as a model that would effect a revolution in education." The school committee could have a whip hand over the masters because teachers did not have tenure and were voted upon annually by the committee. Through active political maneuvering Sumner and Howe received nominations by the Whig party as two of their candidates for the school board, and Howe was elected. Although the reformers were not a majority, their impact was strong. Two of them, including Howe, managed to get themselves appointed to examine the grammar schools. Contrary to custom, they gave written examinations with questions previously unknown to the teachers. On the basis of these examinations they published a scathing indictment of the Boston grammar schools in their annual report. They tried hard to prevent the re-hiring of some of the offending masters, and they obviously made life uncomfortable and insecure for a number of them. Indeed, although the most offensive master was not fired, he was transferred (temporarily as it turned out) to another school. There were even reports that corporal punishment was discontinued in Boston; and other reforms were started. The most important was the consolidation of the administrative system through elimination of the separate, unwieldy primary school board, followed in a few years by the appointment of a city superintendent of schools, one of the reformers' primary goals. Administrative changes in general enhanced and tightened central supervision at the expense of the virtual autonomy the masters had previously enjoyed.[77]

It is hard to imagine that corporal punishment really disappeared from the schools, or that the masters changed their minds on the topics of controversy. In fact, evidence from the 1870's reveals that even if corporal punishment had once been abolished, it had returned; that even if the masters had once been silenced, they could still cause trouble.[78] Yet for this period it is important to remember that it had been demonstrated how unwise it was to oppose the reformers, how brutal and vindictive they could be, how they could heap public scorn on anyone who fought them. For a schoolmaster to resurrect the hard line would be to commit professional suicide. Teachers were not about to do this, and those teachers who wrote in the 1850's found different tactics for increasing the respect of the community for the work of the educator.

5. GOD'S GARDENER: STRATEGIES OF TEACHER MOBILITY

"It is not easy to account for the fact," complained a writer in the *Massachusetts Teacher*, "that the calling of a teacher is generally ranked, not only below the other professions, but even below some of the more common industrial pursuits." [79] Easy to account for the fact or not, no one dissented from the conclusion that the social status of teachers was dreadfully low. If money had become the measure of all things, as social critics maintained, then the rank of teachers was no mystery; teachers were paid very poorly.

In 1843, "in one of the most cultivated towns in the Commonwealth," the author of an article in the *Common School Journal* had set out to determine "the wages of journeymen, shoemakers, carpenters, blacksmiths, painters, carriage-makers, wheelwrights, harness-makers, cabinet and piano-forte makers, and some others." His conclusions were distressing. Every trade received more: "some of them received fifty, and a few one hundred per cent more than was paid to any of the teachers of the district schools of the town." [80] Similarly, nine years later, in 1852, the enlightened school committee of Cambridge complained: "The largest salary paid to a public teacher in Cambridge is not equal to that of a confidential clerk in a commercial establishment; it is about half as large as the salary of the Cashier in a Boston Bank; while the lowest salaries paid in the Alphabet and Primary Schools are less than the wages of a good cook, and not more than as much as can be earned by a tolerable needle-woman. A fashionable music teacher or dancing master easily makes an income superior to the combined salaries of all the teachers in the Cambridge High School together." [81] There were reasons of substance as well as pride for teachers to seek to raise their status and to educate the public concerning the importance of the common schools.

The teachers themselves consciously adopted strategies designed to raise their standing within the community. The improvement of status was the motive, for instance, behind the founding, in 1847, of the Massachusetts Teachers Association and the establishment of its journal, the *Massachusetts Teacher,* in the following year. The first issue of the journal explained that the people, in the present age of equality, were "fast taking the reins in their own hands," and were "driving on, by motive powers entirely their own, — *Association* and the *Press*." Although both association and the press had been used by religious and political groups with great success, educators still lagged behind the times in their failure to use the most modern means of mass influence. The article concluded, "If we wish the teacher in Education to rank beside the teacher in Religion and Government, we must use the same means that they employ." [82]

One strategy for the improvement of teacher status was to remove the blame for educational failure from the school to the home. Articles in the *Massachusetts Teacher* reminded readers of the power of parents to increase the teacher's influence or, on the other hand, to undermine his efforts. For instance, some parents complained of the severity of school discipline; but, chided an article, all too often children learned disrespect for authority, especially for the school, at home. "If parents were sufficiently faithful in . . . home preparation, the necessity for stringent discipline would be greatly diminished, and the moral influence of the teacher . . . greatly enhanced." [83]

The editor of the *Massachusetts Teacher* commended the views of a speaker at a recent teachers' meeting to "the careful consideration of our readers." "Ought not teaching," the speaker asked, "to be raising [sic] to the rank of a liberal profession, distinctly recognized as such?" To accomplish this end persons entering teaching from "caprice" or temporarily from financial motives should be barred in the future. Professionalization would be assured by "a high standard of preliminary requisition," "emoluments corresponding to its true dignity and value," and protection "from the intrusions of the incompetent and unskillful." The time had arrived for the employment and evaluation of teachers to be freed from "the verdict of men engaged in other occupations"; the teaching force had to secure "its own professional faculty, or appropriate body, of whatever name, competent and empowered to grant professional certificates, licences or diplomas." [84] To the speaker, and apparently to many other teachers as well, the hallmark of a profession was control over entry. Through control over entry teachers hoped to become permanent, well qualified, and prestigous professionals.

Teachers' recognition of the importance of permanency and qualification implied the necessity of special training. Thus, in contrast to the earlier response of the Boston schoolmasters, the Massachusetts Teachers Association in the 1850's allied itself with the normal schools and with educational innovation. One author of an article in the *Massachusetts Teacher* employed an analogy that would be used, in the future, with increasing frequency: "The man who imagines himself a teacher, qualified for the responsible duties of an instructor, merely because he has seen others teach in a particular way, is just as much an empiric, as a pretender in medicine, who occasionally walks through the wards of a hospital." "The day for quack pedagogues is passed." Certainly, "no person" could "excel as an instructor" who failed to "make some special preparation for his work, and acquaint himself with the philosophy of teaching, and the art of conducting and governing a school." [85] Theory and normal schools became allies of the teachers in their drive for status. They provided the mystery that would set teachers apart from the rest of mankind. Theory and special preparation contained the potential to make schoolteaching a profession.

The denial of responsibility for failure, the desire to gain control over entry, and the emphasis on proper preparation were all important strategies of occupational mobility; but none were as dominant, or as basic, as the continual repetition of the absolute superiority of the teacher and his calling to all other men and jobs. The *Massachusetts Teacher* repeatedly printed articles concerned with the compensation of the teacher. What was this compensation? What could compensate for the absence of money and respect, the absence of any of the usual criteria of success in a materialistic society? Simply this: the teacher was above money. He served not the spirit of materialistic gain; in fact, it was he who counteracted the sordid tendencies of his age; on his shoulders lay the burden of inculcating a respect for the spiritual in place of the sensual, of fostering the internalization of restraint, of preserving morality and social cohesion. In short, the teacher, God's emissary, was responsible for the future of the human race. An article in the *Massachusetts Teacher* pointed out the teacher's elevated position:

An employment is elevated in dignity in proportion to the importance of its subject, or the materials with which it has to do. The magistrate, or the commander of an army, ranks above the herdsman, for the one governs brutes, the other, men. The maker of chronometers takes rank above the blacksmith, because he is employed with more costly and delicate materials.

Upon this principle, the work of teaching, especially if we include in this term the work of the ministry, surpasses all other occupations in point of dignity. The farmer, the mechanic, the merchant, are employed with material and perishable things. The legal profession is busied with forms and precedents, and with crimes and penalties, and, with the exception of its pleading, it has but little to do directly with the mind. Medical skill is employed almost exclusively upon the outer man, the temporary habitation of the soul. But the subject of the teacher's work is the mind, the masterpiece of the great Architect, delicate in structure, transcendent in value, immortal in destiny.[86]

Similarly, a stanza from "God's Gardener," written expressly for the *Teacher,* exhorted:

> Magnify your office, teacher!
> Higher than the kings of earth; —
> Are you not the prophet, preacher,
> To the future giving birth? [87]

Regardless of the opinion of the community, the teacher at least had the compensation of knowing that his was the most important office on earth.

Teachers took seriously the notion of their moral influence; to them an attack on that notion was a personal assault of the gravest danger. This was the threat that provoked the attack on Cyrus Peirce at the annual meeting of the American Institute of Instruction in 1853. In that year the Institute awarded the prize for its annual essay contest to Peirce for an essay entitled "Crime, its Cause and Cure." On Wednesday, August 17, 1853, in the afternoon, Mr. Peirce read his essay before the assembled educators. The point of the essay, according to Peirce, was that secular instruction by itself was no guarantee against crime, and in his plea for increased moral instruction he pointed out that an increase in crime had accompanied the increase in the provision of formal education. He cited surveys purporting to show that convicts were often better educated "than the generality of their class." [88]

The educationists responded with fury. To them Mr. Peirce had not only denied the moral efficacy of the common schools but had implied that they contributed to crime. Mr. Bishop of Boston complained that "he felt called upon, as having spent his whole life in the Common School cause, to say that we ought not to be told that for thirty years we have been doing the public an injury, by a defective system of education. He denied it." Dr. Hooker of Hartford commented on Peirce's statistics; he admitted he had no evidence but nonetheless declared, "There must be some mistake." Even Barnas Sears, renowned for his urbanity and conciliatory tact, "remonstrated against sending out such a prize essay as this. It was a libel upon the Common Schools of New England." [89]

The Institute did not allow the essay to be made public, voting instead to return the essay to its author but to allow him to keep the prize money.[90] Peirce's mild doubts and strictures had threatened the very foundations upon which the educationists based their existence. With its most august solemnity the synod found him guilty of heresy. Facts were irrelevant; teachers knew they were above the rest of mankind; they knew that, in the last analysis, they alone were responsible for the future of civilization; whatever statistics might show, they knew they were succeeding. Else, how could they continue to live in penury and submit to the scorn of society? If their interpretation of Peirce's essay was correct, and if they accepted this interpretation as true, then in forsaking business for teaching, in scorning the market place, teachers would be not saints but failures.

Moreover, teachers' salaries might be threatened by Peirce's criticisms. Although teachers' salaries were low by comparison with other occupations, they had risen substantially in the years between 1840 and 1853. And the increase was a real one since the cost of living had remained relatively stable (see tables in

Appendix A). One conclusion that teachers could draw was that the public was buying the ideology of reform and slowly accepting the central role of the pedagogue in shaping the future of society. What would happen if Peirce's notions became public? What would happen if teachers were exposed as impotent or hurtful? Surely there were financial as well as emotional reasons for the Institute to turn its fury upon a former champion of its cause.

The new urban pedagogy in which the teachers invested so heavily could not reach its goals. Within educational ideology contradictory perceptions of the new society were fused into a set of goals that were sometimes logically incompatible, nearly always implausible. To join the best of the past with the dynamism of the future, to permeate a landscape of cities and factories with the social and moral virtues of the countryside — all this, as the Lawrence experience, especially, has revealed, was more than education could do, more, probably, than any set of institutions could accomplish. At its core the ideology was soft; the threads that joined the dualistic goals of schoolmen were woven of the flimsiest logic. Schools were to unleash and contain the forces of industrialism, to push social attitudes into a shape that fit the mold of the future and the contours of the past, to send forth individuals supremely equipped both to resist the degenerating tendencies of modern life and to hasten their development. Throughout educational ideology ran deep fissures straining always to split into chasms; but schoolmen leaned ever more heavily upon their construct and refused to see its flaws.

Cyrus Peirce had been right. Despite the common school revival, crime had increased.[91] Educators' paranoiac response, their categoric denial of what had really happened, set the tone for the future. Educators were developing their own world. They had associations and training schools to impart their own version of the truth. Soon teachers would win the certification laws that they asked for in the 1850's; teaching had acquired a core of career professionals — high school principals and administrators — that would expand in size until it controlled all aspects of local school affairs except the committees themselves.[92] Soon teachers would have a machine so large that they would be able to talk only to each other. And to talk to each other would become increasingly necessary. Because they built the rationale for their own existence and their increasing command of community resources upon an implausible ideology ever more divorced from reality, educators had to turn inward; they had to avoid a hard look at the world around the schools and at their own work; they had to retreat into an ideology that became a myth. By the 1850's educators had helped set the stage for the rigid, sterile bureaucracies that soon would operate most urban schools.

The work represented by these institutions [reform schools] has represented more fully the idea of state education than has the work of any other part of the educational system.

David Snedden, 1907

Most of you, indeed, cannot but have been part and parcel of one of those huge, mechanical, educational machines, or mills, as they might more properly be called. They are, I believe, peculiar to our own time and country, and are so organized as to combine as nearly as possible the principal characteristics of the cotton-mill and the railroad with those of the model state's prison.

Charles Francis Adams, Jr., 1880

Part III. Compulsory Education and the Urban Delinquent: The State Reform School

1. REFORMERS AGAINST THE REFORM SCHOOL

The report of the Massachusetts Board of State Charities for 1865 must have surprised many people. Samuel Gridley Howe and Frank Sanborn, prominent and eclectic social reformers, were attacking the state reform school. Their attack undoubtedly came as somewhat of a shock because seventeen years earlier the school had been started with the ardent support of the very reformist circles that Howe and Sanborn represented. To many, the reform school was a paragon of scientific penology, a landmark in the progress of man's enlightened treatment of his fellows, a beacon radiating throughout the land the modern liberality of the commonwealth. Why, then, did Howe and Sanborn heap blame upon this institution less than two decades after its founding? When we can answer this question, we will see much more clearly the fate of mid-nineteenth century reform.

One reason for including the reform school in this study is that aspects of its early history help to clarify and evaluate several salient features of the whole movement for educational reform. But there are other reasons equally important. Educators saw the reform school as part of the commonwealth's system of public education. The words *reform* and *school* had very specific meanings and were chosen with care; most Massachusetts educators would probably have agreed with the authority who wrote in 1907

that reform schools represent "more fully the idea of state education than . . . any other part of the educational system." [1] Thus,
in a study of the early reform school we are not looking at an
institution intended to be penal but at one designed to be educational. Themes that are muted and implied throughout most of
the rest of the literature of educational reform are explicit in dis-
cussions related to the reform school. When Massachusetts reformers talked about the re-making of urban delinquents, they
took off their velvet gloves, and the fact that education was to be a
key weapon in a battle against poverty, crime, and vice became
explicitly, even stridently, clear. Furthermore, the study of one
institution, like the analysis of a particular town, lets us see more
clearly how assumptions about the powers of education fared when
confronted with social reality. Finally, the reform school is important because it was the first form of state-wide compulsory
education in the United States.

2. DELINQUENCY AND THE GRADING OF PRISONS

Educational reform was one aspect of a widespread effort of
government, both state and local, and private philanthropy to
create a network of institutions capable of restraining the effects
of the onset of large-scale manufacturing and increasing urbanism.
Besides establishing the reform school, the state, between the
1830's and 1865, altered its poor laws and established state
almshouses; it built hospitals for different classes of paupers and
criminals; it passed labor laws; and, more dramatic, it created a
central agency whose duty was to coordinate the mid-nineteenth
century war on poverty and crime. As a result of the recommendation of a legislative committee that in 1858 surveyed the public
charitable institutions of the state, the legislature created the Board
of State Charities in 1863. The new body was modeled on the
Board of Education and had a permanent secretary and an appointed, rotating membership. Its duty was to investigate, publish

its findings, and make recommendations to the legislature. The reports of its secretary provide a comprehensive view of the problem of crime and poverty in the commonwealth and a shrewd assessment of the state's institutions.[2] The first secretary, whose initial five-hundred-page historical and analytic report was for the times a truly remarkable social investigation, was Frank B. Sanborn, poet, transcendentalist, intimate and disciple of Emerson. Sanborn provides a link between the idealistic transcendentalists and the social problems of the day; indeed, his work suggests that historians, such as Arthur Schlesinger, Jr., who have argued that the transcendentalists isolated themselves from the crucial issues of the time, have been in error. Perhaps Ralph Waldo Emerson was the T. H. Green of the early and mid-nineteenth century.[3]

Private as well as state philanthropy increased markedly in the decades preceding the Civil War. Between 1815 and 1830, according to one estimate, private philanthropy in Boston averaged $100,000 per year; between 1830 and 1845 the figure was $133,-000; and in the year 1864–65 a cautious estimate revealed an increase to $500,000.[4] But public and private philanthropists did not act in isolation. One significant joint venture was the first normal school;[5] another was the first reform school.

In 1846 two petitions to the State legislature urged the creation of a state manual labor school.[6] The committee appointed to investigate the petitions reported favorably, and a commission was appointed to select and purchase a site.[7] The prospects and prestige of the project were enhanced by an anonymous gift of $10,000 from Theodore Lyman, who promised an equal sum in the future. Lyman, ex-mayor of Boston, had a particular interest in reform schools since he had been influential in establishing a private one on Thompson's Island off the coast of Boston.

In 1814 the Boston Asylum for Indigent Boys had been created through private philanthropy. The asylum never became, strictly speaking, a reform school since its inmates had not been convicted of a crime. Rather, it took orphans and other neglected children "to restrain" them "from vicious courses by a judicious system of education." In 1831, when the asylum, encountering severe financial difficulties, started a public appeal for funds, a group of philanthropists were also soliciting donations to establish a farm school, and with the money collected they purchased Thompson's Island. The boys in the asylum were transferred to the farm school and the two charities combined; for a number of years the president of the directors of the farm school was Theodore Lyman. In 1846 Lyman proposed that the school be enlarged to accommodate boys from communities outside Boston; but the other directors did not accept his proposal, "and, (perhaps in consequence,) General Lyman directed his munificence" toward the state reform school at Westborough.[8] Lyman continued his generosity by willing it $50,000.

The legislative commissioners' report and land purchase were received favorably by the legislature, which passed a law ordering the erection of a reform school, a term the commissioners preferred to manual labor.[9] The governing body of the school was a board of seven trustees responsible to the governor, and in 1863 it was placed under the surveillance of the Board of State Charities. The power of committing boys was vested in each magistrate in the commonwealth, a system later radically altered. Building proceeded rapidly, and on December 7, 1848, the first state reform school officially opened, first definitely in the United States and England, and probably in Europe.

Writers concerned with the reform school were particularly proud that Massachusetts was the first state to establish an institution specifically designed for the reformation of juveniles. Municipalities, however, had anticipated the state. In 1825 the New York House of Refuge was opened through private philanthropy. The city granted increasing sums for its maintenance, and after 1830 "the institution was entirely supported by public appropriations." [10] The other reformatory preceding Westborough was the

Boston House of Reformation, opened in 1827. By 1865, however, the Boston institution and its municipal counterpart, opened
at Lowell in 1851, differed from the state school, since the former
were "mainly, if not exclusively, devoted to the reception of
Truants," whereas the inmates of Westborough were usually committed on different charges.* A number of other municipal reform, really truant, schools were established following the passage
of a state truant law in 1862 that required each city and town to
provide suitable accommodations for children convicted of habitual truancy.[11]

The two concerns that combined to form the argument that the
commonwealth should create a reform shool were the evils of
mixing juvenile delinquents with mature criminals in the same jail
and apprehension at an increase in crime. Each of the two petitions sent the state legislature in 1846 stressed one of these
concerns. The first petition came from the second jury of trials in
Norfolk County. The foreman of the jury was Francis George
Shaw. Shaw was a wealthy businessman and litterateur active at
Brook Farm and in the affairs of Roxbury. He again provides a
link between transcendentalism and social reform. The second
petition, from the selectmen of the town of Roxbury in Norfolk

* The relation of the state reform school at Westborough to municipal
reformatories and truant schools is somewhat complex. When the reform
school was opened in 1848, truancy was not a legal offense and boys actually imprisoned for truancy were convicted on other charges, usually "stub-
borness." The first law making truancy an offense was passed in 1850.
Surprisingly, truancy became a punishable offense two years before attendance at school became compulsory! Truant laws of 1850 and 1852 forced
a differentiation in reform institutions. Truants could only be given sentences of first one, then two years. Boys could only be sent to the reform
school for the duration of their minority. Thus, if a magistrate convicted a
boy of truancy he had to send him elsewhere than to Westborough. Changes
in the pattern of offenses for which boys were sent to municipal institutions
were reflected in the Boston House of Reformation. At first this took boys
for all sorts of offenses. After the passing of the truant law, truancy gradually gained prominence among the offenses of boys committed until the
school became primarily a truant school.

County, was sent "in aid of the petition of F. G. Shaw." The petition of the Norfolk jury argued its case succinctly: "The House of Correction in this County is not a fit or suitable place for the confinement and detention of juvenile offenders . . . there is or can be no suitable employment provided . . . they are necessarily exposed to the contaminating influence of convicts already hardened in crime . . . they are therefore depraved rather than reformed . . . and consequently when discharged, fitter subjects for detention than when they were committed." [12]

The answers to questions asked of selected individuals by the legislative committee reinforced this argument. Judge Emory Washburn of Worcester replied that he had "always felt . . . serious objections to committing boys . . . to a jail or house of correction" because it placed "a stigma upon the character of the boy, which is a serious clog to his success in life." Moreover, the policy afforded a boy little opportunity for either an intellectual or moral education, and, most serious, it allowed him "to see and hold intercourse with the older prisoners." Moses Grant of Boston put the matter even more bluntly. "Boston jail," he wrote, is "as great a school of vice as can be well imagined, and eminently calculated to harden" boys "in crime." In their report the legislative committee echoed the petitions and responses. By the present penal policy, the report claimed, a boy was forced "for a short time to associate with desperate and hardened criminals, and . . . then returned upon the community with feelings hardened, his moral sense blunted, and the spirit of revenge burning in his bosom, it may be, against those whom he considers the instruments of his degradation." [13]

Judge Washburn, in his speech at the opening of the reform school, considered penal policy in the light of other criteria. Improvement in the treatment of criminals, he claimed, was one sign of the advance of civilization. "For some reason, criminal justice seems to have been almost always behind the age in which it was administered." To treat young and old offenders alike violated "one of the first principles of the science of prison discipline, as well as of common humanity." [14] Washburn's remarks highlight two important aspects of mid-nineteenth century reform. First was the consciousness that altered social conditions required altered social institutions. In part the high school was to bring the system of public education into line with economic progress; the reform school was to bring the penal system into line with scientific and moral advance. Second was an increased sensitivity to differences in the age and condition of individuals. The theory of educational reform urged an almost child-centered pedagogy; the theory of penal reform urged a child-centered prison. (In this period, special institutions were also established for the insane, the blind, the deaf, and for teachers.) The theory of educational reform urged the grading of schools; the theory of penal reform urged the grading of prisons.

The desire to provide distinct and humane treatment for children was only one of the concerns behind the founding of the reform school. The other was an increase in crime, especially juvenile crime. In their petition the Roxbury selectmen complained:

> We have been called upon frequently to take charge of boys and give them a place in our Alms House, who have been in the habit of lodging in barns and sheds, and exposed to everything which is bad, and dangerous to society, who have no friends to direct them and if they have cannot control them — We have noticed the most profligate and profane, who are strolling about the streets, who never go to school because they have no one to make them, who are fitting themselves for the most dangerous [sic] in society, growing up in hardened guilt, destroying themselves, and poisoning society with their wickedness.[15]

The selectmen included with their petition an extract from the report of the town school committee, which stressed the existence of "a class of large boys, numerous and we fear increasing, who seldom or never go to school and have little or no visible occupation." Without correction, these boys would grow to be "the more perceptible disturbers [*sic*] pests and burdens" of society.[16] Similarly, in answer to the questions of the legislative committee Judge S. D. Parker of Boston asserted "that during the year 1845, there has been a great and alarming increase of juvenile offenders, and the crimes these youths have committed were of a very aggravated nature, including arson, stabbing, shopbreaking, larcenies, etc"; similarly, from Charlestown William Sawyer observed, "I believe the want, exposure, temptation and suffering of some juveniles in this town, would astound those who have never given any attention to it." [17] "Whoever has been familiar with our criminal courts," observed Judge Washburn, "cannot have failed to mark the increase of crime of late, especially among the young." [18] The reform school was a key strategy proposed for dealing with the alarming increase in crime; but it was a strategy based on certain assumptions about the nature of crime and poverty, assumptions for which reformers thought they had good evidence.

3. FROM FAVORABLE IMPRESSIONS TO IMPERFECTION OF THE STOCK: THE THEORY OF CRIME AND POVERTY

In the lexicon of reformers the first fact about crime was its urban nature. The legislative commission of 1847 asserted confidently, "We know that most of the inmates will come from populous places";[19] and their prediction was fulfilled. In 1850, for instance, 101 of the 311 inmates came from Suffolk County, 63 of the boys from Essex and 59 from Middlesex. These were the most densely populated and industrial counties. Only 30 were sent "from the five western counties." From these figures the superintendent concluded that "the greater proportion of commitments are from the manufacturing portion of the State, and from that section containing the large towns and cities; and but few from the

THE URBAN DELINQUENT | 171

agricultural part of our community." [20] Likewise, in 1864 the

agricultural part of our community." [20] Likewise, in 1864 the
trustees of the reform school noted, "We see a large number of
boys in the State, most of them in the cities and larger towns, who
unless early placed in some such school as this, must inevitably
become a very dangerous class." [21] The relationship assumed between cities and crime was reflected in popular literature as well
as in reformist tracts. David Brion Davis writes:

> During the 1840's fictional descriptions of city crime increased
> to astonishing proportions. In 1853 George Lippard presented,
> against a general backdrop of New York poverty, prostitution,
> and violent death, vivid accounts of six rapes, seven adulteries,
> and twelve murders. In the works of Ingraham, Buntline, Henri
> Foster, and Lippard, the "true" nature of the city was revealed
> to the American people. Under the bustling activity, the growing
> commerce, the glittering stores, and the finery of dress, they
> beheld an incredible social decay. If one cared to leave the
> main thoroughfares and walk into Boston's Ann Street or New
> York's Five Points, one would find a darkened area of poverty
> and oppression, where ragged children begged for pennies, where
> haggard prostitutes desperately solicited trade, where strangers
> suddenly disappeared, and where corpses stiffened in doorways
> and gutters, arousing neither sympathy nor attention.[22]

But how did cities cause crime? Nathan Crosby, justice of the
police court of Lowell, related to the legislative commission the
chilling, if melodramatic, fate of many nice New England farm
girls who came to work in the model city. Often, he claimed, girls
between fifteen and seventeen years old came to Lowell with only
enough money for a week's board. If they failed to find work, they
were ejected from their boarding house and sought another, "to
be again turned away. In the mean time, cab-drivers and others
take advantage of their necessities and ruin them." Still others were
"decoyed away in cabs and long walks, till their boarding houses"
were closed, and after a repetition of such "delinquencies," were

permanently turned away, only to be "taken up by the watchmen as *night-walkers.*" Indeed, the town had "*many* young girls who spend their nights in unfinished and old houses, in the woods, etc., and are supplied with food by the rascals who have ruined them." Here, most graphically, was a need for reformation, and Crosby pleaded, unsuccessfully, that the new reform school be coeducational.[23] Aside from facilitating the seduction of innocent girls, cities promoted crime by bringing together large numbers of potential offenders. "Leagued together for plunder, and in some instances, the accomplices of adult rogues," they raided property and either evaded the law or received short sentences. In short, they "were accelerated in a vicious and criminal career." [24]

In the reformers' view, crime, poverty, immigration, and urbanism were inextricably woven together; Massachusetts, Emory Washburn wrote, was a state

> with a population more dense than that of any of her sister states; with a metropolis ranking, in point of numbers, among the first class of the cities in our country; with cities and villages scattered all over her territory, and teeming with active life, gathering within its crowded masses those poisonous seeds of vice, which by some strange law of our nature, germinate most surely where men do most congregate; with hosts of foreigners crowding to our shores, and bringing with them the habits and associations of foreign lands; with intemperance, that great mother of poverty, and vice, and crime, spreading out her lures on every side.[25]

Within this appalling urban society, observed the superintendent of the reform school in 1850, recurred a typical pattern through which boys became delinquents. The first crime was often truancy from school. The truant became familiar with "*horse racing, the bowling saloon,* the theatrical exhibitions, and other similar places of amusement, debauchery and crime." In the bowling alley, "initiated by being employed in setting pins," he soon acquired the "desire to act the man" and became "a juvenile gambler. Profanity, drunkenness, and licentiousness" soon followed, "hurrying him forward in the path of crime and ruin." [26]

Essentially, the boy became a criminal because he yielded to temptation; he had not "moral principle sufficient to restrain him." [27] But for two reasons the boy himself could not be blamed for his depravity; he was innately neither vicious nor weak, but the victim of poverty and familial failure.[28] Between poverty and crime, reformers held, was an intimate connection; the worst boy came from "the lowest stratum." [29] The unity of crime and poverty was stressed by Frank Sanborn, secretary of the Board of State Charities. "This," he asserted, "is a point which cannot be too strongly urged." "No less than three-fourths of what is technically called crime . . . is the *direct* result of poverty and its attendant evils." "Of the thousands committed to our prisons during the past year, not more than one in ten has ever owned property to the value of a thousand dollars, and the great majority have never owned anything that could well be called property." [30]

One reason cities bred crime is that they bred poverty. The legislative committee on charitable institutions observed, "It is in the cities and large towns that the greater proportion of our State paupers are found." Of the 7,100 inmates in the state almshouses in 1858, 2,719 were from Boston and 480 from Lowell. The cities that sent most paupers, asserted the committee, were the most industrial; immigration sponsored by industrial corporations had caused the alarming increase in the bill for public charity: "monster corporations import by the shipload the employees who fill their mills, do the base drudgery of their workshops and their degrading, ill paid, menial services in every branch of business. They allow them to erect in their cities and towns the most miserable shanties for dwellings, or else the capitalists, who profit by their labor, do it in their stead. In them are made the paupers of the state." According to the committee the foreign population of the five cities leading in the production of paupers was: Boston, 61.75 percent;

Lawrence, 71.66 percent; Lowell, 54.17 percent; Roxbury, 63.70 percent; and Chicopee, about 33 percent.[31]

The nature of the urban family was one of the "attendant evils" of poverty most conducive to criminality. A "family whose parental instructors are ignorant, inefficient and immoral," wrote the chaplain of the reform school in 1859, "is quite sure to make a disastrous failure of the education of the little ones committed to its care." [32] Since pedagogical theory held that the shape of the essentially plastic character of the child was determined by the models from which it gained impressions and direction, it was, said Dr. S. B. Woodward of the State Lunatic Hospital in Worcester, "absolutely important that the young be subjected to favorable impressions, and be trained in the course of virtue and of duty, or the tendency will be unfavorable, and great hazard be run, of a career of vice with individuals whose moral and intellectual culture has been neglected in childhood and early youth." [33] The parental models, the impressions provided in cities, were the worst possible. Charlestown, claimed William Sawyer, "is no worse than other large places, where children are suffered to grow up without any moral culture, and what is worse, amidst scenes of drunkenness, debauchery, and other crime." Judge Sawyer continued:

there is seldom a case of a juvenile offender, in which I am not well satisfied that the parents, or persons having the child in charge, is most blamable — they take no pains to make him attend school — they suffer him to be out nights without knowing or caring where; and, in many instances, they are incapable of taking care of themselves, much less their children; they have no home fit for a child; their residence is a grog shop; their companions drunkards and gamblers or worse; they bestow no thought upon their child, until he falls into the hands of an officer and is brought before a court.[34]

In his introduction to the information presented here as Table 5 the superintendent of the reform school commented, "The follow-

ing facts have been gathered, to throw some light upon the causes of crime as developed in the commitments to the Reform School." The facts served to reinforce the connection reformers asserted between the nature of the family and juvenile delinquency. Some inaccuracy is probable since the figures were "based on the acknowledgments of the boys themselves," but the general shape of the picture remains, and from this table the superintendent concluded the first cause of crime was "orphanage," the second, "parental inefficiency." The impression of urban delinquents presented by observers, a picture of boys reared in poverty and subject to no parental control, exposed to drunkenness, truant from school, leading a wild existence that led to a replication of parental behavior — such a picture was more than a figment of the imagination.[35]

Yet unproven are observers' assertions of a connection between crime and immigrants and of an increase in delinquency. In 1850 41 percent of the inmates of the reform school were Catholics (most of whom of course were either Irish immigrants or their children);[36] the foreign-born population of Massachusetts as a whole was 18.93 percent.[37] The superintendent argued that the number would have been even disproportionately larger were it not for the different attitudes of Protestant and Catholic families toward the reform school. Eager for the state to try to reform their sons, Protestant parents, he claimed, often voluntarily committed their children whereas Catholic parents resisted any attempt to incarcerate their children in the reform school.[38] One reason for the hostility of Catholic parents undoubtedly was the explicitly Protestant nature of the reform school, until April 1862 under the supervision of a resident Evangelical Protestant chaplain, who conducted the compulsory prayers and chapel and worked actively for the spiritual regeneration of the individual boys. This "well-meant, though compulsory and unjust, enforcement of a system of religious instruction," asserted a newspaper, "excited jealousy and alarm, especially among the Catholic families of the boys, which more than neutralized, in many cases, whatever moral influence the school would bring to bear." [39]

Figures relating to the crime rate are both unreliable and hard to find. More figures, though also highly questionable, exist for pauperism, as measured by persons in receipt of state and local aid. The committee investigating state charities and Frank Sanborn both made a persistent effort to gather historical data on poverty. Their figures, while not accurate, probably can be accepted as representing trends. Between 1826 and 1831 pauperism actually decreased; from the early thirties until 1845 pauperism (and immigration) increased slowly, but both increased dramatically in the late forties and reached a peak in 1858. If one accepts the contention that crime was directly related to poverty, then the assertion that crime was increasing can very likely be regarded as valid.[40]

The Civil War had a curious effect on crime and poverty. Many of those who might have become paupers served in the army, and male crime and pauperism diminished. On the other hand, female and juvenile crime increased alarmingly. The nature of this crime was peculiarly disturbing to a generation that preached restraint and the higher pleasures as the paths to social and individual salvation. Frank Sanborn remarked with dismay:

It may not be extravagant to say that one in four of the many children committed to our prisons have near relatives in the army. The same is true of the female prisoners, though probably not in the same proportion. It has been again and again said to me by prison officers that the mothers, wives, sisters and daughters of soldiers are among the numerous additions to the list of female criminals in the past few years; and many of these officers ascribe the increase in female crime to the distribution of State Aid and bounty money. The possession of more money than usual makes these poor women idle and as I have said exposes them to temptation; they drink, and from this they are led on to worse offences; while the absence of their sons, husbands and fathers leaves them without restraint or protection.

Hardly a report to boost morale on the front! Sanborn also warned that the return of peace might bring an increase in both crime and pauperism, a prediction that was verified.[41]

In 1850 two sorts of offenses accounted for most of the committals to the reform school, and the figures for this year were typical of others (see Table 6).

Table 6. Offenses of boys committed to reform school in 1850

Offense	Number
Larceny	109
Stubbornness	106
Idle and disorderly	17
Vagrancy	23
Shopbreaking and stealing	17
Burglary	1
Housebreaking and stealing	2
Shopbreaking with intent to steal	3
Pilfering	7
Having obscene books and prints for circulation	1
Common drunkards	2
Malicious mischief	13
Assault	1
Trespass	4
Arson	2
Runaways	3
Total	311

Source: Senate Document 12, 1850, p. 21.

Most offenses involved stealing under one or another label. The meaning of the obviously important offense, "stubbornness," is however, unclear. Apparently the term puzzled readers of the period, too, because the next year the superintendent tried to provide an explanation. Rather than try to define precisely the amorphous term, he cited case histories of boys committed for "stubbornness":

No. — Has spent most of his time idling about the streets in company with other bad boys, and has been addicted to the use of intoxicating liquors and tobacco; has often been intoxicated, has indulged in lying, profanity, pilfering, and sleeping out.

No. — Was sent to the House of Correction a year since, for stubbornness. For four or five years has been in the habit of pilfering money and small articles from his mother; has been notoriously profane, having formed the habit of lying, and associating with a bad class of boys, often returning to his mother late at night.

No. — Is a notorious truant from school, and home; addicted to the habits of chewing tobacco and profanity. He has associated with the worst class of boys, ran away from home many times, often staying away several days, and even months at a time, sleeping nights in stables, or any place that might afford him shelter. At two different times he was absent three months.

No. — His father died about ten years since. He has often taken money from his mother, and treated her in the most insulting and shameful manner; throwing billets of wood at her, and threatening her life, so that she has been obliged to call in the neighbors and the watchman.

No. — Was once fined for throwing stones at a market man; is a notorious pilferer, having taken money and small articles too numerous to mention; also addicted to the habits of chewing and smoking tobacco, lying, profanity, and Sabbath breaking.

Contained in state law, stubbornness was the "crime" used to incarcerate boys who could be convicted of no other specific offense.

It was, moreover, an offense used by parents to commit their children.[42]

Until the mid-1860's "pauper," "criminal," and "depraved" were closely associated terms; they implied that certain potentialities for evil, present within all men, had been developed at the expense of the more beneficent tendencies. The reformers contended that these potentialities for evil had been cultivated by a pernicious environment. Thus, the theory of crime was profoundly democratic because it implied that all men were inherently equal in moral potentiality; how that potential was realized was determined by the circumstances in which the child lived. In fact, however, the theory explained little. Poverty and crime were related, but each appeared to cause the other; both seemed to occur in cities; both seemed to characterize immigrants. But these are only relationships; the nature of the relationship, the explanation of the visible bonds, was imprecise and remained to be determined.

The stress on environmental causes of deviant behavior was a notable characteristic of the 1840's. For instance, psychiatrists stressed the importance of environment in producing insanity and argued that the tensions accompanying the development of industries and cities were a prime cause of an increase they noted in mental disorder. The belief that insanity was most prevalent in the Northeast, the most urbanized part of the country, was widespread.[43] Likewise, novelists concerned with crime increasingly implied the primacy of environment in moral development,[44] and the same emphasis was characteristic of the theories of reformers concerned with adult prisons. "One manifestation of a sympathetic outlook toward the criminal in the 1840's," asserts W. David Lewis, "was the willingness of many citizens to absolve him from guilt; either wholly or in part, by shifting blame to various environmental deficiencies."[45]

By the mid-1860's another explanation of crime and poverty, and with it a new definition, had appeared. In the second report of the Board of State Charities the new note became blatantly clear.

"The causes of the evil ["the existence of such a large proportion of dependent and of destructive members in our community"] are manifold, but among the immediate ones, the chief cause is inherited organic imperfection, — vitiated constitution, or *poor stock*." [46] The prominence given hereditary rather than environmental causation in the Board's report is explained, first, by the views of its author, the famous educator and social reformer Samuel Gridley Howe. By the 1860's Howe, somewhat discouraged with the results of the Perkins Institute, had begun to believe that the blind were inherently mentally inferior, and a general emphasis on the importance of heredity marked his thought in this period.[47] Howe was not alone in his stress on heredity. By the 1860's the environmentalist theory of insanity had likewise given way to an emphasis upon innate deficiencies,[48] and even popular novels concerned with the causes of crime reflected this trend.[49] The Board of State Charities delineated two kinds of "vitiation or imperfection of the stock": "First, lack of vital force; second, inherited tendencies to vice. The first comes from poor nutrition, use of stimulants, or abuse of functions, on the part of the progenitors. The second comes from their vicious habits of thought and action. The first, or lack of vital force, affects mainly the dependent class, and lessens their ability for self-guidance." The poor and the criminal were no longer merely depraved; they were inferior.

The Board reinforced their contention that characteristics acquired by parents were inherited by children with purportedly scientific evidence from physiologists. Large doses of alcohol stimulate "those organs or those functions" manifest in the "animal passions, and represses those which manifest themselves in the higher or human sentiments which result in *will*." The habit of yielding to the "animal passions" had horrifying consequences for posterity:

> Any morbid condition of body, frequently repeated, becomes established by habit. Once established, it affects the man in various ways and makes him more liable to certain diseases . . .

This liability, or tendency, he transmits to his children, just as surely as he transmits likeness in form or feature . . . It is morally certain that the frequent or the habitual overthrow of the conscience and will, or the *habitual weakening* of them, soon establishes a morbid condition, with morbid appetites and tendencies, and that the appetites and tendencies are surely transmitted to the offspring . . . a father gives to his offspring certain tendencies which lead surely to craving for stimulants. The cravings, once indulged, grow to a passion, the vehemence of which passes the comprehension of common men.

Drink had other dangers, too. "Procreation during drunkenness is rare, but the cases where it is followed by fearful defects, deformities and passions in the offspring are too numerous and well established to admit a doubt of the nature of the cause." Alcohol was particularly insidious, the Board contended, because continued small intakes had more damaging consequences than occasional drunkenness. The body of the habitual, if mild, drinker never rid itself of alcohol. There was little danger that the occasional drunk would sire a legion of potential drunkards since the procreative powers were lessened during drunkenness; but the habitual drinker might because alcohol "taken in small doses" "does not sensibly lessen the period of procreative desires and powers." [50]

All this added up to a difference in native and immigrant stock that the Board felt was proved by Dr. Edward Jarvis' analysis of the registers of burial in "Mount Auburn cemetery, used as a burial place by American families of Boston, in wealthy and comfortable circumstances, and of the three great Catholic cemeteries in Charlestown, North Cambridge, and Dorchester." (See Table 7.) The far more frequent "deaths in infancy and childhood . . . among the foreign population" were partly a product of the "greater skill and care" received by more fortunate children, but also partly a product of hereditary weakness. The impoverished Irishman was not only a foreigner; he was also inferior. Although their argument had pessimistic implications, the Board did not want to induce

despair; "we may, by taking thought, during two or three generations, correct the constitutional tendencies to disease and early
decay."[51] Their attempt at optimism, however, was neither convincing nor precisely and clearly argued. The Board relied on
natural law and contended that the body had certain recuperative
powers; as in the oscillation of the heavenly bodies, the Board
said, a certain margin of error was permissible: that is, if the

Table 7. Number of burials in Mount Auburn and Catholic
cemeteries per ten thousand burials by age of death[a]

Age	Mount Auburn	Catholic cemeteries
Under 1	1163	2877
Under 5	2796	5830
Under 10	3332	6319
Under 20	3979	6713
From 20 to 40	2363	1827
From 40 to 60	1591	975
From 60 to 80	447	252
80 and over	107	0

Source: Board of State Charities, 1866, pp. xix–xxxi.
[a] Note that the first four categories are cumulative, the last four distinct. The
figures show how many of each ten thousand people buried in Mt. Auburn were
in different age categories.

standard deviation of vice had not been exceeded, then the natural
healing powers of the body might control the problem. The Board
rejected the contention that people should be asked to abstain from
marriage, and claimed instead that in "a few generations, with
temperate life and wisely assorted marriage, the morbid conditions
will disappear, — the median line is regained." Tastelessly comparing children to trained dogs, the Board continued: the "in-
temperate and vicious classes do tend to point in the wrong direction, but the tendency is not yet so established that they point
simultaneously. They are still susceptible to the influences of educa-

tion, and of moral and religious training, and these should be brought to bear upon them." [52]

Frank Sanborn felt that the influences of education had not been brought to bear upon the people who needed them most, and he documented his assertion that a relationship existed between crime and illiteracy. In 1854, 73.7 percent of the prisoners in Massachusetts county jails were illiterate, by 1864 only 37.8 percent. What surprised Sanborn was how the Massachusetts figures compared with foreign figures. In England and Wales, which lacked a system of common schools, 33 percent of the prisoners were illiterate, as were 50 percent in Ireland. But in Scotland, where public schooling was a long-standing tradition, "not more than 25 percent" could not read and write. Sanborn felt (although he had very little evidence to support his claims) these figures showed that illiteracy among criminals was much higher than among the population as a whole; it was disappointing, however, that in Massachusetts the drop in the percent of illiterate criminals had not been accompanied by a decrease in crime.[53]

In spite of the gloomy and disheartening theory of the inheritance of acquired tendencies toward vice, the Board retained a faith in the ability of man to control society. The existence of crime and poverty, they said, "is phenomenal — not essential in society . . . their numbers depend upon social conditions within human control." "The important truth, therefore, that the numerical proportion of the dependent and criminal classes to the whole population is subject to conditions within human control, and may be rapidly increased or lessened by the action of society, should be presented in every aspect and on every proper occasion." [54]

The scientific study of heredity had revealed the source of crime; the scientific study of society would reveal the laws of social control. Part of the program the Board advanced to control society was educational, for they shared the belief that education was the best weapon against crime. To increase and diffuse knowledge, Frank Sanborn, in 1865, helped to found the American Association for the Promotion of Social Science. The other aspect of the Board's program was noticeably like the progressivism of the latter part of the century. The Board's second report delineated an ideology for which social Darwinism would be but a veneer, yet the report was used as a springboard for a program stressing increased governmental activity. Paradoxically, the Board used a theory of hereditary vice to argue the need for social medicine based on environmental manipulation. In short, the Board argued the necessity of removing those causes that tempted and predisposed people to acquire pernicious habits that could become hereditary. The Board called for: "improvement of dwellings; encouragement to ownership of homesteads; increased facility for buying clothing and wholesome food; decreased facility for buying rum and unwholesome food; restriction of exhausting labor; cleanliness in every street, lane and yard which the public arm can reach . . . and many other like measures." [55] These new measures were to be added to the battery of weapons in the state's arsenal for the battle against crime and poverty. An older weapon was the state reform school at Westborough.

4. AT ONCE A HOME AND A SCHOOL

In a truly memorable sentence the legislative commissioners of 1847 (one of whom was Robert Rantoul) described the nature and virtues of a reform school: "Of the many and valuable institutions sustained, in whole or in part, from the public treasury, we may safely say that none is of more importance, or holds a more intimate connection with the future prosperity and moral integrity of the community, than one which promises to take neglected, wayward, wandering, idle and vicious boys, with perverse minds and corrupted hearts, and cleanse and purify and reform them, and thus send them forth, in the erectness of manhood and the beauty of virtue, educated and prepared to be industrious, useful and virtuous citizens." [56] The words "reform" and "school" were chosen by the commissioners to convey with precision their idea of the distinctive nature of the new institution.

The purpose of the institution was "the reformation of Juvenile offenders," which the commissioners understood to be distinctly different from punishment. Consequently, the reformatory was "not to be called a prison or a penitentiary"; the commissioners proposed "to give to the external appearance of the buildings as little that of a prison as is consistent with entire security from escape." [57] Likewise, in 1858 the superintendent remarked, "The fact must never be lost sight of that the prime object of the school is the reformation of the boy, and not his punishment . . . It is to prevent him from becoming a criminal, and to make him a man." [58]

In terms of finished products the objects of reformation were the same as the objects of public education: respect for authority, self-control, self-discipline, self-reliance, and self-respect. Without "subjection of will to right control," the superintendent wrote, "no sure reformation can be effected." Indeed, "neglect of restraint" and "unconquered will following depraved inclination" had created "the demand for our institution." But "the erectness of manhood and the beauty of virtue" implied more than abject submission to authority; and self-respect was an important goal of reformation. The properly reformed boy, according to the superintendent, "acquires a fixed character; he finds himself worthy of respect; he finds himself confided in; he respects and confides in himself." [59] The meaning of reform was the total transformation of character.

The commission of 1847 wrote, "In order to secure the desired reformation, the Commissioners propose to call the institution a *school*," meaning a formal institution for learning correct attitudes and useful skills. Because education was as much moral as intellectual, the reformation of character was an educative process. The reformatory was in every sense a school, yet a very special sort of school. "For those who will avail themselves of our schools, open to every child, provision is already made," the commissioners noted. "But for those who, blind to their own interests, choose the school of vicious associates only, the State has yet to provide a compulsory school, as a substitute for the prison, — it may be for the gallows." [60] And this is what their institution was to be: a compulsory school. In fact, the state reform school was the first form of compulsory schooling in the United States. The commonwealth discovered, however, that it had more than the six hundred inmates of Westborough who were "blind" to their own interests, and in the 1850's laws were passed extending compulsory education throughout the state.

The words "reform" and "school" left unsaid a third, crucial part of the definition of the new institution. In their report arguing the hereditary nature of crime and urging social engineering, the Board of State Charities asserted the existence of "a lever for the elevation of the race, more potent than any human instrumentality, to wit, the lever of parental love." [61] Parents who loved their children would see the connection between their own habits and the prospects of their future offspring; such parents would voluntarily reform themselves. But what if the all-powerful force of parental love were missing? What if a child had no family worthy of the name? Then, almost surely, he would come to lead a life of crime and immorality: almost surely, unless he were provided with a home by loving foster parents. This assumption dictated one of the major strategies for the reform of youth. At the inauguration of a new superintendent in 1857, George Boutwell said, "This institution is at once a home and a school." [62]

"The State must supply the place of a lost, or what is worse, a drunken parent," wrote the committee of 1846,[63] and this assumption was echoed in virtually all the literature surrounding the reform school. The first step in the strategy of reform was for the state to become the actual parent of the boy. In terms of the prevalent conception of crime the state had no other choice; reformers believed statistics proved that familial viciousness or weakness was the most direct cause of crime. But the assumption of a parental role was not to be deplored; indeed, educational theory stressed that the state should be parental. The reform school, claimed Emory Washburn, "presents the State in her true relation, of a parent seeking out her erring children." The reform school marked the beginning of an epoch; it represented the first time "in our country whereby a state, in the character of a common parent, has undertaken the high and sacred duty of rescuing and restoring her lost children, not so much by the terrors of the law, as by the gentler influence of the school." [64]

Thus, as Superintendent Joseph A. Allen emphasized in 1861, "The great design of the school should be to make it, as much as possible, like a family, — to have the boys stand to the officers in the relation of children to parents." [65] A distinguished group of men, including John Philbrick, superintendent of schools in Boston, visited the reform school in 1863 and observed, "Here is a *real* home, not costly, but comfortable and satisfying." [66] The parental manner was to extend to discipline, to cause each to feel that he has a "personal interest in the welfare of all." [67] The ideal was never entirely attained, but in 1861 the trustees noted with pleasure progress in "bringing about a near approach to a parental government, and the abandonment of all corporal punishment and restraint." "The government is intended to be parental and kind, and the law of love should be the ruling element in all the discipline of the establishment." [68]

The trustees' pleasure in 1861 resulted from the recent and successful introduction of the family system of organization:

The experiment of subdividing the institution, and establishing separate households, has been fully tried during the year, and with most gratifying results. The farm house and garden house, having been prepared for the accommodation of thirty boys each: that number was selected from the most deserving, and sent out to colonize. Each house is under the charge of a gentleman and his wife, who have control and management of the boys, subject to the general rules of the institution, and subordinate to the Superintendent. They form, in reality, separate institutions.

They have their own domestic arrangements, and their own school; and the boys come into the main building only for Chapel services on Sunday, and for occasional lectures. They are under no physical restraint or confinement. Being employed mostly upon the farm they can run away at any time, if they like.[69]

The family system of organization did not originate at Westborough; its earlier and successful introduction at the commonwealth's Industrial School for Girls at Lancaster, had spurred its establishment in the school for boys. The family system was an administrative reform based on three important assumptions.

The family system clearly was the logical outcome of the contention that delinquency stemmed from the lack of a real home; it represented in part a concrete attempt to make reform familial in nature as well as intent. A second and related contention was "boys are not reformed in masses but by laboring with them individually." [70] Large, impersonal institutions reflected the industrial development of the time: "Partiality to them is fostered by a false analogy between material and moral forces. We see the effect of organization, discipline, and combined effort for any material enterprise, and infer that it is necessary for reformation. Congregation in numbers, order, discipline, absolute powers of officers and entire submission of soldiers, are essential to the efficiency of an army; and are supposed to be so in reformatories; but the object of armies is to make machines; in reformatories it is to make men." [71] The Board of State Charities may have mixed its metaphors, but its point was clear. Reform schools were to counteract, not reinforce, the worst tendencies of the time. The size of cities; the materialism of greedy corporations that imported and exploited labor; the problems of industrial communities: these were causes of crime; at no cost should reform schools ever be thought of as "moral machinery."

A third contention influential in the institution of the family system was the conception of the family as the "social unit."

Without the family there would be "no real society, but a multitude of individuals who harden into selfishness as they grow older." The family "must be at the foundation of all permanent social institutions . . . by no human contrivance should any effectual substitute be found for it." The conclusion was obvious: "We shall find in our public institutions, that, other things being equal, the nearer they approach to the family system the better, and the contrary." [72] Still, the family units created at the reform school were contrived, not real. To obtain the full impact of virtuous, familial influence it was necessary to place the boy "in the quiet circle of a New England family"; and to give boys this experience, as well as to place them "under the steady parental control of a master," was a primary purpose of apprenticeship.[73] To find a boy a true New England family with a foster father was the best strategy of reform.

The location of the foster family, however, was critical. Because crime was an urban phenomenon, its cure could not take place in the city. Throughout the theory of reform ran the nineteenth century's idealization of the countryside; the countryside became a weapon in the battle against juvenile delinquency. Most simply put, "The farmer's life is beset with fewer temptations than most mechanical employments, as they are usually more retired from large villages." [74] The experience of private reformatories had indicated that "a much greater proportion of the cases where boys . . . have fallen back into their former vices, are from among such as have been put to places in cities, or large, compact villages." The assumption of the virtues of the countryside and the influence of landscape upon character were apparent in the description the 1847 legislative commission provided of the site selected for the reform school:

It is situated on the borders of Chauncey Pond, which makes its boundary on one side. The pond is of clear, pure water, about thirty feet in depth, and covering one hundred and seventy-eight acres of land. The ground rises, by a gentle acclivity, from the shore of the pond, to a height which overlooks this beautiful sheet of water, and an extent of country beyond, embracing, in part, the village of Westborough, and gives a very pleasing prospect. There are no manufacturing villages in the vicinity, and the farm-houses are not more numerous than in most of the agricultural towns in the State, in proportion to the area. The situation, therefore, is sufficiently retired.[75]

Like "a mother who kisses while she chides," rhapsodized Emory Washburn, the state offers "hope, and the assurance of favor" to the deserving; but "it does more; it rears for them this refuge from temptation. It offers them this landscape, and spreads before them these pleasant fields, and bids its own servants to watch over their temporal and eternal interests." [76] Juvenile nature was plastic: "I have generally found," asserted Moses Grant of Boston, "that what have been considered in this city the worst of boys, when placed in a more favorable circumstance to the development of their character, have often done well and become useful men." [77] Children were molded by the influences around them; thus, an essential part of the theory of reform was a change in circumstances, and few, if any, aspects of the circumstances were more important than the physical. Exposure to the uplifting influence of the country became a key strategy of reform.

The stress on reformation through kindness and a proper environment was no more a unique characteristic of institutions for juveniles than was the environmental theory of delinquency. For example, in the 1840's a reform movement reached adult prisons. In New York state, according to W. David Lewis, prison reformers rejected the belief that rehabilitation should be sought "by breaking the spirit of a man, subjecting him to a hard and humiliating discipline, and literally burying him from the world." For this harsh conception reformers substituted "a more positive approach of attempting to bring out the best in an inmate through the use of kindness and the extension of privileges." [78] In mental institutions moral therapy (as opposed to physical therapy), "that is, the creation of a complete therapeutic environment — social, psychological, and physical," had been growing in importance since the early nineteenth century, largely as a result of the influence of European writers. During the late 1830's and 1840's innovations spurred by a belief in moral therapy entered asylums, which claimed "annual recovery rates of 80 to 90 percent of patients brought in soon after falling ill, or 40 to 60 percent of all patients admitted in a single year." [79] Such innovations in adult and juvenile penal institutions and mental hospitals were the attempted realization of the "soft line" discussed in the previous part of this study. They were the counterparts of common school reformers' attempts to reduce corporal punishment, to recast the role of the teacher in a humane and benevolent mold, and to introduce pedagogical techniques proceeding from the interests of the children. Joseph Allen, apparently the most successful superintendent of this period, shared the views of the soft line educators, as Frank Sanborn noted: he believed "first in making his pupils happy, and then leading them, by affection rather than affliction, along the path of learning and virtue." [80] Like the common school reforms, other institutional innovations reflected the paradox of trying to instill restraint and prevent or cure deviant behavior through appealing to the affections, the very faculties whose indulgence allegedly bred immorality, crime, and insanity.

Another strategy of juvenile reform was the intellectual education offered the boys. Education, some said, was the best weapon against crime. It was, at any rate, a weapon that Superintendent Allen tried to wield with skill. From the inception of his tenure the classes, attended four hours a day, were graded; and the trustees and previous superintendents claimed their school was comparable to high schools in the large cities and towns of the state. Allen, however, cast doubt on the efficacy of his predecessors as educators; when he arrived, the schools "were found entirely ungraded and over-crowded — each teacher having about eighty pupils, many not provided with desks. The principal teacher had given his notice . . . he having been attacked by the boys, and somewhat injured." Nevertheless all superintendents made a persistent effort to obtain the best teachers available, and Superintendent Allen, who was especially well versed in modern educational theories, introduced object teaching and oral instruction. Allen's goal "was to give the boys thorough elementary instruction, sufficient to make them good citizens, not great scholars; and to inspire them with a love of learning." [81]

The feminization that characterized the teaching force of the state also marked the staff of the reform school: "Experience teaches that these boys, many of whom never had a mother's affection, or felt the kindly atmosphere of woman's love, need the softening and refining influence which woman alone can give, and we have, wherever practicable, substituted female officers and teachers for those of the other sex." [82] The reform school, however, required different duties of teachers than the public schools. In the reform school the teacher, like a real mother, was to establish intimate relationships with the boys in a variety of activities; "teachers are required to oversee the boys in the yards during hours of recreation, and to take charge of them in part, during out-door and in-door labors." On the "Sabbath, when the boys are kept within the limits of the building and yards, the teachers have charge of them in their respective school rooms, except during chapel hours." "The relation of the teacher . . . to his or her class, is very intimate." Yet feminization, noted Allen, who promoted the policy actively, was not without dangers: "Women sometimes get too much interested in the work. One of the most self-sacrificing and excellent women was so much interested in the welfare of the boys, that her sympathy for them, in general, passed beyond a philanthropic, into a particular interest, more than Platonic." [83]

The comprehensive role of the teacher suggests an analogy between the reform school and a boarding school, or even a British public school; the analogy is not far-fetched. The superintendent's comment that "our best boys become active assistants in sustaining order and a good degree of decorum among themselves" suggests the introduction of a modified prefect system.[84] In 1861 the superintendent commented that boys living in one of the recently created "families" were "not even subject to any more strict discipline or supervision than is desirable in well-managed boarding schools." The reform school was not intended as a penal institution; it was to be an academy for delinquents.[85]

Authority, kindness, enlightenment of conscience, and constant employment, the superintendent observed in 1858, were four of the most important means of reform. The agency for employing the first three means was the combination of kindly parental discipline, the family system, and female teachers. But the fourth, constant employment, was equally essential; "the old couplet hath truth, if not poetry, 'Satan finds some mischief still/For idle hands to do.'" Labor, however, was more than busy work to keep boys out of mischief:

> Labor, to employ the hands, and busy the mind, and awaken ingenuity, and produce results, is a demand of our constitution; is needful to the maintenance of virtue; and surely is needful to the recovery of the dissolute and vicious. Without this, the other means of discipline would fail, or would only half complete their work. The health of both body and mind is dependent on the purpose and the exertion of labor. And the habit of industry, nurtured and strengthened by years of trial in our institution, will not only be a safeguard to the youth when he goes forth from us, but will be his assurance of independence and position in his after life.[86]

A precise and tightly packed daily schedule provided one means of assuring that no hands would be idle.[87] Another was to engage the boys in productive labor. Farming, it was generally agreed, was the best possible occupation; but only the most reliable boys could be trusted on the school farm. Until 1860 shoemaking was the occupation in which the largest number of boys was employed; but in the 1860's it was dropped and chairmaking emphasized in its place. In 1863 roughly 20 percent of the boys worked on the school farm; this comprised 75 percent of those living in the farm houses. About 30 percent "were employed in sewing and knitting," about 22 percent in "chair-work," and roughly 22 percent in "various domestic avocations." The chairmaking was performed for a contractor who paid the school only one and one-quarter cents per hour for the labor of each boy.[88]

The strategies employed within the reform school were a means of attacking the problems of crime, poverty, and social disorder through re-making the individual delinquent. But by the mid-1860's the reports of the trustees of the reform school and the Board of State Charities reflected a realization that social reform must come through "enlightenment of conscience" of the prosperous and law-abiding as well as of the individual offender; the trustees and the Board used their reports not only as means for making recommendations to the legislature but also as a spark to kindle social conscience. The trustees concluded their 1865 report with an exhortation more pointed than any they had previously written:

> Think of it, citizens of Massachusetts, who are living in the midst of luxury and splendor, there are boys, perhaps within a stone's throw of your stately residences, whose heads press no downy pillow, who have no resource when the shades of night are creeping on, but to crawl under the shelter of some friendly pile of lumber, by chance to find a more luxurious couch in a hayloft, or in company with criminals, old and young, to seek the station-house. Think of it, mothers, who tenderly provide your beloved daughters with all that money can buy, who bless their slumbers with your prayers, and shield them so far as you may, from every temptation, — there are in the community daughters with souls as white . . . who know not where to lay their heads; who never sit at table to eat an orderly meal; whose ragged dress is insufficient to preserve the remnants of modesty

which have survived evil associations; and whose slumbers are made horrible by oaths and curses, instead of being sweetened by prayers and blessings. What can they do but enter on the road which leads to destruction? [89]

What indeed? The Board of State Charities and Frank Sanborn hinted at an answer. The Board said that they emphasized "having the people understand fully the causes of difference in social condition" so that the people themselves would "take interest and direct action in social improvement, by *levelling from below upward.*" Wherever exists the "degree of poverty which excludes education, which abases and finally destroys self-respect, which breeds diseases, indolence and vice," Frank Sanborn warned ominously, "property is unsafe and morals are weakened." Especially pernicious was the accompaniment of poverty by "a heartless and unscrupulous class of wealthy men, who foolishly suppose their wealth to repose on the degradation of the poor." Against "a society so constituted," continued Sanborn, "the Divine Judge" twice in modern history "issued his terrible decree — in the first French and the last American revolution. If we now fail to read His laws, it is not because they have not been promulgated in fire and blood, with terrors greater than those of Sinai." [90]

Sanborn, in the dislocations immediately following the Civil War, wanted to arouse the people, "to secure fair wages to every laborer, to discourage monopolies, foster education, and promote temperance." [91] To Sanborn it was a question of education, of public enlightenment. If "our people would give as much attention to other principles and laws of sociology, as they have given to the department of politics," he argued, public institutions "would excel" and the conditions of potential social disaster would be eliminated.[92] The fears of the Board and of Sanborn were confessions that the common schools, the reform school, and other charitable institutions had failed. They had been created as strategies for coping with the problems of social and economic transformation, but in spite of often lavish expenditure of money and rhetoric the problems mounted in scope and intensity. Some of the reasons for the failure of public charitable institutions to perform miracles are illustrated by the problems encountered in the reform school. In fact, the problems of the reform school revealed the outer limits of achievement for innovations based on the flawed theories of mid-nineteenth century reformers.

Size was the first major problem of the reform school. It was designed for three hundred, but the enrollment quickly exceeded this number and an extension had to be constructed. Even the extension was overcrowded; in 1857 and 1858, the years of maximum enrollment, there were over six hundred inmates. The problem of accommodating and managing the enrolled boys was intensified in 1859 when Daniel Creeden, one of the inmates, burned the new extension to the ground.[93] The burning highlighted another problem. Boys were usually committed to the reform school for their minority, but given the alternative of a shorter sentence in a prison. A sentence of this length was particularly onerous because boys were committed, for the most part, between the ages of ten and fourteen.[94] Frequently boys tried to appear so incorrigible that they would be ejected from the reform school and sent to the prison, from which they would be released in considerably less time. Creeden had been deliberately trying to be thrown out. The fire prompted changes in the legislation concerning committal. The alternative sentence was abolished, and to alleviate the size problem the power of committal was removed from local magistrates and placed solely with the county and probate courts.[95]

Finding suitable apprenticeships was another problem. Part of the difficulty, as the superintendent pointed out in 1851, was that older modes of apprenticeship were changing. Previously the apprentice had lived as a son with the family, which was concerned with his intellectual and moral, as well as occupational, training. Now masters treated apprentices like any other employees; they could live where they liked and, outside of working hours, do as they pleased. This kind of situation scarcely provided the parental restraint and familial influence the reformers sought from apprenticeship.[96] One town particularly singled out for poor treatment of apprentices was Marblehead, where quite a number of former inmates were placed. In Marblehead the boys were left virtually unsupervised and provided with almost no form of intellectual or moral education; such a situation was conducive to a return to old, vicious habits and could undo the work of the reform school.[97]

Simply finding enough people to take apprentices was also a problem, and most difficult of all was locating sufficient farmers. Those who ran the school argued that the location of suitable and sufficient apprenticeships and the visiting of apprenticed boys required the appointment of an additional member to the staff. In their proposals the origins of the parole officer were evident. Others proposed that the state should offer to pay families willing to take and care adequately for a boy. The payments, proponents held, would be less than the cost of the boy's upkeep within the reform school; thus, the proposal offered an economical way of increasing the amount of familial influence, the best strategy for the reformation of the boy.[98]

Depression and the Civil War also brought problems. During the depression of 1857 the superintendent had difficulty finding paid employment for the boys, and idleness resulted.[99] The situation persisted, and some years later Frank Sanborn, visiting the reform school, was horrified to find large numbers of boys with absolutely nothing to do. The Civil War did not bring economic problems; but the public agitation reached the reform school, which then had to cope with a sudden spurt of escapes.[100]

Another non-economic problem was discipline. The reform school had four different superintendents in its first sixteen years. Three had left, according to Sanborn, because of differences of opinion with the trustees concerning discipline.[101] Joseph Allen, who became superintendent in 1861, was, by his own account, chosen because several "friends of the school" hoped he could introduce "a more humane system of discipline than ever had been practiced there." William Starr, who served from 1857 to 1861, was the least effectual. Part of Starr's troubles was attributable to the overcrowding, at its peak during his tenure; but his inept and somewhat negligent administration was responsible for the laxity that allowed Daniel Creeden and his five associates to commit arson. At his inauguration Starr had told the boys, "I come here to do you good." Why had he come to do them good? "There can be but one motive to induce a person to enter upon this work with any prospect of success; and that is love, — love of those committed to our charge, love of one another, love of the right, love to God and love to man." [102] Apparently, love was not enough. Three years later Starr's long solitary confinement of a group of boys manacled in dismal, unsanitary cells became a public scandal and grounds for his censure by the Governor's Council. The theory of reform through loving, parental government and constant employment was an ideal; but it was an ideal that the reform school only approximated. In fact, one newspaper wrote of the situation in 1860, "The method of treatment . . . was, in great part, the vulgar and harsh method of convict discipline, enforced by the carrying of bludgeons and loaded weapons by some of the officers . . . At length the 'vicious circle' into which the school had settled, in a sort of despair, was violently broken up by the discovery of a case of discipline so abominably cruel, beyond all limits permitted in a state penitentiary for adults, that a crisis was inevitable." It was in this situation that Allen was brought in through the efforts of "S. G. Howe, George B. Emerson, Samuel J. May, and such men," as well as Governor Banks and his successor Governor Andrews. Allen faced initial opposition because he was a Unitarian, a fact that nearly prevented his appointment; he also faced opposition from the present officers, who were "if not unfriendly, at least not in sympathy"; finally, he had to contend with public sentiment, which had "little faith

. . . that the school would ever be a success." [103] Even under Allen, however, except for the boys who lived in the family units he set up in 1861, the reform school was more like a prison than either a home or a school.

That the reform school faced problems of size, apprenticeship, employment, and discipline is not surprising. Parents posed a more unpredictable difficulty. In 1854–55, for instance, "about four-sevenths" of the boys charged with stubbornness "were committed on the complaint of their parents or relatives, or at their request." To some extent, the following year's report revealed, "the complaint was made, to prevent a more serious charge being preferred by others." [104] But a more malignant reason was unearthed by the committee investigating public charities:

> The experience of nine years shows that it is necessary to adopt some means to prevent abuse of the benevolence of the State, in maintaining the institution at Westborough. The place is styled a 'school,' purposely to relieve its inmates from the stigma of criminals; it follows that parents sometimes are not unwilling to send their sons thither, especially those that are troublesome, in order to save the expense of keeping them at home. If the affection of natural parents always prevented this (which it does not), guardians and step-fathers would still frequently treat their wards thus harshly, in some instances, even, as appeared before us in evidence, actually taking pains to tempt the poor boy into the commission of some technical offense, — assault or theft, perhaps, — in order to be able to carry him before a magistrate and procure his committal to the State Reform School at Westborough. [105]

The Mephistophelean nature of some parents was reflected in still another way; greedy for the money from their children's earnings, they tried either to obtain their release or to lure them away from beneficent apprenticeships. Faced with the grasping natural parent, the state, the adopted parent, asserted its superior claim: "We have felt it to be our duty generally to decline giving them up to their parents, and have placed as many of them as we could, with farmers and mechanics in the country." [106]

Finally, superintendents were troubled by what they considered unfair publicity. Superintendent Allen maintained that Frank Sanborn's report had unfairly claimed that the earnings of the boys had declined and that an over-emphasis was being given to intellectual education. Changes in the nature of contracting and payment, Allen countered, had accounted for the apparent decrease in earnings; the number of hours per day devoted to schooling had remained constant throughout the history of the school. In the past year the State Board of Agriculture had turned over the running of the school farm to the reform school itself. Previously the Board had paid the school ten cents per day for the labor of each boy; now nothing was being received.[107] In all likelihood the attack on the allegedly inadequate earnings of the pupils was an expression of general hostility toward the school in its current form because people like Sanborn and Howe, who urged humanitarian reforms in prisons, rarely advocated making penal institutions pay. This latter position was, in fact, identified with those who took a hard line toward criminals and generally opposed the humanitarian reformers. Perhaps, too, Sanborn was influenced by his close associate Samuel Gridley Howe, who, as noted earlier, wrote the report of the Board of State Charities, and who had serious reservations about the virtues of reform schools.

Superintendents also complained of a lack of public appreciation of the school. Unmindful of the hundreds of boys who had become virtuous, productive citizens, the public, according to the superintendents, pointed with derision at every instance of the re-arrest of a reform school "graduate." [108] In all probability, skeptical taxpayers wanted some assurance that they were receiving value for their taxes. The question behind the taxpayers' complaints is of equal importance to the historian: what were the results of the reform school?

5. THE RESULTS OF REFORM

Six hundred and twenty-nine ex-inmates of the reform school served in the Civil War. The trustees hailed the behavior of some of these soldiers as evidence of true reformation and in their 1865 reports presented a selection of cases:

> J.G., an orphan, not yet seventeen, who had a sister and three brothers, having left the institution, was faithfully working at a trade. When the call for hundred days' men came, he enlisted, served his time out, and then enlisted for the war. His pay and bounties were deposited with responsible parties, and when he was mustered out amounted to quite a sum. Before reenlisting, he sought his sister, found her at work in Boston, and gave her $25. His brothers, aged respectively nine, seven, and five years, he found in an almshouse. He secured a good place for the eldest with his master, with the opportunity of attending school, agreeing to pay his board. He was advised to leave the two youngest where they were for one year longer, when he intends to obtain situations for them. At the close of the war he returned, and is now employed by his former master.

> W.H. enlisted in the 35th Massachusetts Regiment, left his bounty with the Superintendent, and was killed at Knoxville, in 1863. His father died about the same time. The mother would have been left utterly destitute, but for the money left by this son, which was used to purchase her a home.[109]

The other cases reported were similar. In his report for 1857 the superintendent proudly noted that one of the best teachers in the school was an ex-inmate;[110] in the previous year he had noted that three graduates were undertaking a liberal, pre-collegiate education.[111] Surely, too, the superintendent would have considered truly reformed the inmate who wrote to his mother: "It pains me to think how cruel and unjust I have been to you, in disregarding your kind advice. When I think of these things, it makes me feel as if I were unworthy to call you mother; but I hope the time will soon come, when I shall have the pleasure of seeing you *bless* the day, that there ever was such an institution as this." [112] What more could the taxpayers ask? If they inquired about financial advantages, George Boutwell, as usual, had an answer. In his address at the inauguration of the ill-fated Mr. Starr, Boutwell observed that the reform school transformed boys from dependent consumers to producers. The labor of a thousand men "reclaimed," he calculated, estimated for a period of "twenty years only, is equal to the labor of twenty thousand men for one year; which, at a hundred dollars each, yields two millions of dollars." [113]

Superintendents also tried to provide more formal demonstrations of the results of the reform school. After the fire of 1859, William Starr realized that he needed to provide evidence of reform to buttress his appeal to the legislature for funds to rebuild the burned portion of the school. He therefore traced as carefully as he could the subsequent careers of all former inmates. He concluded that out of the 1,653 cases investigated, only 281, or 17 percent, "turned out badly"; 1,372, or 83 percent, had reformed. "Turned out badly" meant getting into difficulties with the law. Surely, claimed the superintendent, this was "a better result . . . than the truest friends of the school . . . ever dared to hope for." [114]

Not everyone was convinced. In 1866 the Board of State Charities wondered if those reformed were not those "who naturally tend to virtue" or "who need only removal from vicious associates in order to become virtuous?" Would not "most of them," asked the Board, "have done quite as well if they had been put in the country, without the long and expensive sojourn of years in the reformatory?" Some people, continued the Board, even claimed that apparently good results were achieved "in spite of, rather than by reason of, the influence of the reformatory." Such a person was Mr. Goodspeed, superintendent of the state almshouse at Bridgewater. Goodspeed, who had personally undertaken the education of many delinquents, said "he would rather take a boy immediately after his sentence by the court, all ragged and dirty, than take the same boy after two or three years' residence in an ordinary house of reformation." [115] Some of Goodspeed's sentiments were very likely shared by Howe, the author of the report. In 1854 Howe had unsuccessfully opposed the creation of a girls' reform school at Lancaster. Gathering a large number of delinquents in one school, Howe felt, would only increase vice.[116] This criticism was, as we have seen, directed at academies as well as reform schools: both were seen as potential breeding grounds for immorality.

In an evaluation of the reform school, the Board concluded, it was impossible to be guided "by any actual results as yet obtained, and we must rely upon well established general principles of education, and apply these to the case in point." The most important general principle was that the "doctrine of repression as an agency in reformation is about exploded." Because it had to control a large number of delinquent boys, a reform school, whatever its intent, had to be a repressive institution. What was needed, said the Board, was a new theory of reformatories. The heart of this new theory was the desire to be "rid of the central establishment altogether; or, at least, to so 'reduce' the number of inmates that they will be merely temporary receiving stations." "The principal feature of the change would be to renounce the attempt to instruct and train the children for any length of time in the reformatory and to commit the charge to private families; or, if they could not be found in sufficient numbers, then to societies of benevolent persons." [117]

The conception of a reform school as solely a reception center had been advocated by Howe in 1854 when he opposed the creation of the girls' reformatory.[118] The reception center concept was related to criticism of the reform school in the same way that the high school idea was related to the criticism of academies. In both instances critics attempted to insure that adolescents would spend only part of their time with peers and that they would have the benefit of the influence and example of a family, the most basic, natural, and virtuous human relationship. The controversies concerning the academy and high school and the nature of reform schools point up again the pervasive concern with adolescence in this period. The proper handling of adolescents, many people seemed to agree, was to prolong dependency, to make sure that the adolescent came into daily contact with a virtuous family. Since morality was internalized by associating with models, not by listening to lectures, it was necessary to provide adolescents with a constant example strong enough to curb the passions of youth. And nothing, it was believed, better exemplified morality than a New England family. Reverend William Barrows, writing in *The New Englander* in 1858, lucidly expressed the prevailing notion of the relation between adolescent behavior, moral development, and the contrasting influence of peers and home.

Early departure from the homestead is a moral crisis that many of our youth do not show themselves able to meet. It comes at a tender age, when judgment is weakest, and passion and impulse strongest. The heart is inexperienced, and peculiarly plastic for impressions. The great outlines of character, the prophecies of the coming man, are being drawn out. If a malformation take place at this period, it is organic. It should be remembered, that, if a home is ever of worth to a child, this is the period when he most needs it . . . Many are so confiding, generous and nobly impulsive, that their character will certainly be shaped by their companions . . . All the glittering promises of catalogues and boarding-school circulars, to watch the manners and morals of the pupil, may prove of less worth than the affectionate sympathy of a sister, the gentle words of a mother, and the approving look of a father.

In brief, under this system, all the power of home can be brought to bear on the child, while he is feeling all the forces and using all the advantages of a good school. The parents can carry forward their system of instruction jointly with the public teacher. So the unnatural, and dangerous, and often fatal divorce of the child from his home is avoided.[119]

The reaffirmation of Howe's reservations in 1866 was, in a sense, a claim by the Board that over the last two decades the state had developed a strategy for dealing with urban juvenile crime that was of uncertain success and unnecessary expense. Two decades of reform schools had not eased the problems of crime and poverty in the commonwealth; indeed, they had increased in intensity. At the close of nearly two decades of expensive administrative reform the parental state was still searching for a satisfactory means of restoring tranquillity and stability to its unruly family.

By the 1860's other institutions had also fared badly. Perkins Institute had become too large and impersonal; state insane asylums built in the flush of optimism had been transformed from therapeutic to custodial institutions;[120] and in New York, at any rate, the prison reform movement was dead.[121]

Writing of the period from 1880 to 1930, Roy Lubove has described the change in social work organization as a transition from cause to function, from the enthusiasm of reformers to the dispassionate performance of professionals circumscribed by bureaucracy.[122] In a sense the transition from cause to function' was the trend that Howe perceived and lamented. In the mid-nineteenth century new institutions started in a blaze of reformist zeal; promoted by talented general reformers like Howe, they expanded more rapidly than any of their founders had anticipated. Expansion was accompanied by the growth of a professional, bureaucratic, managerial group: wardens of prisons, wardens of reform schools, and wardens of asylums and their assistants.[123] In part, bureaucratization was a necessary concomitant of managing large, specialized institutions. But size and professionalism led to the lack of warmth inherent in all large institutions. And it was warmth that was the essential ingredient in the 1840 formulas for the re-making of criminals, delinquents, and the insane. In the absence of warmth and amidst an increase in size, in the transition from cause to function, institutions like Westborough that were not completely overburdened by numbers could still do a routine job. Others, like the state mental hospitals, became mere receptacles for human misery.[124]

The course of the educational reform movement as a whole is not as clear cut as that of one institution. But the same trends were visible. By the 1860's the beginning of educational bureaucracy, routine and sterile, was evident. Moreover, there were other indications that the course of educational reform was losing some of its charismatic charm. During the 1860's measures of innovation and spending, like general economic measures, slackened. Of course the Civil War caused dislocation, but it is likely that the slowing started before the war. Compare, too, Joseph White, appointed in 1860, with the three previous secretaries of the Board of Education. Mann, Sears, and Boutwell had been poor, rural boys whose ambition and skill raised them to state-wide eminence. All three were important public figures throughout the state when they were appointed secretary of the Board; all three went on to eminent, national positions. They were unusual, talented men, in a word, statesmen. White came from a wealthy, urban family. He had been agent for a large cotton mill before his appointment. He was not at the time of his appointment nor afterwards a figure of much importance in the state, let alone the nation, and he was not a man of outstanding talent.

Another evidence of general reformist retreat was the growing importance of heredity in social thought. To stress that a boy fails to reform because he is innately wicked, or to stress that a child fails to learn because he was born stupid, is to admit defeat before even starting. It is a kind of rationalization that excuses educational failure, that lets the teacher or the reform school warden escape blame. It is an assertion that one expects will follow a period of reformist innovations that did not work. Thus, it is no surprise that the environmentalist optimism of the 1840's was followed by the hereditary pessimism of the 1860's and the following decades. The prevalence of social Darwinism and the theories of Francis Galton, especially in the 1870's and 1880's, yielded a heavy stress on the importance of heredity over environment, a stress that professional schoolmen probably found congenial. In the 1890's particularly, the re-awakening of reformist zeal, accompanied by reform Darwinism, brought the older, environmentalist emphasis again into prominence. Reform theorists like Lester Ward, John Dewey, and Jane Addams re-asserted the primacy of environment, though certainly a desire for social reform was by no means always consistently accompanied by a disparagement of heredity. Indeed, the racism of the time was itself a hereditary theory, and racist attitudes somewhat uneasily co-existed with environmentalism in the minds of some theorists, like Ward. Nevertheless, it is true that in the years of most ardent reformist enthusiasm, between roughly 1890 and the First World War, many prominent educational reformers once again urged the environmentalist point of view. The co-existence of reform zeal and an emphasis on environment rather than heredity is not surprising, for environmental stress places the responsibility squarely on the teacher, on the reformer; it is optimistic, it looks to the possible, and it is a call for action. Certainly, the decline of reform sentiment after the War was accompanied, again, by a rising emphasis on heredity, an emphasis strengthened by the growing popularity of psychologists' notions of individual differences, by the use and abuse of intelligence tests, and by the often virulent racism that contributed so much to the passing of immigration restriction legislation.[125] Again, the cycle is upon us: today, during the third great educational reform movement in American history, environment is again the villain. Will the wheel spin fully this time, too?

At the opening of the state reform school on December 7, 1848, the inmates sang a hymn written for the occasion by the Reverend C. Thurber of Worcester. Surely, Mr. Thurber's hymn is the best possible summary statement of the assumptions with which Massachusetts reformers began the re-making of urban delinquents:

> This pleasant home of priceless worth —
>   By friendship's hand is given,
> To train the erring sons of earth,
>   For usefulness and Heaven:
> The place where little wanderers come,
>   And taste the sweets of friends and home.
>
> The hapless boy who has no guide,
>   Or brutal, fiendish one,
> From Virtue's path has stepped aside,
>   Or wicked act has done;
> This nursery home receives with joy,
>   And makes the child a virtuous boy.
>
> Within the home of want and woe,
>   The boy of promise sighs,
> He thinks the haughty world his foe,
>   And quick for vengeance flies;
> This sweet abode unfolds its door,
>   And soothes him till he strays no more.
>
> The wayward youth that spurns control,
>   And in dishonor gropes,
> That wings with grief a parent's soul,
>   And ruins all his hopes,
> Retires beyond the furious storm,
>   And gathers strength for sweet reform.

Kind father, wreathe thy blandest smiles,
Around this sweet retreat,
That it may win from folly's wiles,
The little wanderer's feet;
Then from this guardian home will rise
The good and great, refined and wise.[126]

Mid-nineteenth century Massachusetts reformers could not distinguish clearly between a relationship and a cause. They perceived cities, crime, poverty, intemperance, immigration, parental vice, and lack of education as inextricably bound together. Which factor, if any, underlay the rest? They had, as we do today, no answer; instead, they tried to break the vicious circle by providing the youthful products of urban depravity with a change of circumstances: a combination home and school in a rural setting. A bad environment had produced a bad boy; a good environment would produce a good boy. The theory was overly simple, but at least it was democratic: the moral potential of all boys was equal.

Advocates of the reform school considered their theory proved by statistics that indicated most ex-inmates had not been rearrested. Others perceived the inadequacy of the theory and the supposed proof. Boys were bad only partly because they grew up in unfavorable surroundings; they were bad mostly because they were inferior. They had inherited the pernicious habits and deficiencies acquired by their parents. Yet the reformers who advocated the new theory were not completely pessimistic; they offered a vague optimism based on parental love and the natural recuperative powers of the body. They, too, proposed a change in circumstances as the key to reform. But they perceived the weakness in the statistical evidence offered as proof of the worthiness of the reform school and advocated a more economical and, they predicted, more effective system. In one way the Board of State Charities went beyond the earlier reformers; it called for the removal of those conditions that tempted individuals to acquire vices capable of hereditary transmission. Two or three decades of mounting social problems, reflected in increased rates of pauperization and crime, had given reformers a heightened perception of the evils they needed to combat. But the assumptions they brought to the task of reform limited their effectiveness: all problems became essentially problems of education, education of the public in the laws of sociology, education of the delinquent in the laws of morality. Reformers equated education with all learning and hence with home as well as school. But their writings clearly implied and often stated that the home was the scene of the wrong sort of learning, and the problem of education thus became the marshaling of social resources other than the family for the inculcation of a commitment to virtue. Only in the educational area, in the reform of human nature rather than in the reform of social systems, were reformers willing to apply coercion or conceive radically new solutions. Unfortunately, education by itself was inadequate. More than that, the diffusion of a utopian and essentially unrealistic ideology that stressed education as the key to social salvation created a smokescreen that actually obscured the depth of the social problems it proposed to blow away and prevented the realistic formulation of strategies for social reform.

Conclusion. Educational Reform:

Myths and Limits

Urban education is a fashionable cause today as only twice before in the American past.* The second great outpouring of reform spirit upon the urban schools was the progressive movement of the late nineteenth and early twentieth centuries. The first was the educational revival of the mid-nineteenth century, the movement that has formed the subject of this study. All three movements to improve the urban schools have been part of a broader attempt to solve the problems of industrial society. The extent to which those problems persist forms an ironic epilogue to the story of the optimism and efforts of earlier reformers.

Today, as in the first great reformist outburst, a variety of motives impel reformers, but the similarities between the movements are striking. In much the same way as James Bryant Conant, the earliest urban schoolmen, like Horace Mann, were stirred to action by the "social dynamite" they saw in the slums.[1] In both instances the reform effort has been spearheaded by the socially and intellectually prominent concerned for the preservation of domestic tranquillity and an ordered, cohesive society. In both cases this group has been joined and supported by middle-class parents anxious about the status of their children and, somewhat tardily, for the most part, by the organized schoolmen, who understandably

---

* I omit the Lancasterian phase, first, because I am concerned with movements specifically directed at urban education in periods of industrialization and, second, because my impression is that educational reform then was not as much a part of a larger attempt at social reform, not as much a "cause."

enough have usually evaluated reform theory in terms of its impact upon their own precarious status.[2] Today, of course, the cause of urban reform has been complicated by the racial issue, only tangentially important in the ante-bellum North. Because of the racial issue, many urban middle-class parents have had an ambivalent attitude toward reform, seeking to better their schools but to keep them white, and thus dissenting from one important set of goals formulated by reform leaders. Conversely, spokesmen for minority groups have been far more active in the cause of reform than before.

Yet basic similarities remain. We have still to see a movement driven by a desire to bring joy and delight to the life of the individual, to enrich experience solely for the purpose of making life more full and lovely. The goals of both movements, quite to the contrary, have been extrinsic; they have stressed the needs of society and the economy. They have also been utilitarian, stressing the concrete cash value of schooling to the individual. In both movements goals have been formulated with scant regard to the indigenous culture, even the aspirations, of the working-class groups to be reformed. Very largely both movements of urban reform have been impositions; communal leaders have mounted an ideological and noisy campaign to sell education to an often skeptical, sometimes hostile, and usually uncomprehending working class. The reformers have been determined to foist their innovations upon the community, if necessary by force; when permissiveness failed in the 1840's, the state passed compulsory school laws in the 1850's. Today, as drop-outs ignore the economic statistics supplied by the Office of Education and the Department of Labor, some people call for the extension of compulsory schooling to age eighteen.

The limits of forced and essentially conservative reform have been apparent in both previous attempts to improve urban education. One consequence has been the estrangement of the school from the life of the working-class community. In the mid-nineteenth century reformers harangued the masses, excoriated parents, shuddered at immigrants. Ignoring the reactions of the people to be reformed they forced, fast and hard, new institutions that soon were made compulsory. Out of deference to religious rivalry, sectarian teaching was banned; but the cultural attitudes of the reformers were expressed in their pedagogical theories, in textbooks, in the training they gave to teachers, in their reports — all said to the child and parent from the working class, "You are vicious, immoral, shortsighted and thoroughly wrong about most things. We are right; we shall show you the truth."

Literacy was not required to pick up the message; neither was sophistication. It takes no background in social psychology to imagine the feelings of those who became the objects of reformist diatribes. Little has changed; despite the intellectual's acceptance of cultural relativity, first apparent in the work of many of the intellectual reformers of the progressive era, the mentality of cultural absolutism has persisted. Be it from the outraged cries of professional patriots or the indignant wrath of censors who find pornography on every page, one gets the impression that, supported by the public, most people concerned with schools are as sure they see moral truth as were Horace Mann and the founders of the state reform school.

In both earlier reform movements professionalization had some unfavorable consequences. In the mid-nineteenth century teachers based the rationale for their own existence and their increasing command of community resources on an implausible ideology that assigned them the critical role in the salvation of individuals and of society. As the ideology became ever more divorced from reality, as crime and poverty increased despite the extension of schooling, teachers turned inward, and within a couple of decades their growing network of bureaucracies became private worlds, sterile and rigid. Similarly, Lawrence Cremin has shown eloquently the fate of progressive education when the educators turned inward and deliberately cut themselves off from the coalition of reformers that had been trying to break through the crust of sterility and rigidity in which urban education had become trapped. The roots of the movement shrivelled, and educators again were talking more and more in terms that bore little relevance to the world around them.[3] Once more, in the past few years, education has been infused with an element of zeal; it has once again become a cause as the non-professionals have taken an interest and driven spurs into lethargic bureaucracies. But this movement has just recently begun. Must it follow the course of the last two?

Even if disappointing, it will be fascinating to watch the movement unfold. As we saw in the last part of this study, there exists one especially good indicator of the strength of the reformist cause. In the 1830's and 1840's reform started in a passionate blaze of optimism resting on the assumption that environment has prime influence in forming mind and character. The beginning of disenchantment in the sixties was signalled by the appearance of theories stressing the importance of heredity. Whatever scientific basis new theorizing may have had, clearly it provided a rationalization for failure, an excuse for some relaxation of effort. When reform began anew late in the century, one prominent strand among several was a variant of reform Darwinism that used evolutionary theory to argue the power of mind over nature and the primacy of environment over heredity. When the theory of individual differences and the use of intelligence tests became popular, they were based on scientific experiments; nevertheless, the emphasis was again hereditary, and it would probably be possible to plot a rough curve between their ascendance and the decline of reform. Once again, environment has become the rage, the commitment of reformers. If it again passes from fashion, if we view a strong and pervasive reassertion of hereditary stress, then we shall know that this reform movement has gone the course of its predecessors.

One danger then is disenchantment. Educators have always been too optimistic, especially in periods of reform. Repeatedly we have been asked to believe that education would usher in a new and better society. To ask that a little skepticism and realism temper the messianic tendencies of schoolmen is not to downgrade education. By itself education would not create the morality of an idealized countryside in the heart of the city; but this is a fact that mid-nineteenth century education promoters refused to see, and by refusing to see it they obscured the depth of social problems and became incapable of formulating effective strategies of social reform. Of course, they had reasons for their blindness. Aside from the educators themselves, the most vocal advocates of school reform were the very people providing the talent and money that helped usher in an industrial society. Deeply ambivalent toward the society for which they were responsible, social leaders sought innovations that would simultaneously promote economic growth and prevent the consequences that industrialism had brought in other societies, especially England. Education became the means for achieving this end. To have looked long and hard at the flaws in their ideology, or to have compared the goals of their movement with its achievements, was not possible for these promoters. It would have raised too many haunting doubts, too many questions about the real nature of their own impact upon society. Educators likewise had too great a personal stake in the reform movement to admit the possibility that schools alone were impotent to cure social disease. Thus, reformers and schoolmen treated both the criticisms raised and the genuine alternatives proposed as attacks to be dismissed or, even at the necessity of brutality, suppressed.

Here, then, is another danger. When educational reform becomes too bound up with personal and group interests, it loses the capacity for self-criticism. It can be a dazzling diversionary activity turning heads away from the real nature of social problems. It can become a vested interest in its own right, so pious and powerful that it can direct public scorn to anyone who doubts. But the doubters are essential; for someone must try to keep the claims of education in proper perspective, to loose the hold of interest upon the cause of reform. This has yet to be done. But the notion of a war on poverty, a many-sided attack in which education is a component, not the only weapon, is promising. Still, the educational balloon in America has a way of getting loose from its mooring and sailing high, away from its companions. To keep it on a long and flexible but securely tied string is one of the great problems facing urban reformers today.

The thrust of this study has been to try to dissolve the myths enveloping the origins of popular education in America. Very simply, the extension and reform of education in the mid-nineteenth century were not a potpourri of democracy, rationalism, and humanitarianism. They were the attempt of a coalition of the social leaders, status-anxious parents, and status-hungry educators to impose educational innovation, each for their own reasons, upon a reluctant community. But why pierce such a warm and pleasant myth? Because, first of all, by piercing the vapor of piety we have been able to see certain fundamental patterns and problems in the course of American urban educational reform. We know better of what to beware. Because, second, to confront earlier urban reform is to dispel the kind of nostalgic romanticism present in even so acerbic a critic as Paul Goodman.[4] Our reform movements must not be inspired by a vision of a once vital and meaningful schooling to whose nature if not specific features we must return. We must face the painful fact that this country has never, on any large scale, known vital urban schools, ones which embrace and are embraced by the mass of the community, which formulate their goals in terms of the joy of the individual instead of the fear of social dynamite or the imperatives of economic growth. We must realize that we have no models; truly to reform we must conceive and build anew.

Appendixes

Appendix A. Massachusetts Social, Economic, and Educational Statistics

Table A.1. Growth of Massachusetts population, 1810–1860

Year	Population[a]	Percent increase in preceding decade
1810	472,000	9.3
1820	523,000	8.7
1830	610,000	15.2
1840	738,000	14.0
1850	994,000	30.8
1860	1,231,000	23.8

Source: Percy Wells Bidwell, "Population Growth in Southern New England, 1810–1860," *Quarterly Publications of the American Statistical Association*, New Series, no. 120 (December 1917), p. 813.

[a] To nearest thousand.

Table A.2. Number of alien passengers landed at Boston and Charlestown, 1831–1855

Year	Number
1831	1,417
1835	3,168
1840	5,361
1845	10,281
1850	26,612
1855	17,735

Source: Massachusetts Senate Document 2, January 1859, pp. 142–143

Table A.3. Concentration of population in urban communities, southern New England

Groups	1810	1840	1860
All towns and cities			
Number	437	479	526
Population	811,000	1,157,000	1,866,000
Population over 10,000			
Number	3	9	26
Population	56,000	214,000	681,600
Percentage[a]	6.9	18.5	36.5
Population 3,000–10,000			
Number	49	74	129
Population	210,300	340,000	620,700
Percentage[a]	25.9	29.4	33.8
Population less than 3,000			
Number	385	396	371
Population	545,000	603,000	537,000
Percentage[a]	67.1	52.1	30.1

Source: Bidwell, "Population Growth in Southern New England, 1810–1860," p. 813.
[a] Of total population.

Table A.4. Value of agricultural products as percentage of value of manufactured goods

Year	Percentage
1845	34
1855	17
1865	14

Source: Computed from statistics in John G. Palfrey, Statistics of the Condition and Products of Certain Branches of Industry in Massachusetts . . . 1845 (Boston, 1846); Francis DeWitt, Statistical Information Relating to Certain Branches of Industry in Massachusetts . . . 1855 (Boston, 1856); and Oliver Warner, Statistical Information Relating to Certain Branches of Industry in Massachusetts . . . 1865 (Boston, 1866).

Table A.5. Railroad mileage in Massachusetts, 1835–1865

Year	Mileage
1835	113
1840	318
1845	567
1850	1035
1855	1264
1865	1264

Source: Edward C. Kirkland, *Men, Cities and Transportation: A Study in New England History, 1820–1900* (Cambridge, Mass., 1948), I, 284.

Table A.6. Ratio of value of goods manufactured to capital invested

Type of goods	1845	1855	1865
Cotton	0.65	0.81	1.63
Wool	1.58	1.65	3.28
All types	1.94	2.13	2.91

Source: Same as Table A.4.

Table A.7. Massachusetts educational statistics, 1840-1865

Statistic	1840	1845	Percent change	1850	Percent change	1855	Percent change	1860	Percent change	1865	Percent change
No. public schools	3,072	3,475	13	3,870	12	4,215	11	4,487	11	4,749	6
No. students, winter	142,222	174,270	17	194,403	12	207,709	7	217,334	5	229,514	6
No. teachers	6,306	7,582	20	8,427	11	9,447	12	10,311	9	11,002	7
Male	2,378	2,585		2,442		2,114		1,908		1,377	
Female	3,928	4,997		5,985		7,333		8,403		9,625	
Ratio of male to female teachers	0.61	0.52		0.41		0.29		0.23		0.14	
Av. length schools, mos. and days	7-10	7-25		7-12		7-16		7-18		7-17	
Av. male teacher salary	$33.08	$31.76	-4	$34.89	10	$41.45	19	$50.56	22	$54.77	8
Av. female teacher salary	$12.75	$13.15	3	$14.42	10	$17.29	20	$19.08	10	$21.82	14
No. high schools	18			47		87		102		108	
Percent towns complying with high school law	36.4			55.3		64.2		67.2		68.0	
No. incorporated academies	78	67		67		71		65		59	
No. pupils	3,701	3,726		3,717		4,716		3,561		3,190	
No. unincorporated academies, private schools, etc.	1,368	1,091		845		646		640		682	
No. pupils	28,635	24,318		19,534		17,571		15,933		21,334	
Ratio of all academy pupils to all public school pupils	0.22	0.16		0.12		0.11		0.09		0.11	
Tax receipts (dollars)	$477,221	$611,652		$864,668		$1,137,407		$1,428,476		$1,782,624	
School tax rate (mills per dollar of valuation.)	1.59	2.04	12	1.44	49	1.92	19	1.59	12	1.80	12
Per-pupil expenditure	2.71	3.04		4.52		5.36		6.55		7.36	
Mean average attendance ratio	0.59	0.73		0.72		0.74		0.75		0.73	
Valuation of property in Mass.	$299,878,329			$597,936,995				$897,795,326		$1,009,709,652	
Cost of living index (1913 = 100)	60	54		54		67		61		102	

Source: Most of the figures in the table are from the annual reports of the secretaries of the Board of Education. The figures for high school establishment are from Alexander James Inglis, The Rise of the High School in Massachusetts (New York, 1911), pp. 42–45. The cost of living index is from Historical Statistics of the United States, Colonial Times to 1957 (Washington, 1960), p. 127.

Appendix B. Communities and Education: An Analysis of Variance

Even a cursory examination of Massachusetts educational statistics in the mid-nineteenth century reveals a wide variation among communities. Then as now, some towns expended more of their resources on education than others; some had higher per-pupil expenditures; some introduced more innovations; in some more pupils were in private schools. Today one would expect that these variations among communities were not random. One would look at the kind of town, the nature of the population, the degree of wealth, the economic features; one would look at these characteristics and predict certain associations between them and educational measures. But were there significant associations in the mid-nineteenth century? Were there significant patterns of relationships between educational and social, demographic and economic features of Massachusetts communities? This is the basic question that this appendix attempts to answer.

If one were to investigate the communal correlates of educational measures today, one would predict that certain patterns would emerge. So, too, one can make certain predictions about the associations that will be found in an investigation of the same topic a century ago. This study has revealed that in the state as a whole measures of educational change increased at roughly the same time as measures of urban and industrial growth. Therefore,

The statistical computations in this chapter were partially supported by a National Science Foundation Grant, GP-2723.

one hypothesis is that an increase in measures of educational expenditure and measures of innovation (feminization and high school establishment are the two most susceptible of quantitative analysis) within a community will be positively associated with measures of urban-industrial growth. This hypothesis raises certain questions. Massachusetts was marked by an increase in population concentration, manufacturing, and property valuation. Were all three associated with each other? Were all three related to educational measures in the same way? Were the extent and pace of urbanism and industrialism equally related to educational measures? Were educational measures associated with each other? That is, were the development of high schools, the feminization of the teaching force, and measures of educational expenditure all positively associated? Did high teacher salaries, high per-pupil expenditure, and high school tax rate usually occur together?

The increase in educational measures throughout the state was accompanied by a decrease in the value of agricultural goods produced relative to the value of manufactured articles. It can be predicted, then, that all measures of educational innovation and expenditure will be negatively associated with agricultural variables. Since the number and enrollment of incorporated academies remained relatively stable, an additional hypothesis is that little relationship will be found between these schools and social and economic measures. On the other hand, the number and enrollment of unincorporated academies and private schools dropped markedly during the time that high schools were being established. This suggests that unincorporated academies declined in communities establishing public high schools. But was there a relationship between academies of either type and the absence of a high school in a community? Was there any relationship between any particular occupational group and the presence of academies of either type? A variety of statistical tests provides evidence related to these hypotheses and answers to these questions.

I. HIGH SCHOOL DEFINED

The presence or absence of a high school provides the clearest criterion for dividing communities into categories. In mid-nineteenth century Massachusetts, what was a high school? The Manchester school committee answered precisely. "A High School is no ambiguous thing. It is a term that possesses an exact and well defined meaning. It is neither a primary or a grammar school, nor a compound of the two, without any regard to age or attainment, but a school distinct by itself, to which there is no access except through the two first. Thus, the High School has been defined for years past and this definition of them is recognized in our Revised Statutes (1835) and whenever schools are spoken of, 'for the whole town,' as the saying is." [1] The high school, usually attended by students from fourteen to nineteen years old, was designed as an institution roughly intermediate between the common school and the college.[2] Some people intended the high school to provide, primarily, a terminal education for students entering commercial and technical occupations.[3] Others emphasized preparation for college.[4] However, curricula and school reports indicate that the high school, even in this period, was acquiring both functions. As the Brookline school committee wrote: "The proper functions of a High School would seem to be, first, to continue the education of that portion of the Grammar school pupils of both sexes, whose circumstances allow, and whose talents fit them for further training; and, secondly, to give to those desiring it a thorough preparation for the College, or the Scientific, or the Normal School." [5]

The high school, thus, was defined by its function and place in the hierarchy of the school system. The high school was also defined by law; it was to be open to all the inhabitants of a town and administered by a town committee, as opposed to a district committee. In addition, the curriculum was to include certain specified subjects and the school was to be maintained at least ten months a year, "exclusive of vacations." [6] A Massachusetts law of 1827 contained the first legal provisions for high schools. The law required towns of a certain size to maintain an institution later termed a high school, but the provisions of this law were alternately suspended and reinvoked until 1859 when they became a permanent feature of the state's legislation.[7] According to the 1827 law, there were to be two grades of high schools. Lower-grade high schools were to be established in towns of five hundred or more families and higher-grade ones in towns of four thousand or more inhabitants. In the latter, Latin and Greek were to be included in the curriculum. In 1859 Latin was also required in lower-grade high schools. Alexander Inglis, in his book on the Massachusetts high schools, claims that the definition sometimes was applied rather loosely. "Cases are numerous," he wrote, "where we find the name 'High School' applied to higher grades in various districts"; and "still more frequently . . . the so-called 'High School' did not offer all of the studies prescribed by law."[8] By no means did all towns required to establish a high school comply with the law. The degree of compliance grew steadily, but by 1865 it was still only 68 percent.

The law that established high schools in 1827 fundamentally altered the administrative control of local education. Historians have treated the 1827 law as paradoxical. They have pointed out that the law both weakened the district system by stipulating that the high school was to be administered by the town as a whole and strengthened the district system by permitting each district to elect a prudential committeeman who would have considerable power over the schools in his area.[9] B. A. Hinsdale resolved the contradiction by noting that the 1827 law was retrogressive, for it released all but seven towns from the provisions of the law of 1789, which had required one hundred and seventy-two towns to maintain a school that taught Latin and Greek. To Hinsdale the 1827 law was a victory for the district system.[10] Raymond Culver, however, has pointed out that the 1827 law evolved as a compromise. In the previous year a law had been passed requiring towns to elect school committees to take complete charge of education in each town. But the law was so vehemently opposed that the next year the legislature compromised by allowing the districts to elect prudential committeemen with certain specific privileges and duties.[11] Since most towns did not adhere to the law of 1789 requiring them to maintain a grammar school, the 1827 law was realistic and was probably intended to insure that some public institution of higher learning would exist in the more populous areas. Moreover, the power which the new law gave to town committees combined with the fact that the prudential committees were established as a concession indicates that the purpose of the 1827 law was to modify the district system; hence the law's various provisions were consistent with each other.

State law prescribed curricula as well as administrative organization. Table B.1 lists the legal requirements for the high school curriculum in Massachusetts. Even in this sketchy form the curriculum requirements indicate that the legislature expected the content as well as the administrative form of education to alter. Until after 1835 the curricular requirements reflect the concerns of a pre-industrial, commercial economy; for the emphasis is on mathematics, bookkeeping, and surveying. The addition of the sciences may reflect the perception of the need for additional knowledge related to understanding, controlling, and fostering the economic changes in the state. Civil polity, moral science, political economy and intellectual science reflect the importance attributed to education for character development as well as the fear of social disintegration and the decline of morality. The process of curriculum change seems to have followed the same pattern that has continually marked the growth of the curriculum in America — the process of accretion. Instead of re-thinking the structure and nature of the curriculum as a whole, educators tacked subjects onto the existing course. The high school course at the start of the period, according to Inglis, was generally three years in length and, at the close, commonly four.[12] Most high schools employed, at best, a few teachers; considering this fact, the coverage of the

Table B.1. Subjects legally required in Massachusetts high school curriculum in 1865 by date of requirement

Subject	Date
United States History	1827
General History[a]	1827
Algebra	1827
Geometry	1827
Surveying	1827
Latin[a]	1827[b]
Greek[a]	1827
Logic[a]	1827
Bookkeeping	1835
French[a]	1857
Rhetoric[a]	1857
Natural Philosophy	1857
Chemistry	1857
Botany	1857
Astronomy[a]	1857
Geology[a]	1857
Intellectual Science[a]	1857
Moral Science[a]	1857
Civil Polity	1857
Political Economy[a]	1857

Source: Alexander James Inglis, *The Rise of the High School in Massachusetts* (New York, 1911), pp. 71–73.

[a] Required only in higher-grade high schools (those in towns of 4,000 or over), unless otherwise noted.

[b] Required in all high schools in 1859.

legally comprehensive curriculum must have been skimpy, to say the least.

Part of the reason for the inclusion of Latin and Greek in the curriculum undoubtedly was the entrance requirements of the colleges.[13] The preparation of students for college was, however, not the sole purpose of high schools. In many instances the high school was perceived as an institution directly related to the preparation of students for immediate employment. Finally, the high school was the deliberate creation of a law; and, for those interested in beginnings, the Massachusetts school law of 1827 was the legal origin of the American high school. The American comprehensive high school has three outstanding characteristics: it is free; it is open to all qualified students within a given area; and it caters to both terminal and college-bound students. High schools characterized by these features emerged in Massachusetts well before the Civil War.

A division of towns on the criterion of high school establishment immediately reveals one relationship — size. By 1865 every city or town with a population of 6,200 or more did establish a high school; no town with a population of less than 711 did so. For the purposes of this analysis of the relation between educational and social and economic variables the extremes were eliminated, and the sample became each of the 259 towns between the smallest that had instituted a high school by 1865 and the largest that failed to meet its legal obligation to establish one. These limits were chosen in order to include the possibility of variation within each town. That is, the object was to study the differing patterns of relationships within towns which might or might not have established high schools. Fifty-five of the towns chosen for study were eventually eliminated from consideration because it was not possible to obtain accurate information on all the variables considered. This left a final sample of 204 towns.

Information for each town was gathered for forty-eight variables, listed below. Five principal sources were used to supply statistical data: the United States censuses of 1840 and 1865; the abstracts of Massachusetts school returns for 1840 and 1865; and the Massachusetts state census of industry for 1875.[14]

ROSTER OF VARIABLES

1840

1. Population
2. Density of population per square mile
3. Total employed in manufacturing
4. Total employed in non-agricultural occupations, excluding professionals
5. Total employed in agriculture
6. Ratio of non-agricultural to agricultural employees
7. Per capita valuation
8. Number of incorporated academies
9. Number of unincorporated academies
10. Miles from Boston
11. Dependency rate
12. Females as percent of total number of teachers in winter (feminization)
13. Average monthly salary of male teachers
14. Average monthly salary of female teachers
15. Per-pupil expenditure
16. Mills per dollar of valuation raised for school support through taxes (school tax rate)
17. Number employed in commerce
18. Number employed in navigation
19. Number in professions
20. Number over 16 in public schools

1865

21. Population
22. Density of population per square mile
23. Total employed in manufacturing
24. Total employed in non-agricultural occupations
25. Total employed in agriculture
26. Ratio of non-agricultural to agricultural employees
27. Per capita valuation
28. Number of incorporated academies
29. Number of unincorporated academies and private schools
30. Total number of private schools
31. Dependency rate
32. Females as percent of total number of teachers in winter (feminization)
33. Average monthly salary of male teachers

ROSTER OF VARIABLES (*continued*)

34. Average monthly salary of female teachers
35. Per-pupil expenditure
36. Mills per dollar of valuation raised for school support through taxes (school tax rate)
37. Number of foreign born
38. "Other occupations" (commerce, navigation, some trades)
39. Number of females employed in manufacturing
40. Number over 15 attending public school
41. Number of workers per manufacturing establishment

Increases 1840–1865

42. In population
43. In density
44. In total number employed in manufacturing
45. In total number of non-agricultural employees
46. In total number of agricultural employees
47. In ratio of non-agricultural to agricultural employees
48. High school establishment by 1865 (coded as 1 for non-establishment, 2 for establishment)

The fact that a legal obligation to establish a high school is not included in the roster of variables requires explanation, for it may be asked: was not the law the most important factor in high school establishment? Was not high school establishment generally the reflection of a legal obligation? If the answer to this question is affirmative, then a detailed analysis of the social and economic factors associated with high school establishment is superfluous. It is assumed, however, that the answer to the question is *generally* negative. First of all, law had not been a particularly effective means of insuring the maintenance of certain kinds of schools in Massachusetts towns. Historians agree that throughout the eighteenth and early nineteenth centuries the number of towns maintaining grammar schools as required by the law of 1647 modified by the law of 1789 declined quite markedly and that the law was generally not obeyed.[15]

Second, little evidence of the importance of law is provided by an analysis comparing the date that towns were legally required to establish high schools with the date they actually instituted them, as Table B.2 indicates.[16] Table B.2 includes only those towns and

Table B.2. Comparison of date of legal obligation and date of compliance with high school establishment

Time (years) between legal obligation and establishment of a high school	Number of towns and cities
[a]	29
One	18
Two	3
Three	3
Four	2
Five	3
Six to ten	5
Eleven to fifteen	10
Sixteen to twenty	5
Twenty-one or more	11
Total	89

Source: Inglis, *Rise of the High School*, pp 42–45.
[a] Established before required by law.

cities that by 1865 were required to establish a high school and that met their legal obligation by that date. It does not include those towns and cities that established high schools but were not legally required to do so throughout the period under consideration. Thus, the table, unlike the statistical analysis in the rest of this chapter, is based on all the towns and cities in the state.

Of the towns considered in Table B.2, nearly one third established a high school before becoming required to do so by law. Twenty-nine percent did not comply with the law for ten or more years. If a new legal obligation had an immediate impact, how long would it take for a town to establish a high school? Approximation only is possible here; but three years seems reasonable. Eligibility would be ascertained in a census year; one year later the town might vote on establishment at its annual meeting; during the next year preparations for opening could be made; and a third year may be allowed for exigencies. Twenty-seven percent of the towns fall within the three-year limit.

Nevertheless, establishment of a high school within three years is no evidence that towns acted because of the law. Establishment even in these towns may have been the reflection of some underlying dimension. Population, for instance, is one obviously important factor. Towns of a certain size were required to establish high schools, and legal obligation, therefore, reflects growth. But population growth itself is related to other social and economic measures. In short, no evidence exists that makes it reasonable to assume that legal obligation was *generally* the most important factor in high school establishment. On the other hand, so far there is no evidence that legal obligation was not of prime importance. A town may have complied with the law at a later date because at that time the county court decided to enforce the law more stringently, or, as in the case of Beverly discussed in the text, because a group of townspeople brought suit against the town for non-compliance. Even in cases such as the latter, however, the enforcement by the court or the bringing of suit may reflect, as it did in Beverly, fundamental social and economic alterations within the community. Thus, the role of legal compulsion cannot be tested statistically with any accuracy. It is hard to imagine how compulsion could be entered meaningfully into the roster of variables. More promising, instead, is looking for patterns of relationships between quantitative social and economic measures and high school establishment. If relationships are found, then establishment can more safely be assumed to be primarily the result of factors other than legal compulsion.

Density, population, and their increase will be used as measures of urbanism and urbanization. To define "urban" precisely is, as a recent conference on the historian and the city discovered, probably impossible. Nevertheless, size and concentration of population are aspects of most conceptualizations. A problem is that no precise figure for population size or density can be taken as a minimal standard for urbanism because the term is a relative one. That is, concentrations of population considered urban in one context by virtue of their contrast to surrounding units might not be considered urban in another setting. In this study, "urban" refers to towns that had a relatively larger and denser population than others in the sample.[17]

2. FIRST RELATIONSHIPS

A number of statistical analyses were performed to determine the relationship between the various measures.[*] First, the towns were divided into two groups on the basis of whether or not they had established a high school by 1865. Hereafter these groups will be referred to as high school and non–high school towns. Table B.3 presents the means and standard deviations for the two groups and for the sample as a whole. Table B.3 reveals dramatic differences between the two groups of towns. In brief, high school towns were larger, denser, more industrial, and more commercial. Within these categories there was more discrepancy between the two groups of towns in 1865 than in 1840. In 1840 the high school towns had a mean population 32 percent greater than the others. By 1865 the figure was 77 percent. Similarly, the mean density

[*] Not all the statistical tests performed are discussed in this chapter, which considers only those felt to be most relevant. All analyses discussed in the chapter were performed by computer. For most tests the MSA main link tape and programs were used. For a discussion of these programs and a guide to their usage see Kenneth J. Jones, *The Multivariate Statistical Analyzer* (Cambridge, Mass., 1964). For the correlation and division into means, discussed within this chapter, the SLURP program designed by A. Beaton and H. Glauber was used. The subtraction of one variable from another was performed by means of a program written for the author by Dr. Allan Ellis.

of the high school towns was 54 percent greater in 1840 and 127 percent larger in 1865. For total employed in manufacturing, in non-agricultural occupations, and ratio of non-agricultural to agricultural employees, the 1840 differences were 107 percent, 116 percent, and 126 percent, respectively. By 1865 these differences had increased to 175 percent, 169 percent, and 269 percent. The high school towns also grew more rapidly than did the others; their increases in population, density, number employed in manufacturing, number employed in non-agricultural occupations, and ratio of non-agricultural to agricultural employees were, respectively, 439 percent, 433 percent, 260 percent, 267 percent, and 386 percent greater than the increases in the non–high school towns.

Other related differences could not be measured for both years, but in the year in which they could be gauged similar discrepancies occurred. In 1840 the mean number employed in commerce in the high school towns was 138 percent greater than in the other group; the number in professions in the same year was 45 percent greater, the number employed in navigation 62 percent larger. Similarly, in 1865 the number in the category "other occupations," comprising commerce, navigation, and trades, was 133 percent larger in the high school towns; the number of females employed in manufacturing was 147 percent greater and the number of workers per manufacturing establishment was 93 percent larger.

The groups of towns differed only slightly in per capita valuation; the figure was 9 percent higher in the high school towns in 1840 and 5 percent higher in 1865. The differences in dependency rate were negligible, and only small differences existed in the number employed in agriculture. The mean number of agricultural employees was 5 percent smaller in high school towns in 1840 and 5 percent larger in 1865. In both groups of towns the mean number employed in agriculture declined between 1840 and 1865, but in the high school towns the fall was 37 percent smaller.

High school towns spent on the average slightly more per pupil. The difference in per-pupil expenditure rate was 16 percent in

Table B.3. Means and standard deviations (S.D.) of towns in sample, 1840 and 1865

Variable	Towns that did not establish a high school by 1865 (N = 150)		Towns that did establish a high school by 1865 (N = 54)		Difference[a]	Entire sample (N = 204)	
	Means	S.D.	Means	S.D.		Means	S.D.
1840							
Population	1536	689	2023	817	32	1665	755
Density	61.83	31.24	95.46	68.96	54	70.74	46.68
Total employed in manufacturing	125	105	259	168	1.07	161	138
Total employed in non-agricultural occupations, excluding professionals	168	156	363	314	1.16	219	226
Agricultural employees	287	152	273	140	-.05	283	149
Ratio of non-agricultural to agricultural employees	0.78	1.08	1.77	2.18	1.26	1.04	1.51
Per capita valuation	$245	$65	$269.56	$74.95	0.09	$251.79	$68.56
Incorporated academies	0.17	0.38	0.28	0.45	0.64	0.20	0.40
Unincorporated academies, private schools, and schools kept to prolong the common schools	3.43	3.45	4.59	3.93	0.33	3.74	3.61
Dependency rate	0.35	0.05	0.34	0.02	-.03	0.35	0.04
Females as percent of total teachers in winter	0.23	0.20	0.26	0.20	0.13	0.24	0.20
Average monthly salary male	$24.74	$4.24	$27.65	$5.11	11	$25.51	$4.65

female	$11.71	$2.10	$12.19	$1.98	0.04	$11.84	$2.08
Per-pupil expenditure	$2.00	0.61	$2.32	0.75	0.16	$2.09	0.66
Taxation as mills/dollar of valuation	$2.19	0.70	2.36	0.92	0.07	2.23	0.76
Number employed in commerce	6.84	9.11	16.30	21.01	1.38	9.34	13.92
Number employed in navigation	31.37	102.52	52.02	130.44	0.62	36.84	110.64
Number in professions	6.42	4.00	9.35	5.44	0.45	7.20	4.60
Number over 16 in school	40.95	25.68	42.39	31.50	0.03	41.33	27.27

1865

Population	1728	869	3060	1191	0.77	2081	1127
Density	77.11	57.38	175	138	1.27	103	96
Total employed manufacturing	224	366	616	490	1.75	328	437
Total employed non-agricultural occupations	260	382	700	465	169	376	449
Agricultural employees	218	112	229	152	0.05	221	123
Ratio of non-ag. to ag.	1.79	4.19	6.62	11.65	269	3.07	7.27
Per capita valuation	$471	$151	$498	$171	0.05	$478	$156
Number incorporated academies	0.19	0.40	0.13	0.34	-.32	0.18	0.38
Number unincorporated academies and private schools	1.26	1.56	1.30	1.77	.03	1.27	1.61
Dependency rate	0.31	0.03	0.31	0.03	0	0.31	0.03
Females as percent of all teachers in winter	0.75	0.18	0.81	0.18	0.08	0.77	0.16
Average monthly salary							
male	$30.19	$9.64	$47.17	$14.12	56	$34.69	$13.29
female	$17.44	$2.69	$19.13	$2.43	0.09	$17.89	$2.73
Per-pupil expenditure	$3.79	$1.14	$4.60	$1.53	0.21	$4.00	$1.30
Mills/dollar in taxes	1.85	0.54	2.17	0.42	17	1.94	0.53

Table B.3. (*continued*)

Variable	Towns that did not establish a high school by 1865 (N = 150)		Towns that did establish a high school by 1865 (N = 54)			Entire sample (N = 204)	
	Means	S.D.	Means	S.D.	Difference[a]	Means	S.D.
No. foreign born	195	208	498	355	155	275	287
"Other occupations," trades, etc.	30	118	70	169	133	40.19	133.80
Females employed in manufacturing	85	228	210	232	147	118	235
No. over 15 in school	51	35	72	41	41	57	38
Workers/mfg. establishment	15.76	23.82	29	31	93	19.27	26.64
Increase 1840–1865							
Population	192	549	1037	830	439	416	735
Density	15	39	80	114	433[b]	32	73
No. in manufacturing	99	345	357	406	260	167	379
No. in non-agr. occs.	92	359	338	476	267	157	407
No. in agriculture	−69	143	−44	148	37	−62	144
Ratio non-agr. to agr. occs.	1.00	3.90	4.86	10.27	386	2.03	6.45

[a] Difference represents the ratio obtained by dividing the figure for towns that did establish high schools by the figure for towns that did not.
[b] The difference between ratio increases in population and density reflects the changes in the total area of some towns between 1840 and 1865.

1840 and 21 percent in 1865. Similarly, in high school towns the school tax rate was 7 percent greater in 1840 and 17 percent greater in 1865. Female teachers' salaries, on the average, differed slightly between the two groups of towns; in high school towns the figure was 4 percent greater in 1840 and 9 percent in 1865. Male teachers' salaries differed markedly. On the average, high school towns in 1840 paid male teachers 11 percent more but by 1865 the difference had increased to 56 percent. Although both groups of towns hired increasingly higher proportions of female teachers, the degree of feminization differed little between the two groups. In 1840, 23 percent of the winter teaching force was female in non–high school towns and 26 percent in high school towns; in 1865 the proportions had increased to 75 percent and 81 percent. A more marked difference occurred in the number of older children remaining in public schools. In 1840 the number of children over sixteen years old who attended public school was only 3 percent greater in the high school towns; by 1865 the difference in the number over fifteen who attended was 41 percent.

From a simple division on the criterion of high school establishment, marked relationships emerge. In terms of the grossest distinctions and measures, towns that established a high school were noticeably more urban, industrial, and rapidly expanding than those that did not. This general impression is reinforced by a correlation of high school establishment with the other forty-seven variables. The results of this correlation are presented in Table B.4. Table B.4 is drawn from an analysis in which all the variables were correlated with each other. Hereafter, this inter-correlation analysis of all forty-eight variables will be termed the GCA (general correlation analysis). Table B.4 reinforces the impression gained by comparing mean differences. High school establishment was significantly correlated with each of the social, economic, and demographic measures that had a larger mean in high school towns. In spite of the small mean differences between per-pupil expenditure and school tax rate, these measures were significantly corre-

Table B.4. Rank order of correlation coefficients with high school establishment as dependent variable

Rank	Variable	Correlation coefficient[a]
1.	Average monthly salary, male teachers, 1865	0.5650
2.	Population, 1865	.5223
3.	Increase in population, 1840 to 1865	.5082
4.	Number of foreign born, 1865	.4658
5.	Density, 1865	.4490
6.	Total employed non-agricultural occupations, 1865	.4343
7.	Total employed in manufacturing, 1840	.4286
8.	Total employed in manufacturing, 1865	.3966
9.	Increase in density, 1840 to 1865	.3891
10.	Total employed in non-agricultural occupations, 1840	.3806
11.	Density, 1840	.3186
12.	Increase employees manufacturing, 1840 to 1865	.3020
13.	Number employed in commerce, 1840	.3005
14.	Ratio non-agricultural to agricultural employees, 1865	.2938
15.	Ratio non-agricultural to agricultural employees, 1840	.2880
16.	Population, 1840	.2880
17.	Number in professions, 1840	.2821
18.	Average monthly salary, male teachers, 1840	.2852
19.	Average monthly salary, female teachers, 1865	.2757
20.	Per-pupil expenditure, 1865	.2750
21.	Taxation as mills/dollar for schools, 1865	.2686
22.	Increase total employed non-agricultural occs., 1840 to 1865	.2671
23.	Increase ratio non-agr. to agr. employees, 1840 to 1865	.2637
24.	Number over 15 in school, 1865	.2384
25.	Females employed in manufacturing, 1865	.2350
26.	Number of workers per manufacturing establishment, 1865	.2201
27.	Per-pupil expenditure, 1840	.2142

Not significant at .05 or better

Rank	Variable	Correlation coefficient[a]
28.	Miles from Boston	−.1797
29.	Females as per cent total teachers in winter, 1865	.1590
30.	Per capita valuation, 1840	.1558
31.	Unincorporated academies, private schools and schools kept to prolong common schools, 1840	.1428

Table B.4 (*continued*)

32.	"Other occupations," 1865	.1323
33.	Incorporated academies, 1840	.1150
34.	Average monthly salary, female teachers, 1840	.1038
35.	Dependency rate, 1840	—.0986
36.	Taxation in mills/dollar for schools, 1840	.0970
37.	Number employed in navigation, 1840	.0825
38.	Per capita valuation, 1865	.0771
39.	Increase number in agriculture, 1840 to 1865	.0763
40.	Number incorporated academies, 1865	—.0737
41.	Females as percent teachers in winter, 1840	.0622
42.	Number employed in agriculture, 1840	—.0421
43.	Number employed in agriculture, 1865	.0385
44.	Dependency rate, 1865	.0379
45.	Number over 16 in school, 1840	.0234
46.	Total private schools, 1865	—.0104
47.	Number unincorporated academies and private schools, 1865	.1011

ᵃ Significance: 0.05 = .195; 0.01 = .24.

lated with high school establishment. Measures of agricultural employees remain neutral, apparently by themselves having no significant bearing on high school establishment. Also neutral are academies, both incorporated and unincorporated, and per capita valuation.

3. FACTOR ANALYSIS

A division by means and even a correlation analysis present a somewhat oversimplified picture of the relationships between educational variables and others. The distinction between urban-industrial and non–urban-industrial hides shades of difference that may be very relevant to discerning more precisely the characteristics of the relationships under consideration. To discern the patterns of relationships within the variables more subtly a factor analysis was performed. The factor analysis is a test which asks: what are the underlying dimensions in the data and how much does each variable contribute to each dimension? The factor analysis assumes that underlying a large group of observations are certain fundamental unities, that a seemingly chaotic group of events can be reduced and described by certain underlying traits.[18]

Factor analysis is an extremely important test and is superior, for a large group, to partial correlation since it reduces the number of variables to a manageable size and, in effect, partials out the dimensions or factors of significance. However, the dimensions originally identified by a factor analysis have a drawback. The first factor is always a general one that represents only gross differences and obscures some subtle relationships. To overcome these drawbacks a test known as Varimax rotation was used on the factors. The rotation distributes the loadings (or weights of contribution of each variable) of the general factor among the others and accentuates their differences.

The Varimax rotation deals with a maximum of ten factors. In this analysis, all ten factors rotated were statistically significant in terms of contributing to the variation among towns on the measures under consideration. *Factors, it must be emphasized, should not be taken as literal examples of towns.* No town is characterized exclusively by only one or two factors. What the factors do represent are underlying patterns of relationship among the variables, patterns that combined in different degrees with each town. Many variables appear on more than one factor; that is because the particular variable was associated with the characteristic or trait represented by each factor. For example, population size appears on both the manufacturing growth and the urban growth factors because a relatively large population was associated with both industrialization and urbanism. The ten factors that will be discussed have been labelled: (1) manufacturing growth factor; (2) urban growth factor; (3) wealthy suburban factor; (4) small, static, non-commercial factor; (5) agricultural growth factor; (6) growing agricultural population factor; (7) distance-dependency factor; (8) unincorporated academy factor; (9) incorporated academy factor; (10) low school tax-rate factor.

Table B.5 presents the significant factor loadings for the manufacturing growth factor. This and all subsequent factor tables pre-

Table B.5. Manufacturing growth factor: Significant
factor loadings in rank order

Variable	Loading
Positive	
Increase total number employed in manufacturing, 1840–1865	0.96
Increase total employed in non-agricultural occupations, 1840–1865	.95
Total employed in manufacturing, 1865	.92
Total employed in non-agricultural occupations, 1865	.88
Number of workers per manufacturing establishment, 1865	.74
Increase in population, 1840–1865	.55
Increase in ratio of non-agricultural to agricultural employees, 1840–1865	.47
Number of foreign born, 1865	.44
Population, 1865	.41
Increase in density, 1840–1865	.40
Density, 1865	.34
Total employed in manufacturing, 1840	.29
Female teacher salary, 1865	.26
High school established, 1865	.24
Negative	
None	

sent the factors *after* rotation. The five dominant loadings, it is clear, are measures of industrial growth and industrial size in 1865: increase in manufacturing employees, .96; increase in non-agricultural employees, .95; total employed in manufacturing 1865, .92; total non-agricultural employees, 1865, .88; and number of workers per manufacturing establishment in 1865, .74. Other measures related to manufacturing are also important: the increase in the ratio of non-agricultural to agricultural employees, .47; and the total employed in manufacturing in 1840, .29. Since foreign born is highly correlated with manufacturing measures in the GCA (for instance, its correlation with increase in manufacturing employees is .48), the high loading, .44, of this variable can be explained by the increase in industrial measures. Demographic measures are of importance, though they do not dominate: population increase loads, .55; population in 1865, .44; increase in density, .41; and density in 1865, .40. The two significant loadings for educational variables are female teacher salary in 1865, .26; and high school establishment, .24. The former is significantly correlated in the GCA with industrial variables. Its correlation with increase in number of manufacturing employees, for instance, is .33. High school establishment, it has been noted earlier, is also highly associated with industrial variables. Thus, the significance of these two variables on factor one is understandable.

This factor represents an urban-industrial dimension of a special sort. The most important feature of the factor is industrial growth. Second is industrial size in 1865. Third is growth in population and density, or urban growth. Of lesser importance are the variables for 1840. Indeed, only the number employed in manufacturing in that year is significant. In the GCA manufacturing employees and density in 1865 are significantly correlated, .50, as are the measures for the increase in each variable, .45. Since the loadings of industrial characteristics are so high on this factor, it is probable that these were the dominant characteristics, bringing with them associated growth and magnitude in population and density. Hence, this factor has been termed the manufacturing growth factor.

Table B.6 presents the significant loadings for the urban growth factor. In this factor, as in the former, urban-industrial characteristics are dominant, but their combination reveals a different underlying relationship. In this second factor, first of all, the 1840 variables are more important than in the former factor. The variable with the highest loading, .77, is number employed in manufacturing in 1840. Second in importance is population in 1865; third is another 1840 variable, total employed in non-agricultural occupations, .66. Density, too, is significant. For 1840 its loading

Table B.6. Urban growth factor: Significant factor loadings in rank order

Variable	Loading
Positive	
Total employed in manufacturing	0.77
Population, 1865	.74
Total in non-agricultural occupations, 1840	.66
Foreign born, 1865	.62
Density, 1840	.60
Density, 1865	.58
High school establishment, 1865	.57
Population, 1840	.56
Number in professions, 1840	.56
Number in commerce, 1840	.55
Increase in population, 1840 to 1865	.55
Average monthly salary of male teachers, 1865	.53
Increase in density, 1840 to 1865	.39
Unincorporated academies, 1840	.35
Total employed in non-agricultural occupations, 1865	.34
Total employed in manufacturing, 1865	.32
Ratio of non-agricultural to agricultural employees, 1840	.31
Negative	
None	

is .60, for 1865, .58, and for the increase between the two, .39. Foreign born in 1865, which has a loading of .62, is another important demographic variable. Similarly, population in 1840, .56, and its increase, .55, are significant. Three other variables related to manufacturing have significant loadings: non-agricultural employees 1865, .34; total employed in manufacturing 1865, .32; and ratio of non-agricultural to agricultural employees 1840, .31;

but, it is important to note, no increase in a manufacturing variable has a significant loading. Given the general urban characteristics in 1840 represented by factor two it is not surprising that number of professionals and number in commerce, both with loadings of .56, are significant.

The important educational characteristics of this factor are high school establishment, .56; male teacher salary 1865, .53; and number of unincorporated academies 1840, .35. High school establishment, it has been noted, was significantly correlated with all of the urban and industrial variables of importance in this factor. In the GCA, high school establishment was also significantly correlated with number employed in commerce in 1840, .30, and with number of professionals in 1840, .28. The importance of the social, economic, and occupational characteristics associated with high schools explains the high loading of the latter variable on this factor. Male teacher salary is significantly correlated, .56, with high school establishment in the GCA; and the high loading of the latter undoubtedly contributes to the former's significance on the factor. At first glance, the significance of unincorporated academies is somewhat surprising on a factor containing high school establishment, since academies were considered inimical to the expansion of the public educational system. However, it is unincorporated academies for 1840 — not for 1865 — that is significant. In 1840, the GCA shows, unincorporated academies were significantly correlated with number in commerce, .48, and number in professions, .31. The pattern of relationships of unincorporated academies in 1865 was very different, as will be shown presently, and the differences suggest that the relation of these private institutions to the rest of the community altered markedly in the intervening years. In factor two, finally, both urban and industrial characteristics are present. The size of manufacturing variables in 1840 is, however, more important than their size in 1865, and their growth is not significant. On the other hand, in 1865 demographic, urban variables weigh more heavily than the manufacturing ones and their growth *is* significant. That is, the dominant 1840 characteristics represent manufacturing; the dominant 1865 and growth characteristics represent urbanism. Thus, factor two has been termed the urban growth factor.

Table B.7 lists the significant factor loadings for the wealthy suburban factor. In this factor the dominant loadings are educa-

Table B.7. Wealthy suburban factor: Factor loadings in rank order

Variable	Loading
Positive	
Per-pupil expenditure, 1865	0.80
Per-pupil expenditure, 1840	.78
Average male teacher salary, 1840	.75
Per capita valuation, 1865	.74
Average female teacher salary, 1865	.72
Average female teacher salary, 1840	.58
Average male teacher salary, 1865	.52
Per capita valuation, 1840	.48
School tax rate, 1840	.30
High school established, 1865	.26
Increase in density, 1840 to 1865	.24
Negative	
Miles from Boston	−.45

tional. The two highest loadings are per-pupil expenditure in 1865 and 1840, .80 and .78. Likewise, salaries of both male and female teachers for 1840 and 1865 have high loadings; for male teachers in 1840 the loading is .75, in 1865, .52. For female teachers in 1865 it is .58, in 1865, .72. Significant also in this dimension is communal wealth, represented by per capita valuation with a loading of .74 in 1865 and .48 in 1840. The association of per capita valuation and per-pupil expenditure is predictable from the correlation between the two, .41 on the GCA; but the significant loading of school tax rate in 1840, .30, is surprising because the correlation between tax and per capita valuation is −.46. Thus factor three represents an exceptionally high level of educational expenditure. This conclusion is reinforced by the significance of high school establishment, .26, which in the GCA is significantly associated with measures of educational spending in 1865 and with male teacher salary in 1840.

Particularly revealing in factor three are the significant demographic loading; increase in density, .24; and the significant geographic loading, miles from Boston, −.45. Factor three represents an increasing clustering of population near Boston and probably reflects the growth of suburban areas in this period. This is the dimension most characterized by measures of both educational expenditure and innovation; it has been termed the wealthy suburban factor.

The first three factors represent varieties of urban dimensions. By contrast the next three factors to be considered represent varieties of agricultural dimensions. The significant factor loadings of the small static non-commercial factor are listed in Table B.8. Striking in this factor are the significant negative loadings of both measures associated with urbanism and occupations other than agriculture. Particularly dominant negatively are number employed in navigation in 1840 and "other occupations" in 1865, −.90 and −.81. The ratio of non-agricultural to agricultural employees is also significantly negative, −.73 in 1840 and −.55 in 1865. Not surprisingly, number employed in commerce, −.37, is also significantly negative as is the increase in the total number of non-agricultural employees, −.44. That this is a dimension characterized by small population size and relatively few children is attested by the loadings of population in 1865, −.29, and dependency rate in 1840, −.24. Yet it is not a dimension characterized by a lack of communal wealth since the loading of per capita valuation in 1840 is .38.

Given the dominant social and demographic characteristics of this dimension most of the educational features are predictable from the general correlation analysis. For instance, the correlation coefficient of number employed in commerce in 1840 with male teacher salary in 1840 is .26. In this factor the loading of male teacher salary is negative, −.32. Likewise, the correlation between

Table B.8. Small, static non-commercial factor: Significant factor loadings in rank order

Variable	Loading
Positive	
Per capita valuation, 1840	0.38
Feminization, 1865	.24
Negative	
Number employed in navigation, 1840	−.90
"Other occupations," 1865	−.81
Ratio of non-agricultural to agricultural employees, 1840	−.73
Number over 15 in public school, 1865	−.67
Unincorporated academies, 1840	−.56
Ratio of non-agricultural to agricultural employees, 1865	−.55
Population, 1840	−.52
Total employed in non-agricultural occupations, 1840	−.46
School tax rate, 1840	−.44
Increase in ratio of non-agricultural to agricultural employees, 1840–1865	−.44
Density, 1840	−.41
Number employed in commerce, 1840	−.37
Average monthly salary of male teachers, 1840	−.32
Number over 16 in public school, 1840	−.31
Population, 1865	−.29
Dependency rate, 1840	−.24
Total employed in non-agricultural occupations, 1865	−.24

number over 15 in public school and ratio of non-agricultural to agricultural employees in 1865 is .32; and the loading of the former is negative, −.67. Similarly, the correlation coefficient of per capita valuation and school tax rate in 1840 is −.46, and the loading of the latter is −.44. Feminization in 1865, with a loading of .24, is less readily explicable since there is no significant correlation between this measure and any variable in the GCA. However, the polarity noticeable between feminization and unincorporated academies is a relationship that appears also in another factor and will be returned to. The negative loading of unincorporated academies for 1840, −.56, is understandable in light of its positive correlation with number employed in commerce, .48; average male teacher salary in 1840, .24; and number employed in navigation, .54. It is somewhat surprising that per-pupil expenditure in 1840 is not significantly positive, since this variable was significantly correlated, .41, with per capita valuation. The absence of per-pupil expenditure as positive combined with the negative significance of number over 16 and 15 in school and of school tax rate indicates a low level of expenditure on, and perhaps a lack of interest in, public education as a characteristic of the factor. Besides a low expenditure on public education, the factor represents smallness, an absence of sea-faring and commercial activity and at the least a balance between non-agricultural and agricultural enterprise resistant to change. Thus, it has been termed the small, static non-commercial factor.

Table B.9 presents the significant factor loadings for the agricultural growth factor. The dominant characteristic of this factor is clearly agricultural. Significantly positive are number employed in agriculture in 1865, .79; increase in agricultural employees, .40; and number employed in agriculture in 1840, .40. By contrast the significant negative loadings are, predictably, the ratio of non-agricultural to agricultural employees for 1840 and 1865 and the increase between the two years, with negative loadings of −.32, −.59 and −.59. The negative loadings of density measures indicate the sparseness of population that accompanies agriculture; the loading of density for 1840 is −.26; for 1865, −.50; and for the increase also −.50.

The only significant educational variable in factor six is school tax rate for 1840, which has a negative loading of −.28, a loading expected because of the significant correlation, .50, between it and ratio of non-agricultural to agricultural employees. It is important to note that within this factor measures for 1865 and measures of increase are more heavily weighted than are measures for 1840. No measures of manufacturing, moreover, are associated, even negatively, with this factor. It is an agricultural, not an anti-manu-

Table B.9. Agricultural growth factor: Factor loadings in rank order

Variable	Loading
Positive	
Number employed in agriculture, 1865	0.79
Increase in agricultural employees, 1840–1865	.40
Number employed in agriculture, 1840	.27
Negative	
Increase in the ratio of non-agricultural to agricultural employees, 1840–1865	−.59
Ratio of non-agricultural to agricultural employees, 1865	−.59
Density, 1865	−.50
Increase in density, 1864–1865	−.50
Ratio of non-agricultural to agricultural employees, 1840	−.32
School tax rate, 1840	−.28
Density, 1840	−.26

facturing dimension. Likewise, it is not in itself an anti-education factor, although the low level of school tax rate indicates a tendency toward a low level of educational expenditure. Thus this factor has been named the agricultural growth factor.

The significant factor loadings for factor seven are listed in Table B.10. This factor is also clearly agricultural. The number of agricultural employees and the population in 1840 are negative, −.31 and −.81; but the increase in agricultural employees between 1840 and 1865 is positive. Factor seven, then, represents the emergence of a numerous group of agricultural employees between 1840 and 1865. It will be termed the growing agricultural population factor. Again, only one educational variable, this time number over 16 in public school in 1840, is significant, −.62; and this significance is explicable in terms of its association with agricultural employees in 1840, .31 in the GCA. As in factor six,

Table B.10. Growing agricultural population factor:
Significant loadings in rank order

Variable	Loading
Positive	
Increase in agricultural employees, 1840–1865	0.81
Negative	
Number of agricultural employees, 1840	−.81
Number over 16 in school, 1840	−.62
Population, 1840	−.31

agricultural characteristics by themselves neither fostered nor precluded manufacturing development or a high level of educational spending.

Only one other factor lends itself to a non-educational characterization. Table B.11 lists the significant factor loadings. This factor

Table B.11. Distance-dependency factor: Significant
loadings in rank order

Variable	Loading
Positive	
Dependency rate, 1865	0.75
Dependency rate, 1840	.61
Miles from Boston	.57
Feminization, 1840	.34
Average monthly salary of female teachers, 1840	.32
Feminization, 1865	.26
Negative	
None	

is characterized by a high dependency rate for both 1840 and 1865, .75 and .61; and it is associated with distance away from Boston, .57. The educational characteristics of factor eight all relate to female teachers: the degree of feminization has a loading of .34 in 1840 and .26 in 1865; and the average monthly salary of female teachers in 1840 has a loading of .32. The association of variables in this factor is somewhat surprising in light of the correlation analysis. None of the educational variables are significantly correlated either with each other or with the significant demographic variables. Again, the role of feminization is puzzling, and this variable will be analyzed by itself later in this appendix. This factor has been termed the distance-dependency factor.

The three remaining factors represent educational dimensions. Table B.12 lists the significant loadings for the unincorporated

Table B.12. Unincorporated academy factor: Significant loadings in rank order

Variable	Loading
Positive	
Number of unincorporated academies and private schools, 1865	0.97
Total number of private schools, 1865	.95
Negative	
Feminization, 1865	−.24

academy factor. The dominant characteristic here is unincorporated academies and private schools in 1865, whose loading is .97. This has been termed the unincorporated academy factor. As in the wealthy suburban factor, feminization and unincorporated academies tend to have opposite loadings; and feminization in 1865 has the only significantly negative loading on the factor, −.24.

The significant factor loadings for the next factor are listed in Table B.13. Factor nine is dominated by incorporated academies, which have a loading of .74 in 1840 and .78 in 1865. The significance of number of professionals, .50, is comprehensible from the correlation between it and incorporated academies, .45 in

Table B.13. Incorporated academy factor: Significant loadings in rank order

Variable	Loading
Positive	
Incorporated academies, 1865	0.78
Incorporated academies, 1840	.74
Number of professionals, 1840	.50
Population, 1840	.30
Feminization, 1840	.25
Negative	
None	

1840 and .30 in 1865. Population in 1840, whose loading is .30, is also significantly correlated, .30, with incorporated academies in 1840. Feminization in 1840 has a significant factor loading of .25 but is significantly associated in the GCA with none of the other significant variables in factor nine, which is called the incorporated academy factor.

Table B.14 lists the significant factor loadings for the last fac-

Table B.14. Low school tax-rate factor: Significant loadings in rank order

Variable	Loading
Positive	
Per capita valuation, 1865	0.37
Per capita valuation, 1840	.34
Negative	
School tax rate, 1865	−.82
School tax rate, 1840	−.59
Feminization, 1865	−.26

tor. Dominant in this factor is the low school tax rate in both 1840, −.59, and 1865, −.82. The significantly positive loadings for valuation, .34 in 1840 and .37 in 1865, are predictable from the correlation between valuation and tax measures, −.46 in 1840 and −.42 in 1865. Again, feminization in 1865 has a negative loading of −.26 but is not significantly correlated with any of the significant variables in factor ten, which is termed the low school tax-rate factor.

4. PATTERNS OF VARIANCE

Feminization has been a puzzling variable throughout the analysis of factors. Although its correlations in the GCA for both 1840 and 1865 are almost entirely below significance, it has appeared as a significant variable in five, or half, of the ten factors. Four of the five appearances of feminization suggest that it is associated with a low level of expenditure on public education. Feminization was positively significant on the small, static non-commercial factor, a factor on which two measures of educational expenditure also had significantly negative loadings and none positive. Feminization for 1840 was positively significant on the incorporated academy factor. Since no measures of educational expenditure are significant on this factor and incorporated academies have no significant relationships with such measures on the GCA, these institutions are not associated with high levels of school spending. Feminization was significantly positive also on the dependency-distance factor. Although one measure of educational expenditure, average female teacher salary in 1840, was significant on this factor, distance itself was negatively associated with per-pupil expenditure in the GCA, −.48 for 1840 and −.45 for 1865. Likewise dependency in both years was negatively correlated with per-pupil expenditure, −.25 in 1840 and −.27 in 1865. Thus, in this case feminization appeared with variables noticeably associated with a low level of educational spending. In the low tax-rate factor, feminization for 1865 and school tax rate for both 1840 and 1865 had significantly negative loadings. In part, at least, feminization may be considered a variable associated with a low level of expenditure on public education. Since female teachers' salaries were roughly half as large as those of male teachers, feminization probably represented an educational economy. This conclusion is reinforced by the absence of a clear relationship between feminization and social and economic measures.

Twice feminization has a polar relationship with unincorporated academies in the factor analysis. In the first case, feminization is positive on the small, static non-commercial factor, which suggests an association with agricultural characteristics. This is reinforced by the negative significance of incorporated academies in 1840 on this factor, for in that year the latter were positively associated in the GCA with measures of urbanism and manufacturing. On the other hand, feminization for 1865 is negative on the unincorporated academy factor, in which unincorporated academies for 1865 is significant and positive at an extremely high level. By this year, unincorporated academies had no significant associations with any social and economic measures, and the alteration in their relationships with the latter variables suggests that they were becoming increasingly characteristic of non-urban and non-manufacturing areas. If this is the case, then the negative significance of feminization suggests that it may have been associated with denser and more industrial areas. This conclusion is supported by the positive significance of feminization on the distance-dependency factor, which, it will be argued shortly, was associated with manufacturing measures. Thus, the relationship of feminization to the social and economic characteristics of a community remains ambiguous, and the ambiguity reinforces the conclusion that most important variables related to feminization were measures of educational expenditure.

High school establishment is a less ambiguous variable. Three types of urban dimensions have been identified: manufacturing

growth, urban growth, and wealthy suburban. High school establishment is significantly weighted on each and on no others. It is
most heavily weighted, however, on the second, the urban growth
factor. Although high school establishment is significantly correlated with both urban and manufacturing variables in the GCA,
it is associated rather more markedly with the former. The correlation of high school establishment with population in 1865, .52,
is second only to its correlation with average male teacher salary
in the same year, .56. Its correlation with the increase in population and the density in 1865 both rank ahead of its correlation with
measures of manufacturing employees, and its correlation with
increase in density ranks ahead of its association with the increase
in variables relating to manufacturing employees. Thus, high school
establishment was relatively more associated with urban than with
manufacturing characteristics.

The relationships of school tax rate are less clear. In general,
the wealthier a town in terms of property the lower was its school
tax rate considered as the number of mills per dollar of valuation
raised for school support. In the GCA the coefficient between per
capita valuation and school tax rate is −.42 for 1865 and −.46
for 1840. Similarly, in the school tax-rate factor the two measures
have significant and opposite loadings. Yet, the normal relationship between wealth and tax apparently varied in two kinds of
circumstances. First, a high school tax rate is characteristic of the
wealthy suburban dimension; second, a low school tax rate is part
of the agricultural growth factor.

The relationship of per-pupil expenditure to other variables is
only partly clear. It appears only in the wealthy suburban factor
and there, for both years, its loading is extremely high. This high
loading is understandable in light of the correlation in the GCA of
per-pupil expenditure with per capita valuation, .55 for 1865. The
relationship of per-pupil expenditure to communal wealth is the
opposite of school tax rate. In no factor is per-pupil expenditure
negatively significant, and in the GCA it is negatively and sig-

nificantly correlated with only one variable, dependency rate for 1865, −.27. Dependency rate, in turn, was positively associated with manufacturing and urban variables; its correlation for 1865 with total employed in manufacturing is .20; for foreign born it is .34; for population increase, .30; and for both increase in number employed in manufacturing and total number of non-agricultural employees, .21. Per-pupil expenditure was probably depressed by an increase in dependency rate, which in turn was associated with manufacturing and urban characteristics. It is likely, therefore, that per-pupil expenditure would be relatively low in a town characterized by a rapid and sharp development of manufacturing. The social and economic determinants of both per-pupil expenditure and school tax rate would be clearer if more were known about the relationship of per capita valuation to other variables. Neither

Table B.15. Significant correlations of average male
teacher salary, 1840 and 1865

Variable	Correlation, 1840	Correlation, 1865
Population	0.28	0.52
Density	.35	.52
Manufacturing employees	.29	.32
Non-agricultural employees	.33	.32
Agricultural employees	−.23	a
Ratio of non-agricultural to agricultural employees	.39	.32
Number in commerce	.37	—
Number in navigation	.26	—
Number of professionals	.20	—
Increase in population	.26	.52
Increase in density	.36	.44
Increase total employed manufacturing	a	.23
Increase ratio non-agricultural to agricultural employees	.37	.28

a Not significant.

the factor analysis nor the GCA, however, provides the necessary illumination.

The salary of male teachers was significant and positive on the urban growth and wealthy suburban factors. This suggests that high male teacher salary is relatively more closely associated with urban than with manufacturing characteristics, and this hypothesis is reinforced by the GCA, from which Table B.15 is derived. Table B.15 reveals that male teacher salary has a relatively higher correlation with demographic measures, .52 with density and population in 1865 and .44 and .52 for their increase, than with manufacturing variables, .32 with total employed in manufacturing and .23 with its increase. The urban associations of male teacher salary are likewise reflected in its negative correlation, −.23 for 1840, with agricultural employees and in its negative loading on the small, static non-commercial factor.

Female teacher salary, Table B.16 shows, was also related to

Table B.16. Significant correlations of average female teacher salary in 1865

Variable	Correlation
Population	0.31
Density	.31
Total number employed in manufacturing	.36
Total number employed in non-agricultural occupations	.36
Females employed in manufacturing	.25
Population increase	.35
Density increase	.33
Increase in total number employed in manufacturing	.36
Increase in total employed in non-agricultural occupations	.26

urban and manufacturing measures. Table B.16 indicates that manufacturing variables are relatively more associated with female teacher salary than with male teacher salary in 1865. Female teacher salary's correlations with urban and manufacturing variables are nearly identical. This conclusion is reinforced by the significant loading of female teacher salary on the manufacturing growth factor. The connection of female teacher salary with manufacturing helps to explain its importance on the dependency-distance factor, since in the GCA both dependency and female salary are associated with measures of manufacturing. The significant loading of female teacher salary on the wealthy suburban factor also indicates that it was subject to influences besides manufacturing, namely wealth and high per-pupil expenditure.

Unincorporated academies had a significant loading on three factors: positive for 1840 on urban growth and for 1865 on the unincorporated academy factor and negative for 1840 on the small, static non-commercial dimension. Earlier it was suggested that these weightings reflected a change in the relationship of unincorporated academies to social and economic measures. Table B.17 reinforces this conclusion. In 1840 unincorporated academies, Table B.17 shows, were significantly related to measures of urban-

Table B.17. Significant correlations of unincorporated academies and other private schools with social and economic variables, 1840 and 1865

Variable	Correlation
1840	
Population, 1840	0.36
Density, 1840	.33
Total employed in non-agricultural occupations, 1840	.39
Ratio of non-agricultural to agricultural employees, 1840	.34
Number of people in commerce, 1840	.48
Number employed in navigation, 1840	.54
Number in professions, 1840	.31
Population, 1865	.36
"Other occupations," 1865	.36
1865	
Population, 1865	.22

ism and manufacturing; for instance, their correlation with density was .33, with total employed in non-agricultural occupations, .39. In 1865 unincorporated academies were no longer significantly associated with these measures. Likewise, unincorporated academies were significantly correlated in 1840 with number employed in commerce, navigation, and professions, .34, .48, and .54; but academies in 1865 were not correlated with the variables from the earlier year or with "other occupations" (commerce, navigation, and trades). Unincorporated academies in 1840 were, however, significantly correlated with "other occupations" in 1865, and this suggests that these schools had been discontinued in communities where they had previously existed. Unincorporated academies in 1840 are correlated with variables similar to those associated with high schools in 1865. This suggests that the kinds of communities that sustained an unincorporated academy in 1840 had often established high schools by 1865, and that people employed in commerce and navigation were associated with the movement. These conclusions are reinforced by two additional observations. First, no significant correlation exists between unincorporated academies in 1840 and in 1865. Second, in 1840 male teacher salary was significantly correlated with unincorporated academies, .24; male teacher salary in 1840 was also significantly correlated with high school establishment by 1865, .28; in 1865 unincorporated academies had no correlation whatsoever with male teacher salary, but the correlation between the latter and high school establishment was .56.

The most important associations of incorporated academies have already been discussed. These institutions, unlike the unincorporated ones, were not associated in 1840 with urban-industrial measures. Indeed, in 1840 incorporated academies were significantly correlated, .21, with agricultural employees. The other principal contrast between incorporated and unincorporated academies is their relationship to professionals. Both professionals and people employed in commerce are significantly correlated with unincorporated and incorporated academies in 1840. In 1865, however, the number of professionals in 1840 is significantly correlated only with incorporated academies. Yet both professionals and number employed in commerce in 1840 are correlated nearly identically with high schools, .28 and .30. This suggests that in communities where professionals were numerous in 1840 an incorporated academy often existed and continued to exist through the next two and one-half decades. The correlation between incorporated academies in 1840 and 1865 is .52. In communities where incorporated academies did not exist, however, professionals were often associated with the shift from unincorporated ones to public high schools.

In 1840 the number of children over 16 attending school was associated with agricultural characteristics. In the growing agricultural population factor both school children over 16 and number of agricultural employees were negatively loaded. In addition, the two were significantly correlated, .31, in the GCA, and number over 16 was negatively correlated, −.19, with increase in the number of manufacturing employees. The negative loading of number over 16 in school on the small, static non-commercial factor is, however, somewhat harder to explain since one would predict differently from the general association of the measure with agricultural variables. Two reasons account for its presence on the factor. First, number over 16 was correlated positively, .22, with population, which was also negatively loaded on the variable. Second, it was correlated, .35, with number over 15 attending school in 1865. The latter measure was significantly correlated with population, density, number employed in manufacturing, and ratio of non-agricultural to agricultural occupations in 1840, .47, .23, .35, and .46. Likewise, it was correlated with all of the same variables, except density, in 1865, .39, .29, and .32, and with increase in the ratio of non-agricultural to agricultural employees, .26. This suggests that in both 1840 and 1865 older children often attended school in the larger communities, but that in 1840 more children over 16 years of age attended school in predominantly agricultural communities, whereas the communities in which the largest numbers of children over 15 attended school in 1865 were in 1840, and continued to be in 1865, relatively non-agricultural. This may suggest that in the years between 1840 and 1865 farmers and tradesmen in static communities had to begin taking their children out of school earlier than before. There is little evidence on this point; but the complaints of the Lynn shoemakers, cited in Part I, do support the hypothesis. There, it will be recalled, we noted shoemakers' complaints that technological developments had led to falling prices, a diminution of their income, and hence a need to take their children out of school earlier than was desirable in order to help support their family. Perhaps, these statistics suggest, the experience of the shoemakers was fairly widespread.

5. CONCLUSIONS AND LIMITATIONS

The hypotheses and questions concerning the relationship between educational and social, economic and demographic variables posed at the start of this chapter, have been examined from three directions: by an examination of mean differences between high school and non–high school towns, by the results of a factor analysis, and by an examination of the associations of individual variables within the factor analysis and a correlation analysis. This examination suggests certain conclusions, summarized below.

I. Feminization
1. Feminization was associated with a low level of expenditure on public education.
2. In general feminization was affected by social and economic conditions through their impact on the level of educational spending.
3. In towns distant from Boston feminization was associated with a high dependency rate.

II. High schools
 1. High school establishment was related to all the dominant patterns of urbanism and industrialism.
 2. High school establishment was relatively more associated with urban than with manufacturing characteristics.
 3. People employed in commerce were particularly associated with high school establishment.
III. School tax rate
 1. The greater the per capita valuation of a town the lower, in general, was its school tax rate.
 2. Independent of per capita valuation, a high school tax rate was associated with wealthy suburban characteristics.
 3. Independent of per capita valuation, a low school tax rate was associated with agricultural growth.
IV. Per-pupil expenditure
 1. The higher the per capita valuation of a town the higher was its per-pupil expenditure.
 2. Per-pupil expenditure was often depressed by a high dependency rate.
 3. Per-pupil expenditure was often depressed by the rapid and sharp development of manufacturing.
V. Average male teacher salary
 1. A high average male teacher salary was associated with both urban and manufacturing measures.
 2. A high average male teacher salary was relatively more associated with urban than with manufacturing measures.
 3. A high average male teacher salary was negatively associated with a large number of people employed in agriculture.
VI. Average female teacher salary
 1. A high average female teacher salary was associated nearly equally with manufacturing and urban measures.
 2. Independent of manufacturing, a high average female

teacher salary was associated with high per capita valuation and high per-pupil expediture.

VII. Unincorporated academies

1. In 1840 unincorporated academies were significantly related to measures of urbanism and manufacturing.

2. In 1865 unincorporated academies were not related to measures of urbanism and manufacturing.

3. Unincorporated academies lost their significant association with number engaged in commerce and professionals between 1840 and 1865.

4. Kinds of communities that had sustained an unincorporated academy in 1840 had often established a high school by 1865.

VIII. Incorporated academies

1. In communities where professionals were numerous in 1840 an incorporated academy frequently existed and continued to exist through the next two and one-half decades.

2. In communities where incorporated academies did not exist in 1840 professionals were often associated with the shift from unincorporated academies to public high schools.

IX. Number over 16 in public school in 1840 and over 15 in 1865

1. In both 1840 and 1865 older children attended public school in the more populous towns.

2. In 1840 more children over 16 attended school in predominantly agricultural towns.

3. Towns in which the largest numbers of children over 15 attended school in 1865 were in 1840, and continued to be in 1865, relatively non-agricultural.

4. Farmers and tradesmen in smaller, more static communities were adversely affected by technological developments and, in 1865, had to remove their children from

school at an earlier age than in 1840. (This is quite tentative.)

Although this investigation has yielded significant conclusions, a greatly expanded analysis might produce results both more definitive and more extensive. The analysis could be expanded profitably in three ways. First, additional variables could be added to the study. If the year 1860, as well as 1865, is included then it would be possible to obtain information on additional occupational groups, particularly merchants, shoemakers, and laborers. Moreover, manuscript census records contain the number of church seats claimed by each denomination in each town. The utilization of these data as a rough indication of denominational strength would provide some empirical evidence for the assertions frequently made concerning the role of religion in the mid-nineteenth century educational reform movement. It would be well, too, to include the figures in the 1845, 1855, and 1865 censuses of industry for the value of agricultural and manufacturing (perhaps broken down by categories) goods produced. These measures might illuminate the determinants of communal wealth, a key variable that this analysis has handled most inadequately.

A second way in which the investigation could be profitably extended is through the introduction of more derivative variables. The present analysis has determined that the degree of change between certain variables as well as static differences was of considerable importance. Additional socio-economic as well as educational variables could be likewise derived and important information obtained on topics such as the relationships of the degree of change in per-pupil spending and school tax rate. In all, an expanded analysis could profitably utilize over twice the number of variables in the present study.

A final way in which this study could be extended is through the addition of the very large and very small communities omitted from the present analysis. Ideally, the expanded analysis would consider separately the sample as defined in the present analysis, all the towns and cities for which data are obtainable and the cities and towns in the extreme categories. It would be particularly useful in this connection to study the effect of the pace of urbanism and industrialism on levels of educational spending and on educational innovation. It would be necessary to include the very large cities in order to determine whether, past a certain degree of development, the impact of urbanism and industrialism on education altered. In this connection, a set of graphs should be constructed plotting the relationship between the various educational and socio-economic measures.

No matter how this analysis is extended, no matter what degree of refinement is introduced, the utility of statistics will still have severe limitations. This appendix began with a question: were there significant patterns of association between educational and social, demographic and economic features of Massachusetts communities? The answer is clearly affirmative, and some of the relationships have been discovered. But to discover a relationship is not to explain its meaning. To find the meaning of historical relationships is the task of the historian, not the computer.

Appendix C. Social Composition of High School Enrollment

Table C.1. Town size and estimation of proportion of eligible children attending high school, 1860[a]

Size of town	Population	Proportion attending
Small	1,129	70
	1,348	22
	2,912	28
	3,296	28
	3,333	20
Medium	6,272	20
	7,261	11
Large	14,026	6
	15,376	7
	19,083	7
	24,960	11

Source: Massachusetts state census of 1860 and town school committee reports.
[a] Based on 10 percent random sample of communities with high schools. The proportion was figured as the number of children attending during the winter or third (depending on how the year was divided) session divided by four fifths of the average of children 10–15 and 15–20.

Table C.2. Occupations of fathers of graduates of Chelsea High School, 1858–1864,[a] and of fathers of students entering Somerville High School, 1856–1861[b]

Occupation	Chelsea	Somerville
Upper middle class		
Professional and public employee	2	11
Owner of business, store, manufacturing operation, or financial concern (merchant or broker)	19	44
Business employee	3	8
Master mariner, shipping master, shipwright, shipsmith	5	2
Total	29	65
Middle Class		
Artisan	11	26
Farmer	0	9
Total	11	35
Lower Class		
Operative	0	0
Farm laborer	0	1
Laborer	0	0
Total	0	1
No occupation listed for parent	3	10
Total	43	111

Source: Based on records in possession of Chelsea and Somerville high schools and manuscript census for 1860.

[a] The 43 families in the Chelsea group represent 49 children, 39 girls and 10 boys. These 49 children make up 69 percent of the 71 graduates during the period.

[b] The 111 families in the Somerville group represent 135 children, or 75 percent of the 181 who entered during this period.

A valid question is: did the students about whom no information was obtainable represent a socially marginal group whose inclusion would change the results? My feeling is that the answer is no. Some students were not included because spelling ambiguities in the census and school records made identification too uncertain; the ones who left the high school before 1860, the census year, may have been the most successful graduates in terms of finding good employment in other cities. In general, however, my feeling is that the gaps are random.

Appendix D. Beverly: Analysis of the 1860 Vote on the High School Issue

Table D.1. Residential distribution of vote on high school, Beverly, 1860

District	Votes to retain			Votes to abolish			Total district vote	
	Number	Percent of all votes in district	Percent of all votes in town	Number	Percent of all votes in district	Percent of all votes in town	Number	Percent total vote in town
Grammar	79	57	61	58	43	27	137	40
Cove	5	9	4	52	91	24	57	17
South	22	44	17	28	56	13	50	15
Washington	12	33	9	24	67	11	36	10
Bald Hill	4	30	3	9	70	4	13	4
Bass River	4	22	3	15	78	7	19	5
West Farms	0	0	0	11	100	5	11	3
East Farms	1	5	0.1	19	95	9	20	6

Tables in this appendix are based on Massachusetts state censuses, 1850 and 1860; Censuses of Industry, 1855 and 1865; school returns; town records; and tax books.

Table D.2. Occupational distribution of vote on high school, Beverly, 1860

Occupation	Votes to retain		Votes to abolish		Total	
	No.	Percent of all to retain	No.	Percent of all to abolish	No.	Percent of all votes
Professional and public employees	17	13.18	2	0.94	19	5.56
Gentlemen	4	3.10	0	0	4	1.17
Business	30	23.26	24	11.27	54	15.79
Shoe manufacturers	5	3.88	9	4.23	14	4.09
Merchants or traders	10	7.75	7	3.29	17	4.97
Proprietors of business	1	.78	4	1.88	5	1.46
Business employees	4	3.10	0	0	4	1.17
Retail sales	7	5.43	6	2.82	13	3.80
House to house sales	3	2.33	2	.94	5	1.46
Sea captains and master mariners	8	6.20	1	.47	9	2.63
Artisans	30	23.26	34	15.96	64	18.71
Farmers	7	5.43	37	17.37	44	12.87
Shoemakers	29	22.48	80	36.62	109	31.29
Mariners or fishermen	3	2.33	21	9.86	24	7.02
Laborers or farm laborers	0	0	10	4.69	10	2.92
Unknown	1	.78	5	2.35	6	1.75

Table D.3. Distribution of wealth in high school vote, Beverly, 1860

Category	Vote to retain		Vote to abolish		Total	
	No.	Percent of all to retain	No.	Percent of all to abolish	No.	Percent of total
Value of real estate						
$0–999	75	58.14	108	50.70	183	53.50
$1,000–4,999	38	29.46	99	46.01	136	39.77
Over $5,000	16	12.40	7	3.21	23	6.73
Mean	$1892.09		$1152.70		$1431.59	
Value of personal estate						
$0–999	76	58.91	169	79.34	245	71.64
$1,000–4,999	34	26.36	40	18.31	73	21.35
Over $5,000	19	14.73	5	2.35	24	7.02
Mean	$2107.18		$ 655.59		$1203.12	
Value of total estate						
$0–999	54	41.86	94	44.13	148	43.27
$1,000–4,999	42	32.56	104	48.36	145	42.40
Over $5,000	33	25.58	16	7.51	49	14.33
Mean	$3999.26		$1806.88		$2633.83	

Table D.4. Distribution of dependency and age in high school vote, Beverly, 1860

Category	Vote to retain		Vote to abolish		Total	
	Number	Percent	Number	Percent	Number	Percent
Has no school age children	56	43.41	120	56.34	176	51.46
Number of children 12–17 who attended school past year	45	34.48	52	24.41	97	28.36
Number of children 12–17 who did not attend school past year	16	12.40	30	14.08	46	13.45
Number of children 5–11	91	70.54	105	49.30	196	57.31
Mean age of voter	42.6047		42.5728		42.5848	

Table D.5. Artisans: Wealth and vote on high school, Beverly, 1860

Category	Retain		Abolish	
	No.	Percent of all artisans voting	No.	Percent of all artisans voting
Real estate				
$0–999	21	33	19	30
$1,000–4,999	9	14	13	21
$5,000 and over	0	0	1	2
Personal estate				
$0–999	21	33	25	40
$1,000–4,999	7	11	8	13
Over $5,000	2	3	0	0
Total estate				
$0–999	15	24	17	27
$1,000–4,999	12	19	13	20
Over $5,000	3	5	3	5

Table D.6. Business people: Wealth and vote on high school, Beverly, 1860

Category	Retain		Abolish	
	No.	Percent of all in business voting	No.	Percent of all in business voting
Real estate				
$0–999	13	24	7	13
$1,000–4,999	8	15	12	22
Over $5,000	9	17	5	9
Personal estate				
$0–999	12	22	12	22
$1,000–4,999	12	22	9	17
Over $5,000	6	11	3	6
Total estate				
$0–999	7	13	5	9
$1,000–4,999	9	17	12	22
Over $5,000	14	26	7	13

Table D.7. High school vote of artisans and business people with no school-age children, Beverly, 1860

Category	Retain		Abolish	
	No.	Percent of all voting	No.	Percent of all voting
Artisans (No. = 63)	13	21	22	35
Business (No. = 54)	19	35	16	30

Table D.8. Distribution of votes on high school in
Grammar District, Beverly, 1860

Variable	Vote to retain		Vote to abolish	
	Number	Percent of votes to retain	Number	Percent of votes to abolish
Professional and public employees	12	14.81	2	3.46
Gentlemen	0	0	0	0
Sea captains and master mariners	8	9.88	1	1.82
Business	19	23.46	14	18.18
Shoe manufacturers	3	3.70	5	9.09
Merchants or traders	5	6.17	3	5.45
Proprietors of business	1	1.23	3	5.45
Business employees	3	3.70	0	0
Retail sales	6	7.41	3	5.45
House to house sales	1	1.23	0	0
Artisans	18	22.22	9	16.36
Farmers	0	0	1	1.82
Shoemakers	21	25.93	26	45.45
Mariners or fishermen	2	2.47	5	9.09
Laborers or farm laborers	0	0	1	1.82
Unknown	1	1.23	1	1.82
Value of real estate				
$0–999	50	61.73	30	54.55
$1,000–4,999	20	24.69	24	43.64
Over $5,000	11	13.58	1	1.82
Mean	$2085.19		$1014.55	
Value of personal estate				
$0–999	50	61.73	43	78.18
$1,000–4,999	20	24.69	11	20.00
Over $5,000	11	13.58	1	1.82
Mean	$2232.42		$ 654.00	
Value of total estate				
$0–999	35	43.21	25	45.45
$1,000–4,999	27	33.33	26	47.27
Over $5,000	19	23.46	4	7.27
Mean	$5417.59		$1668.55	
Voters with no school age children	35	43.21	39	70.91
Mean number of children 12–17 in school per voter	3.333		1.455	
Mean number of children 12–17 not in school per voter	1.481		0.909	
Mean number of children 5–11 per voter	6.914		3.818	
Mean age of voter	42.75		41.15	

Table D.9. Distribution of vote on high school in
South District, Beverly, 1860

Variable	Retain		Abolish	
	No.	Percent	No.	Percent
Professional and public				
employees	2	9.09	0	0
Gentlemen	4	18.18	0	0
Sea captains and master				
mariners	0	0	0	0
Business	9	40.91	7	25.93
Shoe manufacturers	0	0	1	3.70
Merchants	5	22.73	3	11.11
Proprietors	0	0	1	3.70
Employees	1	4.55	0	0
Retail sales	1	4.55	2	7.41
House to house sales	2	9.09	0	0
Artisans	4	18.18	7	25.93
Farmers	1	4.55	3	11.11
Shoemakers	2	9.09	5	14.81
Mariners or fishermen	0	0	2	7.41
Laborers or farm laborers	0	0	4	14.81
Unknown	0	0	1	0
Real estate				
$0–999	10	45.45	11	40.74
$1,000–4,999	8	36.36	12	44.44
Over $5,000	4	18.18	4	14.81
Mean	$2042.28		$1848.15	
Personal estate				
$0–999	6	27.27	16	59.26
$1,000–4,999	9	40.91	9	33.33
Over $5,000	7	31.82	2	7.41
Mean	$3263.64		$1274.07	
Total estate				
$0–999	6	27.27	10	37.04
$1,000–4,999	6	27.27	10	37.04
Over $5,000	10	45.45	7	25.93
Mean	$5305.92		$3122.22	
No children of school age	14	63.64	15	55.56
Mean number of children				
12–17 in school per voter	1.818		2.963	
Mean number of children				
12–17 not in school per				
voter	0.455		0.370	
Mean number of children				
5–11 per voter	3.636		3.333	
Mean age of voter	44.68		45.04	

Bibliographical Note　　Notes　　Index

Bibliographical Note

The purpose of this note is to indicate some of the more important sources used in this study. More detailed information is found in the notes and the thesis version of the study. There are surprisingly few original, scholarly treatments of mid-nineteenth century educational reform. Among the more useful are: Frank Tracy Carlton, *Economic Influences upon Educational Progress in the United States,* first published in 1908 and now available in the Teachers College Classics in Education series edited by Lawrence Cremin (New York, 1965); Lawrence Cremin, *The American Common School: An Historic Conception* (New York, 1951); Sidney L. Jackson, *America's Struggle for Free Schools: Social Tension and Education in New England and New York, 1827–42* (first published in 1941; re-issued New York, 1965). Also helpful are the relevant chapters in Merle Curti, *The Social Ideas of American Educators* (first published 1935; reprinted New York, 1959); and Rush Welter, *Popular Education and Democratic Thought in America* (New York, 1962). The work of Jonathan Messerli has been particularly valuable; see his unpublished dissertation "Horace Mann: The Early Years, 1796–1837" (Harvard University, 1963); and his articles, "James G. Carter's Liabilities as a Common School Reformer," *History of Education Quarterly,* 5:14–25 (March 1965), and "Localism and State Control in Horace Mann's Reform of the Common Schools," *American Quarterly,* 17:104–118 (Spring 1965). Three other books with particularly useful data are: Emit Duncan Grizzell, *Origin and Development of the High School in New England before 1865* (Philadelphia, 1922); Alexander James Inglis, *The Rise of the High School in Massachusetts* (New York, 1911); and Raymond Culver, *Horace Mann and Religion in the Massachusetts Public Schools* (New Haven, 1929).

The general literature of the Jacksonian period has been frequently reviewed, and there is no need to review it here. On Massachusetts in the period the work of Oscar Handlin is indispensable. See his *Boston's Immigrants: A Study in Acculturation* (rev. ed.; Cambridge, Mass.,

1959); and, with Mary Flugg Handlin, *Commonwealth: A Study of the Role of Government in the American Economy, Massachusetts, 1774–1861* (New York, 1947). Some other useful works relating to Massachusetts in this period are: Percy Wells Bidwell, "The Agricultural Revolution in New England," *The American Historical Review,* 26:683–702 (July 1921), and "Population Growth in Southern New England," *Quarterly Publications of the American Statistical Association,* New Series, no. 120 (December 1917); Richard D. Birdsall, *Berkshire County: A Cultural History* (New Haven, 1959); Charles C. Bullock, *Historical Sketch of the Finances and Financial Policy of Massachusetts from 1780–1905* (New York, 1905); Donald B. Cole, *Immigrant City: Lawrence, Massachusetts, 1845–1921* (Chapel Hill, 1963); Arthur Darling, *Political Change in Massachusetts, 1824–1865* (New Haven, 1925); Robert W. Kelso, *The History of Public Poor Relief in Massachusetts, 1620–1920* (Boston, 1922); Edward C. Kirkland, *Men, Cities and Transportation: A Study in New England History, 1820–1900* (2 vols.; Cambridge, Mass., 1948); Samuel Eliot Morison, *The Maritime History of Massachusetts, 1763–1860* (Cambridge, Mass., 1921); Charles Persons, "The Early History of Factory Legislation in Massachusetts," pp. 1–129 in Susan M. Kingsbury, ed., *Labor Laws and Their Enforcement* (New York, 1911); Harold Schwartz, *Samuel Gridley Howe, Social Reformer, 1801–1876* (Cambridge, Mass., 1956); Stephan Thernstrom, *Poverty and Progress: Social Mobility in a Nineteenth Century City* (Cambridge, Mass., 1964); Caroline Ware, *The Early New England Cotton Manufacture: A Study in Industrial Beginnings* (Cambridge, Mass., 1931). Of special relevance is Gerald N. Grob, *The State and the Mentally Ill: A History of Worcester State Hospital in Massachusetts 1830–1920* (Chapel Hill, 1966), which appeared after this study was completed.

Six sorts of primary sources were particularly useful for this study; unpublished manuscripts; the reports of the secretaries of the Board of Education and other state documents; local school reports; newspapers and educational journals; miscellaneous pamphlets, books, and speeches; and statistical data.

As for manuscript material, collections of papers are of course very helpful. I found the most useful to be the Horace Mann Papers at the Massachusetts Historical Society and the Rantoul Papers at the Beverly Historical Society and the Essex Institute. At the Massachusetts Historical Society the Appleton Papers were also useful. It is important to point out that sources other than the usual manuscript collections are of great benefit to the historian of education. Among these are town records, school committee books, school registers, and other school records. A particularly valuable collection of such sources exists in the Beverly Historical Society. The Boston School Committee has in its archives complete unpublished minutes and other records since the latter eighteenth century. Oftentimes individual schools have a few very valuable records preserved in their vaults; the same is sometimes true of school superintendents' offices. The Massachusetts State Archives has much vaulable material: the manuscript census schedules, petitions filed with bills, and records of executive bodies like the Governor's Council.

The published reports of the secretaries of the Board of Education, especially those of Horace Mann, have been used by historians before, and they provide an excellent overview of theory and developments. Local school reports, on the other hand, have been used too infrequently. Besides reflecting the general ideology of reform, they provide vivid pictures of the problems encountered by school committees. These, however, must be used with caution. They present only a school committee's view of developments and controversies, and more varied material is necessary to begin to comprehend what is going on within a given town. For this study the reports of the following school committees, usually over a twenty-year span (though with many omissions because of unavailability) were read: Attleborough, Barnstable, Beverly, Bridgewater, Cambridge, Canton, Chatham, Dalton, Dartmouth, Douglas, East Bridgewater, Fairhaven, Falmouth, Gardner, Groton, Harwich, Lawrence, Lincoln, Medway, Monson, Provincetown, Rockport, Salisbury, Townsend, Uxbridge, Watertown, Webster, Wellfleet, Williamstown, Winchendon, Yarmouth.

Many of the documents published as *House Documents, Senate Documents* or *Public Documents* are very helpful. These run the gamut from statistical reports to petitions, to full-scale legislative inquiries (like that on state charities), to reports of state boards. In general they contain a wealth of factual and interpretive data that is crucial for anyone working on the history of the state. Local communities rarely published documents as comprehensive, although Boston is an exception. There are, however, published statistical records and vital statistics for most communities. Critical to the history of communities are the local newspapers. These were consulted for the towns studied in depth. Often the hometown paper tried very hard to be inoffensive and was maddeningly short on reporting. Anyone who criticizes modern newspapers would do well to look at these nineteenth century sheets to realize just how far journalism has come, despite its many shortcomings. Nevertheless, patient reading turns up an occasional insight obtainable in no other way. At the state level, the educational journals, the *Common School Journal* and the *Massachusetts Teacher,* have scarcely been touched by historians; and I have, although drawing heavily on them, barely scratched the surface of their potential utility. These journals were usually edited by men prominent and experienced in educational affairs, and my impression is that many of the anonymous authors were practicing teachers. These journals provide an extraordinarily clear picture of leading pedagogical attitudes, and their reports tell what went on at teachers' institutes, conventions, and other important educational gatherings. Without doubt they are a key source for the period.

Among the most useful of the many miscellaneous primary sources for the study of Massachusetts education in this period are: *American Normal Schools: Their Workings and Their Results, as Embodied in the Proceedings of the American Normal School Association, Held at Trenton, New Jersey, August 19 and 20, 1859* (New York, 1860); Joseph A. Allen, *Westboro' State Reform School Reminiscences* (Boston, 1877); Association of Masters of the [Boston] Public Schools, *Remarks on the Seventh Annual Report of the Honorable Horace Mann* . . . (Boston, 1844), and *"Rejoinder" to the "Reply"* . . . (Boston, 1845); George Boutwell, *Thoughts on Educational Topics and Institutions* (Boston, 1859); Charles Brooks, various lectures delivered on educational reform; James G. Carter, *Essays upon Popular Education* (Boston, 1826); [George B. Emerson], *Observations on a Pamphlet Entitled "Remarks"* . . . (Boston, 184[4?]), and "The Schoolmaster," in Alonzo Potter and George B. Emerson, *The School and the Schoolmaster: A Manual for the use of Teachers, Employers, Trustees, Inspectors, etc. etc. of Common Schools, in Two Parts* (New York, 1842); Silas L. Loomis, *Record of the Holliston Academy, 1836–1844* (Washington, D.C., 1876); Horace Mann, *Answer to the "Rejoinder" of Twenty-Nine Boston Schoolmasters* . . . (Boston, 1845), *Lectures on Education* (Boston, 1845), and *Reply to the "Remarks" of Thirty-one Boston Schoolmasters* . . . (Boston, 1844); [Massachusetts Teachers Association], *Abstract of the Proceedings of the Massachusetts Teachers' Association, 1845–1880* (Boston, 1881); Andrew Norton, ed., *The First State Normal School in America: The Journals of Cyrus Peirce and Mary Swift* (Cambridge, Mass., 1926); Henry K. Oliver,

Lecture on Teachers' Morals and Manners . . . (Boston, 1851); N. A. Scott, *A Plea for the Bible in the State Reform School* . . . (Boston, 1862); *Services at the Inauguration of William E. Starr, esq., as Superintendent of the State Reform School* . . . (Boston, 1857); Emory Washburn, *An Address at the Dedication of the State Reform School* . . . (Boston, 1849); Joseph M. Whightman, *Annals of the Boston Primary School Committee* . . . (Boston, 1860); Leonard Withington, *Penitential Tears* . . . (Boston, 1845).

Statistical information provided the other primary source used. From censuses of industry and population, state documents, and school reports comes a wealth of statistical information, again mined most inadequately in the past. In addition to the federal censuses, the researcher should not overlook the valuable state censuses, particularly those of 1855, 1865, and 1875. The censuses of industry were published in 1837, 1845, 1855, and 1865. After that they were incorporated in the general state census. One question that immediately arises concerning these statistics is their accuracy. Without doubt they contain inaccuracies, but they do reflect differences and trends that make minor inaccuracies unimportant. Indeed, since inaccuracies are random, the fact that statistically significant results are obtained in tests that use the figures indicates that they are generally correct, for inaccuracies would tend to lower the significance of the results.

A particularly valuable source of statistical information is the manuscript census mentioned earlier, which is obtainable either at the Library of Congress or the Massachusetts State Archives. This provides some information, such as the number of church seats of various denominations and farming conditions, that was not tabulated in published census abstracts. As well, it provides a wealth of demographic and social information concerning individuals in specific towns and is essential for certain tasks, such as analyzing a vote or determining the social composition of schools.

Notes

In the notes all references to the various annual reports of the Massachusetts Board of Education will be abbreviated and include only the number and the word "report," *e.g., Nineteenth Report.* The full title would be *Nineteenth Annual Report of the Massachusetts Board of Education together with the Nineteenth Annual Report of the Secretary to the Board.* Report number one is dated 1838. Reports of school committees from the same town changed titles frequently. Here they will be referred to in this manner: *Groton, 1851–52,* p. 5.

Introduction. Educational Reform: The Cloud of Sentiment and Historiography

1. As an example of the standard version of educational reform in the mid-nineteenth century, one of the most widely read social histories of the period claims: "It was not until the common man became conscious of the privileges of which he had been deprived and used the suffrage he had acquired to demand education for his children that the state turned to a consideration of the common school. This movement was in accord with the humanitarianism of the time, and the reformers joined the workingmen in seeking remedies for the defects in the educational system." Alice Felt Tyler, *Freedom's Ferment: Phases of American Social History to 1860* (Minneapolis: University of Minnesota, 1944), p. 233.

2. Jonathan Messerli, a leading historian of the revival of education in Massachusetts, has applied one version of the consensus interpretation to the events of the period. Messerli suggests that the concept of fundamental educational controversy is not valid and that we must look upon educational history in this period more as the pragmatic efforts of individuals to meet certain glaring deficiencies in the provisions for learning and to alter the schools to meet new social obligations. "Controversy and Consensus in Common School Reform," *Teacher's College Record,* May 1965, pp. 749–758. A good review of

the consensus literature is Dwight Hoover, "Some Comments on Recent United States Historiography," *American Quarterly*, 17:299–318 (Summer 1965).

3. *Twentieth Report*, pp. 35–36. Boutwell was the third secretary of the Massachusetts Board of Education.

4. *Massachusetts Teacher*, 17:34 (January 1864).

5. *Twentieth Report*, p. 5.

6. *Ibid.*, pp. 5–6.

7. On the complexity of this era see Leo Marx, *The Machine in the Garden: Technology and the Pastoral Ideal in America* (New York: Oxford University Press, 1964); Marvin Meyers, *The Jacksonian Persuasion* (Stanford, Calif., 1957); William R. Taylor, *Cavalier and Yankee: The Old South and American National Character* (New York, 1961); Arthur P. Dudden, "Nostalgia and the American," *Journal of the History of Ideas*, 22:515–530 (October–December 1961); Daniel H. Calhoun, *Professional Lives in America: Structure and Aspiration, 1750–1850* (Cambridge, Mass., 1965).

8. For a biography of Horace Mann see Jonathan C. Messerli, "Horace Mann: The Early Years, 1796–1837," unpub. diss., Harvard University, 1963.

9. Tables showing relevant economic and population statistics are included in Appendix A. On population and its concentration see the illuminating article by Percy Wells Bidwell, "Population Growth in Southern New England, 1810–1860," *Quarterly Publications of the American Statistical Association*, New Series, no. 120 (December 1917), pp. 813, 816.

10. Samuel Eliot Morison, *The Maritime History of Massachusetts, 1783–1860* (Boston, 1921); Caroline Ware, *The Early New England Cotton Manufacture: A Study in Industrial Beginnings* (Cambridge, Mass., 1931), p. 118.

11. *Massachusetts Senate Document 2*, January 1859, pp. 142–143; Francis DeWitt, *Abstract of the Census of the Commonwealth of Massachusetts . . . 1855* (Boston, 1857), pp. 230–233; and Oliver Warner, *Abstract of the Census of Massachusetts . . . 1860* (Boston, 1863), p. 335.

12. Bidwell, "Population Growth," p. 816. For a different, more quantitatively sophisticated, and precise approach to the urban-industrial development of the Northeast than mine see Jeffrey G. Williamson, "Antebellum Urbanization in the American Northeast," *Journal of Economic History*, 25:592–614 (December 1965). I have been

encouraged to find that this paper generally supports the positions taken here about the *extent* of structural change, its pace and the relation of urban to industrial development.

13. Ware, *Early New England Cotton Manufacture,* pp. 50–59.

14. Bidwell, "Population Growth," pp. 830–833; Ware, *Early New England Cotton Manufacture,* pp. 79–118.

15. Computed from the statistics in John G. Palfrey, *Statistics of the Condition and Products of Certain Branches of Industry in Massachusetts . . . 1845* (Boston, 1846); Francis DeWitt, *Statistical Information Relating to Certain Branches of Industry in Massachusetts . . . 1855* (Boston, 1856); and Oliver Warner, *Statistical Information Relating to Certain Branches of Industry in Massachusetts . . . 1865* (Boston, 1866). These will hereafter be referred to as the Censuses of Industry.

16. Ware, *Early New England Cotton Manufacture,* pp. 64–65, 199, 228–232.

17. Victor S. Clark, *History of Manufactures in the United States* (Washington, 1916), p. 429; Ware, *Early New England Cotton Manufacture,* p. 630.

18. Clark, *History of Manufactures,* pp. 407–408, 423, 434, 444.

19. Quoted in Marx, *Machine in the Garden,* pp. 194, 196.

20. Quoted in *ibid.,* p. 196.

21. Edward C. Kirkland, *Men, Cities and Transportation: A Study in New England History, 1820–1900* (Cambridge, Mass., 1948), I, 284.

22. Charles Kennedy, "Railroads in Essex County a Century Ago," *Essex Institute Historical Collections,* 95:142 (April 1959).

23. Percy Wells Bidwell, "The Agricultural Revolution in New England," *The American Historical Review,* 26:687–689, 690–693 (July 1921). On agriculture in this period see also Paul W. Gates, *The Farmer's Age* (New York: Holt, Rinehart and Winston, 1960). On p. 269 Gates claims, "Too much emphasis has been placed upon 'rural decline and farm abandonment' in the Northeast, and too little attention has been given to the growing agricultural specialization and readjustment that took place in the area."

24. Bidwell, "Agricultural Revolution," p. 696.

25. Quoted in *ibid.,* p. 700.

26. Thomas C. Cochran, "Business Organization and the Development of an Industrial Discipline," in Harold F. Williamson, *The*

Growth of the American Economy: An Introduction to the Economic History of the United States, 2nd ed. (New York, 1951), pp. 279, 294. The best economic history of this period is George Rogers Taylor, *The Transportation Revolution, 1815–1860* (New York, 1951).

27. Oscar and Mary Flugg Handlin, *Commonwealth: A Study of the Role of Government in the American Economy, Massachusetts, 1774–1861* (New York, 1947), *passim.*

28. Figures from the abstracts of the state censuses, cited above, note 9.

29. Figures computed from the Censuses of Industry.

30. *Historical Statistics of the United States, Colonial Times to 1957* (Washington, 1960), p. 127. In general the trends in the Massachusetts economy do not refute Thomas Cochran's conclusion "that the Civil War retarded American industrial growth." "Did the Civil War Retard Industrialism," in Thomas C. Cochran, *The Inner Revolution* (New York, 1964), p. 48. In Massachusetts, at any rate, all the characteristics of an industrial society had developed by the mid-50's and little expansion, indeed, some decline, occurred between the mid-50's and 1865. Whether the Civil War retarded industrial growth or whether the declining growth rate reflected the inevitable leveling off of an earlier spurt is a question beyond the scope of this study.

31. Except where specifically noted all statistics in the introduction are from the reports of the secretaries of the Massachusetts Board of Education.

32. The figures for high school establishment are from Alexander James Inglis, *The Rise of the High School in Massachusetts* (New York, 1911), pp. 42–45.

33. On the first normal school see Andrew Norton, ed., *The First State Normal School in America: The Journals of Cyrus Peirce and Mary Swift* (Cambridge, Mass., 1926).

34. *Massachusetts Statutes,* 1852, chap. 283.

35. *Twenty-Ninth Report,* p. 18.

36. Many of the innovations are listed in George H. Martin, *The Evolution of the Massachusetts Public School System* (New York, 1894), *passim.*

37. Merrill D. Peterson, *The Jefferson Image in the American Mind* (New York: Oxford University Press, 1960), p. 21. On ideology see also Karl Mannheim, *Ideology and Utopia* (New York, 1936).

On the formulation of inquiries in the social sciences see R. M. MacIver, *Social Causation* (New York, 1942), a work that has contributed greatly to my construal of the problem of this study.

38. One example of the kind of economic approach against which I am arguing is provided by Theodore Shultz, "Education and Economic Growth," in Henry B. Nelson, ed., *Social Forces Influencing American Education* (Chicago, 1961); see also Frederick Harbison and Charles A. Myers, *Education, Manpower and Economic Growth: Strategies of Human Resource Development* (New York, 1964). For the Marxian approach see Benjamin Higgins, *Economic Development Principles, Problems, and Policies* (New York, 1959), pp. 107–121. For a critique of the approach of many economists see David C. McClelland, *The Achieving Society* (Princeton: D. Van Nostrand Co., 1961), p. 8; for a good brief statement of the factors important in economic development see Richard T. Gill, *Economic Development: Past and Present* (Englewood Cliffs, N.J., 1963), pp. 3–20.

Actually, the hypothesis that in any sense an investment in education "caused" the economic growth of Massachusetts can be rejected from the outset. Without any change in the educational level of the population Massachusetts presented· as ideal a situation as one can conceive for the rapid transformation from an agricultural-commercial to an industrial economy. Population was increasing; food was abundant and the Malthusian dilemma could be avoided; land and water were plentiful; technology could be imported; capital was seeking an outlet and the government was fostering the development of manufactures.

39. On religious controversies see Raymond Culver, *Horace Mann and Religion in the Massachusetts Public Schools* (New Haven, 1929); on politics see Rush Welter, *Popular Education and Democratic Thought in America* (New York, 1962), pp. 45–123; on foreign influence see John Davies, *Phrenology: Fad and Science, a Nineteenth Century American Crusade* (New Haven, 1955); and Newton Edwards and Herman G. Richey, *The School in the American Social Order* (Boston, 1963), pp. 306–310.

40. Lawrence Cremin, *The Wonderful World of Ellwood Patterson Cubberly: An Essay on the Historiography of American Education* (New York, 1965); and Foreword to Frank Tracy Carlton, *Economic Influences upon Educational Progress in the United States* (New York, 1965).

41. Meyers, *Jacksonian Persuasion;* Walter Huggins, *Jacksonian*

Democracy and the Working Class (Stanford, 1960); Lee Benson, *The Concept of Jacksonian Democracy: New York as a Test Case* (Princeton, 1961); Chilton Williamson, *American Suffrage from Property to Democracy, 1760–1860* (Princeton, 1960).

42. Carlton, *Economic Influences;* Sidney L. Jackson, *America's Struggle for Free Schools: Social Tension and Education in New England and New York, 1827–42* (New York, 1965); Lawrence A. Cremin, *The American Common School: An Historic Conception* (New York, 1951).

Part I. Reform by Imposition: Social Origins of Educational Controversy

1. *Beverly Citizen,* March 17, 1860, p. 2.

2. The tax books are in the Beverly City Hall. These are useful because they group the tax assessment lists by school district. The manuscript census of 1860 is in the Massachusetts State Archives.

3. I was able to judge district density and location from a map in the possession of the Beverly Historical Society.

4. For biographical details on Rantoul see Frederick A. Ober, "Beverly," in D. Hamilton Hurd, ed., *History of Essex County, Massachusetts, with Biographical Sketches of Many of its Pioneers and Prominent Men* (Philadelphia, 1888), I, 728–729.

5. Robert S. Rantoul, "Some Material for a History of the Name and Family of Rentoul-Rintoul-Rantoul," *Historical Collections of the Essex Institute,* 21:261 (October–November–December 1884); "Mr. Rantoul's Youth and Apprenticeship," *ibid.,* 5:193–196 (October 1863); Robert Rantoul, Sr., "Autobiography" MS., Beverly Historical Society, Beverly, Mass., pp. 275, 415; his collection of *Hunt's* . . . is in the possession of the Beverly Historical Society. His will is in the Essex County Court House, Salem.

6. Robert Rantoul, "Lecture on Economy," delivered before the Beverly Lyceum, December 8 and 15, 1836, MS. in the Beverly Historical Society.

7. "Autobiography," pp. 219, 365. Rantoul started to compile his autobiography in 1848 and made additions until his death ten years later. It draws heavily on extracts from his diary, record books, and letters and is, therefore, much more than the senile musings of an old man.

8. Ober, "Beverly," p. 749.

9. Edwin Stone, *History of Beverly, Civil and Ecclesiastical, from its Settlement in 1630 to 1842* (Boston, 1843), p. 307.

10. Ober, "Beverly," p. 749.

11. *Beverly Citizen*, March 12, 1864; April 1, 1863; November 5, 1859; all p. 2.

12. Rantoul, "Autobiography," pp. 194, 365.

13. Robert Rantoul, "Lecture on Agriculture," read at Beverly Lyceum, February 11, 1841, MS. in the Beverly Historical Society.

14. Rantoul, "Autobiography," unnumbered page.

15. The papers of Robert S. Rantoul are at the Essex Institute in Salem. Also there are some papers of Robert Rantoul, Sr., and many of the papers of Robert Rantoul, Jr.

16. Given Rantoul's transition from Federalism to democracy the stress on social unity is to be expected, as is clear from Shaw Livermore, Jr., *The Twilight of Federalism: The Disintegration of the Federalist Party, 1815–1830* (Princeton, 1962).

17. Horace Mann, *Life and Works of Horace Mann* (Boston, 1867), IV, 259; VIII, 109.

18. For biographical details on Boutwell see the article by Henry G. Pearson in the *Dictionary of American Biography*, II, 489–490; Samuel A. Green, *An Historical Sketch of Groton, Massachusetts, 1655–1890* (Groton, 1894), *passim;* and George Boutwell, *Reminiscences of Sixty Years in Public Affairs*, 2 vols. (New York, 1902).

19. *Twentieth Report*, pp. 36–37. For Barnas Sears's comments on the relation of education and economic growth see *Nineteenth Report*, p. 51.

20. Horace Mann to J. A. Shaw, March 7, 1840, MS., Massachusetts Historical Society.

21. *Winchendon, 1852–53*, p. 15. For Robert Rantoul on this point see his "Resolution offered at Town Meeting, 1837," MS., Beverly Historical Society.

22. Brookline report abstracted in *Eighteenth Report*, p. 205.

23. "Mr. Rantoul's Connexion with Town and Parochial Affairs — His Views on Religion," *Historical Collections of the Essex Institute*, 6:82–84 (April 1864).

24. *Winchendon, 1852–53*, p. 15.

25. Report of Rufus Putnam as superintendent of schools in *Beverly, 1853–54*, pp. 24–26.

26. Rantoul, "Autobiography," p. 229.

27. Albert Boyden, *Here and There in the Family Tree* (Salem, 1949), p. 113. The draft of the petition, in Rantoul's handwriting, is in his papers, Beverly Historical Society.

28. On both the demise of the academy and the proprietor-trustee controversy see Rantoul, "Autobiography," pp. 221–223; and Ober, "Beverly," p. 722.

29. The resolution forming the Republican party in Beverly, together with the signatures of the ten founders, is reproduced in Boyden, *Here and There in the Family Tree,* opposite p. 116.

30. Boyden, *Here and There in the Family Tree,* pp. 16–17. The account of Boyden is taken from this source, which is a genealogy composed partly of narrative and partly of generous excerpts from family papers.

31. *Ibid.,* p. 17.

32. *Ibid.,* pp. 23–24.

33. *Ibid.,* pp. 22–23. The fragment of a letter concerning the high school is on pp. 117–120.

34. *Ibid.,* p. 119.

35. *Massachusetts House Document 49,* "Report on the Education of Children in Manufacturing Establishments," March 17, 1846. On Carter's background and the reasons why Mann rather than he was chosen secretary of the Board of Education see the illuminating article by Jonathan C. Messerli, "James G. Carter's Liabilities as a Common School Reformer," *History of Education Quarterly,* 1:14–25 (March 1865).

36. Jesse H. Jones, "Henry Kemble Oliver," in Commonwealth of Massachusetts, *Seventeenth Annual Report of the Bureau of the Statistics of Labour,* March 1886 (Boston, 1886), pp. 3–47.

37. Stone, *History of Beverly,* pp. 150–154.

38. Report of the meeting accompanies a letter from William Ellery Channing to Nathan Appleton, June 10, 1834, in Appleton papers, Massachusetts Historical Society. Neither the letter nor the report states where the meeting was held.

39. *Dalton, 1859–60,* p. 8.

40. Abstract of the Athol report, *Eighteenth Report,* pp. 64–65 (of abstracts).

41. Seymour Martin Lipset and Reinhard Bendix, *Social Mobility in Industrial Society* (Berkeley and Los Angeles, 1959), pp. 203–226.

42. These results, shown in tabular form in Appendix C, are based on manuscript records kept in the respective high schools and on manuscript census returns for 1860.

43. Mann, *Life and Works*, IV, 245, 250.

44. Mann, *Life and Works*, IV, 248–250; and letter to J. A. Shaw, March 7, 1840, MS., Massachusetts Historical Society.

45. [Horace Mann], *The Massachusetts System of Common Schools being an Enlarged and Revised Edition of the Tenth Annual Report of the First Secretary of the Massachusetts Board of Education* (Boston, 1848), pp. 84–86.

46. See Alvah Hovey, *Barnas Sears: A Christian Educator* (Boston, 1902); and Earle Huddleston West, "The Life and Educational Contributions of Barnas Sears," unpub. diss., George Peabody College for Teachers, 1961.

47. *Nineteenth Report*, pp. 41–50.

48. *Twenty-First Report*, p. 61; and *Twenty-Third Report*, p. 55.

49. Mann, *Massachusetts Common Schools*, pp. 18–31, 147. Sears's comment is in *Nineteenth Report*, p. 50.

50. *Twenty-First Report*, p. 66.

51. *Twenty-Ninth Report*, p. 87. For biographical detail on White see *A Tribute to the Memory of Joseph White* (no place, no date).

52. *Winchendon, 1852–53*, pp. 17–18.

53. *Twenty-Eighth Report*, pp. 83–84.

54. *Lincoln, 1853–54*, pp. 6–7.

55. *Barnstable, 1860–61*, pp. 27–28. See also *Watertown, 1856–57*, p. 5: "Common modesty is often shocked in the neighborhood of the playground, by indecencies of language and conduct, which seem to be the prevailing dialect and manner of life: and which it is manifestly the duty of somebody to reform. Peaceable travelers, whose habiliment or equipage is not of the approved pattern or construction, are hooted at, and persons quietly pursuing their daily avocations, are pelted with snowballs." See also the following reports: *Barnstable, 1857–58*, p. 19; *Fairhaven, 1863*, pp. 7–8; *Dartmouth, 1859–60*, pp. 3–4; *Groton, 1850*, p. 5; *Townsend, 1861–62*, pp. 11-12; *Webster, 1855–56*; *Monson, 1857*, p. 17 and *1859*, p. 14; *Dalton, 1858–59*, pp. 1–2; *Rockport, 1854–55*, p. 5.

56. *Eighteenth Report*, p. 59.

57. James G. Carter, *Essays upon Popular Education* (Boston, 1826), p. 8.

58. Abstract of Hadley school report in *Eighteenth Report,* p. 178.

59. *Dalton, 1859–60,* p. 8, claims that at academies children were exposed to "temptations and vice." See also *Attleborough, 1862–63,* p. 4, which charges that children who attended academies "because they have nothing else to do, to spend father's money, or simply to gratify the earnest wish of their parents to have them educated, are better off at home . . . They are much less likely to fall into bad practices under parental restraint, than among strangers, mingling with the giddy youths that are usually found at academies."

60. *Winchendon, 1852–53,* pp. 16–17.

61. *Twentieth Report,* pp. 43–45.

62. Boutwell in *Twentieth Report,* pp. 43–45.

63. *Twenty-Eighth Report,* p. 83; *Watertown, 1855–56,* p. 16.

64. See, *e.g., Twenty-Ninth Report,* p. 14, where the Board of Education wrote that they hoped communities, at their next town meeting, would vote "the total abolition of the cumbrous and unwieldy district system, which has so long clogged the progress of educational improvement in the towns where it has been suffered to remain. Reason and fact alike condemn it as a fruitful source of inconveniences and evils. It perpetuates poor schoolhouses, inefficient teachers, and neighborhood feuds and jealousies. It prevents the equalization of school advantages, and stands in the way of a proper classification of pupils. As compared with the town system, it is at once expensive and inefficient." See also George H. Martin, *The Evolution of the Massachusetts Public School System* (New York, 1894), pp. 114–115.

65. For Boutwell on districts see *Twenty-First Report,* pp. 49–51; and *Twenty-Third Report,* pp. 76–78. Boutwell's views on districts went through an interesting evolution. When he began his work as secretary he believed that districts were harmful but that they could not be abolished within the century, and he consequently urged some modifications in the system. A few years later, however, he openly reversed his former position and declared that districts were much worse than he had imagined and had to be abolished as soon as possible.

66. Sears, in *Nineteenth Report,* p. 53, wrote, concerning the opposition of districts to high schools: "Local prejudices already existing will come in to increase the difficulty. Instead of lookng dispassionately at the benefit of the whole, and favoring that arrangement which will accomplish the greatest good with the least sacrifice, parties will

sometimes be induced by the arts of selfish and designing men, to consult only their own passion and prejudices, and refuse to advance any other interest than their own."

67. See, *e.g.*, *Lincoln, 1852–53*, p. 5.

68. See *Eighteenth Report*, p. 56; *Dartmouth, 1865–66*, p. 7; and *Dalton, 1860–61*, p. 7.

69. *Beverly, 1857–58*, pp. 4–12.

70. For a long and thorough discussion of grading see John Brubacher, ed., *Henry Barnard on Education* (New York, 1931), pp. 96–104. See also abstract of Marshfield report in *Eighteenth Report*, p. 229: "Grading schools brings scholars of similar attainments together; the number of classes is diminished, and the amount of instruction which the scholar receives directly from the teacher is correspondingly increased."

71. George B. Emerson, "Address on Education," *Common School Journal*, 10:321–326 (1848). Robert C. Waterston, *Memoir of George Barrell Emerson* (Cambridge, Mass., 1884), p. 8. Emerson's claim as first high school teacher rests on the fact that he was first teacher at Boston English, usually considered the first high school. Arthur O. Norton, ed., *The First State Normal School in America: The Journals of Cyrus Peirce and Mary Swift* (Cambridge, Mass., 1926), pp. 99–100.

72. See, *e.g.*, *Fairhaven, 1851–52*, p. 12; and *Twenty-Eighth Report*, p. 81.

73. The suitability of females as teachers of the young was, of course, related to the period's idealization of women and their alleged inborn virtues; on this subject see Barbara Welter, "The Cult of True Womanhood: 1820–1860," *American Quarterly*, 18:151–174 (Summer 1966).

74. Abstract of the Braintree report in *Eighteenth Report*, p. 203.

75. *Twentieth Report*, pp. 42–43.

76. Silas L. Loomis, *Record of Holliston Academy, 1836–1844* (Washington, D.C., 1876), pp. 7–8, 30–61, is the source from which this information was compiled.

77. Charles William Eliot, "Wise and Unwise Economy in Schools," *Atlantic Monthly*, 35:715 (June 1875).

78. H. J. Habakkuk, *American and British Technology in the Nineteenth Century: The Search for Labour-Saving Inventions* (Cambridge, Eng.: Cambridge University Press, 1962), pp. 25, 45–48.

79. George Boutwell, *Reminiscences of Sixty Years in Public Af-*

fairs (New York, 1902), I, 35. John P. Bigelow, *Statistical Tables: Exhibiting the Condition and Products of Certain Branches of Industry in Massachusetts for the year ending April 1, 1837* (Boston, 1838), p. 28.

80. *Groton Mercury*, December 18, 1851, p. 3; January 15, 1853, p. 2; June 15, 1854, p. 2.

81. *Groton Herald*, March 27, 1830, p. 2. The *Herald* was published from 1828 to 1830.

82. *Groton, 1841–42*, pp. 3–4; *1847–48*, pp. 11–14.

83. *Groton, 1847–48*, pp. 11–14.

84. Samuel A. Green, *An Historical Sketch of Groton, Massachusetts, 1655–1890* (Groton, 1894), pp. 91–93.

85. Letters from Joshua Green to Amos Lawrence, April 19, 1841 and December 2, 1843, Lawrence MSS., Massachusetts Historical Society.

86. Green, *Historical Sketch*, pp. 91–93.

87. Curriculum details are included in the various editions of the *Catalogue of the Trustees, Instructors, and Students of Groton (later Lawrence) Academy;* hereafter referred to as *Catalogue.*

88. *Catalogue*, 1845, p. 9; 1849, p. 10; 1850, p. 20.

89. *Groton Mercury*, January 1852, p. 2.

90. *Groton, 1847–48*, p. 16.

91. *Groton, 1849–50*, pp. 15–16.

92. *Ibid.*, pp. 22–23.

93. *Catalogue*, 1851, p. 18.

94. Lists of students were printed at the front of the catalogue each year.

95. *Groton Town Records*, 1839 and 1840, pp. 77, 90, 92; 1847, p. 221. The town records are on file in the town clerk's office.

96. *Town Plan Book No. 12*, town plan map of Groton, 1830, p. 17. The town plan books are on microfilm in the Massachusetts State Archives.

97. *Groton, 1851–52*, pp. 7–8.

98. *Ibid.*, pp. 8–10.

99. *Ibid.*, pp. 10–11.

100. *Ibid.*, p. 12.

101. *Groton Town Records*, 1853, p. 374; 1854, p. 407.

102. *Groton, 1851–52*, p. 12.

103. *Groton Town Records*, 1851, pp. 526; 1854, pp. 407, 421, 429, 431.

104. *Groton Town Records*, 1855, p. 433.

105. *Groton Town Records*, 1857, pp. 456, 1.

106. *Groton Town Records*, 1859, pp. 73, 85.

107. *Groton, 1853–54*, p. 8.

108. *Groton, 1854–55*, pp. 10–11.

109. *Catalogue*, 1855, p. 15.

110. *Groton, 1854–55*, pp. 11, 10.

111. *Groton, 1856–57*, pp. 11–12.

112. *Groton, 1858–59*, p. 8.

113. *Groton Mercury*, July 20, 1855, p. 2; January 15, 1857, p. 2.

114. *Ayer, 1871–72*, pp. 8–9.

115. *Groton Mercury*, July 20, 1855, p. 2.

116. *Catalogue*, 1859, p. 16.

117. *Groton, 1861–62*, pp. 8–9.

118. George Rogers Taylor, *The Transportation Revolution, 1815–1860* (New York, 1951), pp. 284–285.

119. J. Leander Bishop, *A History of American Manufactures from 1608 to 1860* (Philadelphia, 1866), II, 509–510; Victor S. Clark, *History of Manufactures in the United States, 1607–1860* (Washington, 1916), p. 444; Blanche Hazard, *The Organization of the Boot and Shoe Industry in Massachusetts before 1875* (Cambridge, Mass., 1929), *passim;* and *Lynn Reporter*, March 31, 1860, p. 3, and March 10, 1860, p. 3: "There are too many shoemakers, and millions of cheap, miserable things have been manufactured, through the aid of machinery, and the employment of a vast number who are novices in the art." It is difficult to determine exactly how much the wages of shoemakers had been cut, and, thus, how far their objective situation had deteriorated. All sources, however, agree that there had been a substantial pay reduction. Perhaps most important, the shoemakers *believed* that their situation had deteriorated, and it was on this belief that they acted.

120. I followed the course of the strike in two newspapers, the pro-strike *Lynn Bay State* and the anti-strike *Lynn Reporter*. The former was Democratic, the latter Republican.

121. *Lynn Bay State*, March 15, 1860, p. 2.

122. *Ibid.*, March 1, 1860, p. 2.

123. *Ibid.*, March 15, 1860, p. 1.

124. *Ibid.*, March 8, 1860, p. 2.

125. Insofar as the strike was a protest against replacement of a craft skill by machinery there is a similarity to Luddism. Yet, unlike

the Luddites the American shoemakers protested peacefully. Even hostile accounts did not report the wrecking of machinery or deliberate physical assaults. On Luddism see George Rude, *The Crowd in History, 1730–1848* (New York, 1964), pp. 79–92. On p. 226, Rude notes the particular hostility of the pre-industrial crowd to "capitalist innovation." Luddism and the attitudes of the working class during the period of the first industrialization in England are portrayed sensitively in E. P. Thompson, *The Making of the English Working Class* (New York, 1964). A comparable study for the United States would be a major contribution. The interpretation stressing "displaced aggression" is supported by psychological theory of various schools. See Calvin S. Hall and Gardner Lindzey, *Theories of Personality* (New York, 1957), pp. 47–49, 449–453.

126. See *e.g.*, *Fairhaven, 1858–59*, p. 4; and *Lincoln, 1853–54*, pp. 4–5.

127. See, *e.g.*, *Webster, 1859–60*, pp. 4–5.

128. See, *e.g.*, *Fairhaven, 1860–61*, pp. 9–10.

129. See, *e.g.*, *Watertown, 1861–62*, pp. 9–10.

130. *Massachusetts Teacher*, 14:329 (September 1861).

131. See, for example, Oscar Handlin, "The Modern City as a Field of Historical Study," in Oscar Handlin and John Burchard, eds., *The Historian and the City* (Cambridge, Mass.: M.I.T. Press, 1963), pp. 14–15: "The complex interrelationships of life in the modern city called for unprecedented precision. The arrival of all those integers who worked together, from whatever part of the city they inhabited, had to be coordinated to the moment. There was no natural span for such labor; arbitrary beginnings and ends had to be set, made uniform and adhered to. The dictatorship of the clock and the schedule became absolute. No earlier human experience had made such demands. The urban factory was conceivable only well in the nineteenth century when it was possible to imagine that a labor force would come to work regularly and dependably." Writing of the clock as "Thoreau's model of the capitalist economy," Leo Marx (*The Machine in the Garden, Technology and the Pastoral Ideal in America* [New York: Oxford University Press, 1964], p. 248n) notes: "Thoreau's response to the mechanization of time reflects the heightened significance of the clock in the period of the 'take-off' into full scale industrialism. With the building of factories and railroads it became necessary, as never before, to provide the population with access to the exact time. This was made possible, in New England, by the transformation of the

clockmaking industry. Before 1800 clocks had been relatively expensive luxury items made only by master craftsmen. Significantly enough, the industry was among the first to use machines and the principle of interchangeable part manufacture. By 1807, in Connecticut, Eli Terry had begun to produce wooden clocks in large numbers, and before he died in 1852 he was making between 10,000 and 12,000 clocks a year sold at $5.00 each."

132. *Fifth Report,* pp. 93–94; *Twenty-Third Report,* pp. 44–45.

133. See, *e.g., Fairhaven, 1864–65,* p. 5.

134. *Groton, 1864–65,* p. 13.

135. For the emphasis on teacher-training in high schools see, *e.g., Chelsea, 1858,* pp. 27–28. The statistics on employed females are from the 1865 state census.

136. Nathan Appleton, *Introduction of the Power Loom and Origin of Lowell* (Lowell, 1858), p. 15. On the early manufacturing cities and the ideas they represented see Stephan Thernstrom, *Poverty and Progress: Social Mobility in a Nineteenth Century City* (Cambridge, Mass., 1964), esp. pp. 60–61; Donald B. Cole, *Immigrant City: Lawrence, Massachusetts, 1845–1921* (Chapel Hill, 1963), esp. chap. 2; and Charles L. Sanford, "The Intellectual Origins and New-Worldliness of American Industry," *Journal of Economic History,* 18:1–16 (Spring 1958).

137. Appleton, *Introduction of the Power Loom,* p. 16.

138. Cole, *Immigrant City,* pp. 21, 26. On the history of Lawrence see also Maurice B. Dorgan, *History of Lawrence with War Records* (Lawrence, 1924).

139. *Lawrence Courier,* March 6, 1847.

140. Letter from Charles Storrow to Horace Mann, February 8, 1848, Mann Collection, Massachusetts Historical Society.

141. Dorgan, *History of Lawrence,* pp. 83, 89.

142. *Lawrence, 1848–49,* pp. 3–7.

143. *Lawrence Courier,* April 11, 1856, p. 2.

144. *Lawrence Courier,* April 24, 1853; December 11, 1854; January 1, 1855; January 8, 1855; July 10, 1855; April 11, 1856; January 9, 1857; February 18, 1857; October 16, 1857; August 9, 1860; and *Lawrence Sentinel,* February 9, 1861.

145. *Lawrence Courier,* December 25, 1855.

146. *Merrimac Courier,* November 21, 1846; *Lawrence Sentinel,* August 27, 1864.

147. *Lawrence Courier,* January 16, 1857; February 3, 1859.

148. *Lawrence Courier*, August 26, 1853. See also *Lawrence Sentinel*, August 19, 1865.

149. *Lawrence, 1852–53*, pp. 20–21.

150. *Ibid.*

151. *Lawrence, 1854–55*, p. 6.

152. *Lawrence, 1857–58*, pp. 43–44.

153. *Lawrence, 1858–59*, pp. 67–72.

154. *Lawrence, 1848–49*, p. 8; *1850–51*, pp. 19–20; *1852–53*, p. 6.

155. *Lawrence, 1856–57*, pp. 5, 27; *1857–58*, p. 8; *1859–60*, p. 5.

156. *Lawrence, 1852–53*, p. 12; *1860–61*, pp. 11–12; *1861–62*, pp. 12–13; *1862–63*, pp. 11–12; *1864–65*, p. 12.

157. *Lawrence, 1847–48*, p. 9; *1850–51*, pp. 7–8.

158. *Lawrence, 1858–59*, pp. 22–24.

159. *Lawrence, 1859–60*, p. 11.

160. *Lawrence, 1860–61*, pp. 14–15; *1861–62*, pp. 10–12.

161. *Lawrence, 1863–64*, p. 18; *1864–65*, p. 17.

162. *Lawrence Courier*, July 11, 1854.

163. *Ibid.*, June 9, 1854; June 16, 1854.

164. *Lawrence, 1853–54*, pp. 8–12.

165. On the problem see *Lawrence, 1854–55*, pp. 7–9; *1859–60*, pp. 9–12; *1860–61*, p. 12.

166. *Lawrence, 1859–60*, pp. 9–12.

167. *Lawrence, 1862–63*, p. 23.

168. *Lawrence Sentinel*, January 26, 1856.

169. On the controversies over Williams and Fairfield see *Lawrence Sentinel*, January 26, 1856; March 15, 1856; May 17, 1856; September 16, 1856; *Lawrence American*, January 19, 1856; February 2, 1856; November 2, 1856; and *Lawrence, 1855–56*, pp. 13–14.

170. On private schools in Lawrence see *Merrimac Courier*, April 17, 1847; *Lawrence Courier*, October 31, 1854; *Lawrence Sentinel*, June 26, 1850; April 13, 1861; *Lawrence Daily Journal*, November 14, 1861; *Lawrence American*, April 16, 1864; February 4, 1865.

171. *Lawrence, 1864–65*, p. 22.

172. *Lawrence, 1857–58*, p. 48.

173. *Lawrence, 1856–57*, pp. 38, 59.

174. *Lawrence, 1857–58*, pp. 48, 59.

175. *Lawrence, 1852–53*, p. 16; also *1856–57*, p. 63.

176. *Lawrence, 1856–57*, pp. 57–59.

177. *Lawrence, 1855–56*, p. 24; *1857–58*, pp. 25–27, 73–75.

178. *Lawrence, 1862–63*, p. 12.

179. *Lawrence, 1857–58*, pp. 31, 33; *1860–61*, pp. 20–21.

180. *Lawrence, 1857–58*, p. 38; *1859–60*, p. 18; *1861–62*, p. 15; *1862–63*, pp. 14–15. The rationale for this sort of curricular change is treated in Part II of this study.

181. *Lawrence, 1860–61*, pp. 21–22; *1862–63*, p. 25; *1863–64*, pp. 14–15; *Lawrence Daily Journal*, March 23, 1861.

182. *Lawrence Courier*, November 1, 1855.

183. *Lawrence, 1852–53*, pp. 23–24; *1856–57*, pp. 42, 54.

184. An experienced educator looking back on the results of the style of educational reform practiced for the last half century told the N.E.A. Department of Superintendence in 1883 that the "very success" of the public school "tended to remove it further from the very class of children for whose benefit it was originally established. Theoretically, the public school is for all; practically, it is conducted with less regard to the very lowest stratum of society than is desirable. Our public schools are now the best schools to be found, but they are surrounded by a set of rigid rules, customs, and traditions which have a tendency to keep out the very children that these schools were established to educate." M. A. Newell (principal of the State Normal School, Baltimore, Maryland), in *Journals and Proceedings of the National Education Association . . . 1883* (Boston: Department of Superintendence, 1884), p. 79.

Part II. The Uses of Pedagogy: Teachers and the Educational Process

1. *Massachusetts Teacher*, 6:310–312, 320–322 (October, 1853). For biographical details on Peirce (1790–1860) see Samuel J. May, "Memoir of Cyrus Peirce," *American Journal of Education*, 4:275–308 (December 1857).

2. *Massachusetts Teacher*, 12:347–349 (September 1859).

3. *Massachusetts Teacher*, 2:167 (June 1849).

4. *Common School Journal*, 12:236 (August 1850).

5. *Massachusetts Teacher*, 2:213 (July 1849).

6. *Massachusetts Teacher*, 15:364 (September 1862).

7. *Massachusetts Teacher*, 17:46–47 (February 1865).

8. *Massachusetts Teacher*, 1:83–84 (March 15, 1848).

9. *Massachusetts Teacher*, 10:103 (March 1857). Similarly, a writer in the *Common School Journal*, 3:168 (May 15, 1841), claimed, "We must rub off the rust that sticks to us at home."

10. *Common School Journal*, 7:226 (August 1, 1846).

11. *Boston, 1857–58*, pp. 10–11.

12. On the nature of desired character traits see also Francis Wayland, *The Elements of Moral Science*, ed. Joseph Blau (Cambridge, Mass., 1963); and Ruth Miller Elson, *Guardians of Tradition: American Schoolbooks of the Nineteenth Century* (Lincoln, 1964). For a revealing and striking comparison note the social values prevalent in Britain as stressed in Walter E. Houghton, *The Victorian Frame of Mind, 1830–1870* (New Haven, 1957).

13. *Boston, 1857–58*, p. 50.

14. *Massachusetts Teacher*, 2:139 (May 1849).

15. Quoted in Robert W. Lovett, "From Social Library to Public Library: A Century of Library Development in Beverly, Massachusetts," *Essex Institute Historical Collections*, 88:231 (July 1952).

16. Lovett, "From Social Library to Public Library," p. 231.

17. *Massachusetts Teacher*, 1:81–84 (March 15, 1848). See also *Essex Institute Historical Collections*, 1:243 (August 15, 1848); 2:139 (May 1849); 2:168 (June 1849); 2:211 (July 1849); 2:33 (February 1851); 14:329 (September 1861).

18. *Common School Journal*, 2:373–374 (December 1, 1840).

19. *Massachusetts Teacher*, 4:35 (February 1851).

20. *Common School Journal*, 2:49 (February 15, 1840).

21. Newspapers in this period carried advertisements for numerous alleged birth-control and abortion-producing pills. The most widely advertised were Dr. Cheesmen's Female Regulating Pills. A typical advertisement for these proclaimed:

> The combination of ingredients in these Pills are the results of a long and extensive practice. They are mild in their operation and certain in correcting all irregularities, painful menstruations, removing all obstructions, whether from cold or otherwise, headache, pain in the side, palpitation of the heart, disturbed sleep, which always arise from interruption of nature. They can be successfully used as a preventive. These Pills should never be taken in pregnancy, as they would be sure to cause a miscarriage. . . .

On the relation between status anxiety and an explicit emphasis on sexual restraint see D. E. C. Eversley, *Social Theories of Fertility and the Malthusian Debate* (Oxford, 1959), pp. 89–162. On status anxiety see also Oscar Handlin's essay "The Horror," in his *Race and Nationality in American Life* (Boston, 1950), esp. p. 125; and Theodore

Parker, *The Collected Works of Theodore Parker,* ed. Frances Power
Cobbe (London, 1864), VII, 105, 123, 194.

22. *Common School Journal,* 14:85 (March 15, 1852).

23. *Massachusetts Teacher,* 14:121–124 (April 1861), and 9:106–
107 (March 1856).

24. *Common School Journal,* 12:236 (August 1, 1850).

25. *Massachusetts Teacher,* 12:350 (September 1859).

26. *Massachusetts Teacher,* 1:193 (July 1, 1848).

27. *Massachusetts Teacher,* 2:49 (February 1850).

28. *Common School Journal,* 5:7 (January 1, 1843).

29. *Massachusetts Teacher,* 1:198 (July 1, 1848).

30. *Massachusetts Teacher,* 2:143 (February 1853).

31. *Massachusetts Teacher,* 1:199 (July 1, 1848).

32. *Common School Journal,* 8:366–367 (December 1, 1846).

33. *Common School Journal,* 1:4 (January 1843).

34. *Massachusetts Teacher,* 1:120–121 (April 15, 1848).

35. *Common School Journal,* 10:371 (December 15, 1848).

36. *Massachusetts Teacher,* 1:121 (April 15, 1848).

37. *Lawrence, 1861–62,* pp. 19–20. See also, *e.g., Massachusetts
Teacher,* 4:119 (February 1851): "Fellow Teacher . . . your hands
are daily shaping that which shall bear your impress forever."

38. *Massachusetts Teacher,* 9:105–107 (February 1856).

39. The case is reported in *Massachusetts Teacher,* 2:257–262
(September 1849). On the nature of the moral lessons to be inculcated
by schools see also Elson, *Guardians of Tradition,* which reveals the
similarity between the preaching of schoolmen and the content of
textbooks.

40. *Boston 1859–60,* pp. 56–57.

41. *Common School Journal,* 2:63 (February 15, 1840).

42. *Massachusetts Teacher,* 1:134 (May 1, 1848).

43. *Ibid.*

44. *Ibid.*

45. *Massachusetts Teacher,* 13:416 (November 1860). For a discussion of object teaching see Charles J. Brauner, *American Educational Theory* (Englewood Cliffs, N.J., 1960), pp. 36–48.

46. *Massachusetts Teacher,* 1:113–115 (April 15, 1848).

47. *Ibid.*

48. *Massachusetts Teacher,* 5:168–174 (June 1852).

49. *Massachusetts Teacher,* 9:398–403 (September 1856). For

biographical information on Sherwin see John D. Philbrick, "Thomas Sherwin," *Education*, 1:388–392 (March 1881).

50. *Massachusetts Teacher*, 9:398–403 (September 1856).

51. See *Beverly, 1863–64,* pp. 6–8, on the virtues and introduction of physical education; *1864–65,* pp. 6–7, on object teaching; and *1865–66,* p. 7, on music. These passages clearly show that the ideas advocated on the state level had finally seeped down to Beverly.

52. Letter from Rufus Putnam to Beverly School Committee, March 26, 1827, MS., Rantoul Papers, Beverly Historical Society.

53. Quoted in Edwin Stone, *A History of Beverly, Civil and Ecclesiastical, from its Settlement in 1630 to 1842* (Boston, 1843), pp. 150–154. There is no evidence of a direct confrontation between Stone and Putnam, but given the divergence in their views and their activity in the same period, it is not unlikely that the issue of emulation was discussed by the school committee. There is, likewise, no evidence to support or contradict Stone's assertion that the schools discarded emulation. By this he may have meant that teachers ceased to give tangible rewards for good behavior and outstanding achievement.

54. *Common School Journal,* 15:242–243 (August 1, 1844).

55. [Boston Association of Masters of the Public Schools], *Remarks on the Seventh Annual Report of the Honorable Horace Mann, Secretary of the Massachusetts Board of Education* (Boston, 1844), pp. 45–47, 84–87.

56. *Ibid.,* pp. 84–87, 126–127.

57. *Ibid.,* pp. 126–127.

58. *Ibid.*

59. *Ibid.,* pp. 128–129.

60. [Boston Association of Masters of the Public Schools], *Rejoinder to the "Reply" of the Hon. Horace Mann . . . to the "Remarks" of the Association of Boston Masters . . .* (Boston, 1845), 4th pt. (Joseph Hale), p. 60.

61. *Remarks,* p. 134.

62. [Leonard Withington], *Penitential Tears; or a Cry from the Dust, by "The Thirty-one," Prostrated and Pulverized by the Hand of Horace Mann, Secretary, &c.* (Boston, 1845), p. 56.

63. *Remarks,* p. 13.

64. George B. Emerson to Horace Mann, July 16, 1844, Mann Papers, Massachusetts Historical Society.

65. *Remarks,* p. 17.

66. *Ibid.*, p. 29.

67. For a discussion of religious controversy see Raymond Culver, *Horace Mann and Religion in the Massachusetts Public Schools* (New Haven, 1929).

68. Withington, *Penitential Tears*, pp. 51–52. *Massachusetts House Document 49*, 1840, "The Expediency of Abolishing the Board of Education and the Normal Schools," Allen Dodge, chairman.

69. *Massachusetts House Document 49*, pp. 3–4.

70. *Ibid.*, p. 4.

71. *Ibid.*, pp. 5, 6, 7–11.

72. *Ibid.*, pp. 11–12.

73. *Massachusetts House Document 49*, 1840, p. 2.

74. W. David Lewis, *From Newgate to Dannemora: The Rise of the Penitentiary in New York, 1796–1848* (Ithaca: Cornell University Press, 1965), p. 201.

75. David Brion Davis, *Homicide in American Fiction, 1798–1865: A Study in Social Values* (Ithaca, 1957), p. 299.

76. Norman Dain, *Concepts of Insanity in the United States, 1789–1865* (New Brunswick, 1965), pp. 148–164.

77. The discussion of the political finale of the Mann-Masters controversy is taken largely from Harold Schwartz's excellent book, *Samuel Gridley Howe, Social Reformer, 1801–1876* (Cambridge, Mass., 1956), pp. 120–136. On the primary school board see also Mary Ann Connolly, "The Boston Schools in the New Republic, 1776–1840," unpub. diss., Harvard University, 1963. Unfortunately, this thesis ends just when events in Boston become most exciting and interesting. See also Joseph Whightman, *Annals of the Boston Primary School Committee, from its First Establishment in 1818, to its Dissolution in 1855* (Boston, 1860).

78. The problems of Boston in the 1870's have not been treated by historians; evidence is from my own research now in progress.

79. *Massachusetts Teacher*, 6:109 (April 1853).

80. *Common School Journal*, 5:355 (December 1, 1843).

81. *Cambridge, 1851–52*, p. 6.

82. *Massachusetts Teacher*, 1:4 (January 1, 1848). On the founding of the Association see also *Abstract of the Proceedings of the Massachusetts Teachers' Association, 1845–1880* (Boston, 1881).

83. *Massachusetts Teacher*, 1:277 (September 15, 1848).

84. *Massachusetts Teacher*, 9:58–60 (February 1856).

85. *Massachusetts Teacher*, 4:37 (February 1851).

86. *Massachusetts Teacher*, 6:109–110 (April 1853).
87. *Massachusetts Teacher*, 10:261–263 (June 7, 1857).
88. *Massachusetts Teacher*, 6:310–312 (October 1853).
89. *Ibid.*, pp. 310–314.
90. *Ibid.*, pp. 320–322.
91. For data on crime see Part III.
92. The Massachusetts Teachers Association started in 1847, the National Teachers Association in 1857. The first meeting of the American Normal School Association was in 1859, the first meeting of the association of superintendents in 1865. See Edgar B. Wesley, *N.E.A. The First Hundred Years: The Building of a Profession* (New York, 1957), p. 44; *American Normal Schools: Their Theory, Their Workings and Their Results, as Embodied in the Proceedings of the American Normal School Association, Held at Trenton, New Jersey, August 19 and 20, 1859* (New York, 1860).

Part III. Compulsory Education and the Urban Delinquent: The State Reform School

1. David Snedden quoted in Edward A. Krug, *The Shaping of the American High School* (New York, 1964), p. 265.
2. See "Public Charitable Institutions," *Massachusetts Senate Document 2*, January 1859, hereafter referred to as Public Charitable Institutions. The two reports considered in this part are the *First Annual Report of the Board of State Charities to which are added the Reports of the Secretary and the General Agent of the Board, Public Document 19*, January 1865 and *Second Annual Report . . .* , January, 1866. These will hereafter be referred to as Board of State Charities, 1865 and 1866, respectively.
3. See Arthur M. Schlesinger, Jr., *The Age of Jackson* (Boston, 1950), pp. 380–382. On the influence of T. H. Green see Melvin Richter, *The Politics of Conscience: T. H. Green and His Age* (Cambridge, Mass., 1964). For an intriguing comparison of the influence of Green and Garman of Amherst see George E. Peterson, *The New England College in the Age of the University* (Amherst, 1964), chap. 7, "The Whole Man as Reformer." If the comparison with Emerson is valid, then the fact that Emerson did not hold a university appointment suggests in itself the change in the nature and role of universities in the late nineteenth century.

4. Board of State Charities (Secretary's Report), 1865, pp. 210–212. Comparisons of Massachusetts and English administrative reform, institutional development, and private philanthropy during this period are striking. See David Roberts, *Victorian Origins of the British Welfare State* (New Haven, 1960); and David Owen, *English Philanthropy, 1660–1960* (Cambridge, Mass., 1964), pp. 91–208. Owen discusses reform schools on pp. 152–155. On aspects of the organization of American philanthropy see Clifford S. Griffin, *Their Brothers' Keepers: Moral Stewardship in the United States, 1800–1865* (New Brunswick, 1960).

5. On normal schools see particularly Jonathan C. Messerli, "Localism and State Control in Horace Mann's Reform of the Common Schools," *American Quarterly,* 17:104–118, esp. pp. 114–115 (Spring 1965).

6. The petitions in manuscript form are on file in the Massachusetts State Archives, under Resolves, 1846, chap. 143, "for the erection of a State Manual Labor School."

7. *Senate Document 86,* March 27, 1846; hereafter referred to as First Legislative Report.

8. Board of State Charities (Secretary's Report), 1865, pp. 97–100.

9. *Senate Document 10,* January 1847; hereafter referred to as Second Legislative Report.

10. Blake McKelvey, *American Prisons: A Study in American Social History Prior to 1915* (Chicago, 1936), p. 14. For an account of a different method of handling delinquents see Miriam Z. Langsam, *Children West: A History of the Placing-Out System of the New York Children's Aid Society, 1853–1890* (Madison, 1964).

11. Board of State Charities (Secretary's Report), 1865 (*Public Document 19,* 1866), pp. 108–109. See also: City of Boston, *Report of the Standing Committee of the Common Council on the Subject of the House of Reformation for Juvenile Offenders* (Boston, 1852), pp. 5–7; City of Boston, *Houses of Industry and Reformation* (*City Document No. 14,* Boston, 1844), p. 20; *Massachusetts Statutes,* 1850, chap. 294; 1852, chap. 283; United States Bureau of Education, *Truant Schools* (chap. 111 of the report of the Commissioner of Education, Washington, 1901); John William Perrin, *The History of Compulsory Education in New England* (Meadville, Pa., 1896).

12. From the MS., Massachusetts State Archives. For biographical details on Francis George Shaw see James Grant Wilson and John

Fiske, eds., *Appleton's Cyclopedia of American Biography* (New York, 1888), L, 486.

13. First Legislative Report, pp. 9–11, 14, 2.

14. Emory Washburn, *An Address at the Dedication of the State Reform School at Westborough, December 7, 1848* (Boston, 1849), pp. 88–92.

15. From the MS., Massachusetts State Archives.

16. *Ibid.*

17. First Legislative Report, pp. 16, 6–7.

18. Washburn, *Address,* p. 102.

19. Second Legislative Report, p. 10.

20. *Senate Document 12,* 1850, p. 17. This and all future references cited as *House Document, Senate Document,* and *Public Document* refer to the annual reports of the trustees and superintendent of the reform school, published under different titles.

21. *Public Document 20,* October 1864, p. 3.

22. David Brion Davis, *Homicide in American Fiction, 1798–1860: A Study in Social Values* (Ithaca: Cornell University Press, 1957), p. 259.

23. Second Legislative Report, pp. 60–61. The state did establish a reformatory for girls in 1854 at Lancaster.

24. *House Document 20,* 1856, p. 37.

25. Washburn, *Address,* p. 102.

26. *Senate Document 12,* 1850, pp. 21–22.

27. *Ibid.*

28. On poverty in this period see Robert H. Bremner, *From the Depths: The Discovery of Poverty in the United States* (New York, 1956), chap. 1.

29. *House Document 2,* 1856, p. 37.

30. Board of State Charities (Secretary's Report), 1864 (*Public Document 19,* 1865), p. 409.

31. Public Charitable Institutions, pp. 81–82.

32. *Public Document 23,* 1859, p. 44.

33. First Legislative Report, p. 4.

34. *Ibid.,* pp. 7–8.

35. *House Document 14,* 1851, pp. 24–25.

36. *Public Document 23,* 1858, p. 51.

37. My computation from census figures.

38. *Public Document 23,* 1858, p. 51.

39. Quoted in Joseph A. Allen, *Westboro' State Reform School Reminiscences* (Boston, 1877), p. 5. Allen was one of the school's superintendents, and his reminiscences make a wise and often delightful book that is still relevant. For a comment on the importance of the role of the chaplain see the speech of the out-going one, Rev. N. Scott, *A Plea for the Bible in the State Reform School at Westboro', Mass. A Farewell Discourse Delivered April 4, 1862* (Boston, 1862). This is hardly an unbiased source, but it does offer insight into the role of chaplain and an extreme statement of the necessity of Protestant evangelicalism in the reform school.

40. Public Charitable Institutions, pp. 39, 131.

41. Board of State Charities (Secretary's Supplementary Report), 1865, p. 77.

42. *House Document 14, 1851*, pp. 18–19; (Mass.) *Revised Statutes . . . 1836*, title III, chap. 143, sec. 5.

43. Norman Dain, *Concepts of Insanity in the United States, 1789–1865* (New Brunswick, 1964), pp. 85–90.

44. Davis, *Homicide*, pp. 43–44.

45. W. David Lewis, *From Newgate to Dannemora: The Rise of the Penitentiary in New York, 1796–1848* (Ithaca, 1965), p. 231.

46. Board of State Charities, 1866, pp. xxii–xxiii.

47. Harold Schwartz, *Samuel Gridley Howe, Social Reformer, 1801–1876* (Cambridge, Mass., 1956), pp. 271–272, 275–276.

48. Dain, *Concepts of Insanity*, p. 110.

49. Davis, *Homicide*, p. 82.

50. Board of State Charities, 1866, pp. xxiii–xxix.

51. *Ibid.*, pp. xix–xxxi.

52. *Ibid.*, pp. xxxi–xxxvii.

53. Board of State Charities (Secretary's Report), 1865 (*Public Document Supplementary, No. 19*), pp. 71–72.

54. *Ibid.*, p. xxii.

55. *Ibid.*, pp. xxxvi–xxxvii.

56. Second Legislative Report, pp. 12–13.

57. *Ibid.*, pp. 5, 11. The desire of the commissioners not to have the reform school considered a penitentiary is ironical in view of the fact that in the late eighteenth and early nineteenth centuries "penitentiary" denoted an advanced, enlightened kind of penal institution. See Lewis, *From Newgate to Dannemora*.

58. *Public Document 23*, 1858, p. 7.

59. *Ibid.*, pp. 9, 11.

60. Second Legislative Report, p. 17.

61. Board of State Charities, 1866, p. xxxvi.

62. George Boutwell, "Speech at the Inauguration of Mr. Starr," in *Services at the Induction of William E. Starr, Esq., as Superintendent of the State Reform School at Westboro', January 15, 1857* (Boston, 1857), p. 13.

63. First Legislative Report, p. 10.

64. Washburn, *Address,* pp. 85, 100–101.

65. *Public Document 24,* 1861, p. 35.

66. *Public Document 23,* 1863, p. 10.

67. *House Document 2,* 1854, p. 28.

68. *Public Document 24,* 1861, p. 7.

69. *Ibid.,* pp. 4–5.

70. *Public Document 24,* 1862, p. 37.

71. Board of State Charities, 1866, lxiii–lxiv.

72. *Ibid.,* xlv–xlvi.

73. *Senate Document 14,* 1851, p. 16.

74. *Ibid.*

75. Second Legislative Report, pp. 53, 6–7.

76. Washburn, *Address,* p. 108.

77. First Legislative Report, p. 14.

78. Lewis, *From Newgate to Dannemora,* p. 201.

79. Dain, *Concepts of Insanity,* pp. 13, 119–120.

80. Allen, *Reminiscences,* p. 41.

81. *Ibid.,* pp. 12, 14. On formal education in the reform school and its importance see *Senate Document 6,* 1849, pp. 9–10, which gives the daily routine; *Public Document 15,* 1857, p. 6, which emphasizes the effort to obtain the best available teachers; *Public Document 23,* 1858, p. 13, which claims the school is as good as most high schools; *Public Document 24,* 1862, p. 5, which discusses the introduction of object teaching and oral instruction; *Public Document 23,* 1863, p. 8, which discusses the grading of the school; *Public Document 20,* 1865, which also discusses grading and reports good progress.

82. *Public Document 20,* 1865, p. 8.

83. *Public Document 23,* 1858, p. 14; Allen, *Reminiscences,* p. 54.

84. *Report of the Superintendent for 1852,* p. 28 (not numbered as a state document).

85. *Public Document 24,* 1861, p. 5.

86. *Public Document 23,* 1858, pp. 8–10.

87. *Senate Document 6,* 1849, pp. 9–10.

88. Board of State Charities (Secretary's Report), 1864 (*Public Document 19*, 1865), p. 176.

89. *Public Document 20*, 1865, p. 14.

90. Board of State Charities (Secretary's Report), 1865 (*Public Document 19*, 1866), pp. 217–218.

91. Board of State Charities (Secretary's Report), 1864 (*Public Document 19*, 1865), p. 410.

92. Board of State Charities (Secretary's Report), 1865 (*Public Document 19*, 1866), p. xviii.

93. On the size issue see Second Legislative Report, p. 11; *Senate Document 12*, 1850, p. 3; *Public Document 15*, 1857, p. 4; *Public Document 23*, 1859, pp. 3, 7–10.

94. In its early years the school had accepted many boys aged 15–17 and some under 8. By 1864–65 the school took only boys 8–14, concentrating on those 11 and older. The shift was deliberate, for it was increasingly felt that the reform of boys received over the age of 14 was nearly impossible. *Public Document 20*, 1865, p. 37.

95. *Public Document 19*, 1864, pp. 185–186.

96. *Senate Document 12*, 1850, p. 19.

97. *House Document 2*, 1857, p. 42.

98. *House Document 2*, 1857, p. 42; and Public Charitable Institutions, pp. 14–16.

99. *Public Document 23*, 1858, p. 15.

100. *Public Document 24*, 1862, pp. 4–5.

101. Board of State Charities (Secretary's Report), 1864 (*Public Document 19*, 1865), p. 177.

102. Allen, *Reminiscences*, p. 4; and *Services at the Induction of William E. Starr*, pp. 8–9.

103. Allen, *Reminiscences*, pp. 84–87. The report to the Governor's Council is in "Records of the Governor's Council," 1860, pp. 205–207, MS., Massachusetts State Archives. This vividly documents the physical and psychological brutality of Starr's punishment as well as his attempt at evasion. That this was excessively brutal treatment by the standards of the time was testified to in the same source by Nathaniel Banks, who had visited most of the jails in the state.

104. *House Document 2*, 1856, p. 36.

105. Public Charitable Institutions, p. 15.

106. *Public Document 20*, 1864, pp. 3–4.

107. Sanborn's charges are in Board of State Charities (Secretary's

NOTES TO PAGES 201–207 | 315

Report), 1864 (*Public Document 19,* 1865), pp. 174–176. Allen's answer is in *Public Document 20,* 1865, p. 9. Allen claimed that the decrease in earning was the result of the fact that the State Board of Agriculture turned over the running of the school farm to the reform-school itself.

108. For complaints about unfair popular opinion see *House Document 2,* 1856, p. 22.

109. *Public Document 20,* 1865, pp. 12–14.

110. *Public Document 15,* 1857, p. 7.

111. *House Document 2,* 1856, p. 39.

112. *Senate Document 12,* 1850, p. 40.

113. George Boutwell, "Speech at the Inauguration of Mr. Starr," pp. 11–12.

114. *Public Document 23,* 1859, p. 6.

115. Board of State Charities, 1866, pp. lxxv–lxxvi.

116. Schwartz, *Samuel Gridley Howe,* pp. 273–274.

117. Board of State Charities, 1866, pp. lxxvi, lxxvii, lxxviii.

118. Schwartz, *Samuel Gridley Howe,* pp. 273–274.

119. Quoted in Carrol D. Wright, *The Results of the Massachusetts Public School System* (Boston, 1879), pp. 66–67.

120. Schwartz, *Samuel Gridley Howe,* p. 272; and Dain, *Concepts of Insanity,* p. xiv.

121. Lewis, *From Newgate to Dannemora,* p. 256.

122. Roy Lubove, *The Professional Altruist: The Emergence of Social Work as a Career, 1880–1930* (Cambridge, Mass., 1965), *passim.*

123. For instance, the first two superintendents of Westborough left to become superintendents of newly founded reform schools elsewhere. Board of State Charities (Secretary's Report), 1864 (*Public Document 19,* 1865), p. 175. Four of the teachers who served under Allen had moved up to superintendencies of other reform schools by 1877. Allen, *Reminiscences,* p. 51. Likewise, Dain, in *Concepts of Insanity* reports the development of a self-conscious group of psychiatrists, then meaning superintendents of insane asylums.

124. In fact, it was probably the good fortune of having an exceptional man like Allen at its head that kept the reform school from degenerating even more quickly, as the mental hospitals seemed to do. After Allen left in 1866, the situation at the school apparently deteriorated steadily until, in the 1870's, the newspapers were again full of accounts of riots sparked by the cruel and stupid administration

of the badly overcrowded institution. See, *e.g., Boston Evening Transcript,* March 30, 1877, p. 4; April 6 and 13, 1877, both p. 4; December 7, 1877, p. 4.

125. See Thomas F. Gossett, *Race: The History of an Idea in America* (Dallas, 1963), pp. 144–197, 339–408; Richard Hofstadter, *Social Darwinism in American Thought,* rev. ed. (Boston, 1955), *passim;* and Daniel Levine, *Varieties of Reform Thought* (Madison, 1964). See particularly Levine's chapters on Jane Addams and Albert J. Beveridge as well as his "Conclusion." My hunch about the attitude of schoolmen in the 1870's and 1880's is based on some of my own research now in progress. There is at present no study of the attitude of educators toward the environment-heredity question.

126. The poem is inserted between pp. 440 and 441 of Robert Rantoul's "Autobiography," MS., Beverly Historical Society. In Rantoul's handwriting on the poem is, "Sung by the boys (inmates) at the dedication of the house at Westborough, December 1848."

Conclusion. Educational Reform: Myths and Limits

1. James Bryant Conant, *Slums and Suburbs* (New York, 1961), p. 2.

2. Two prominent educators who are exceptions to the "tardy" generalization are James Carter and Francis Parker.

3. Lawrence A. Cremin, *The Transformation of the School: Progressivism in American Education, 1876–1957* (New York, 1961). See, *e.g.,* p. 350.

4. Paul Goodman, *Compulsory Mis-education* (New York, 1964), pp. 178–180.

APPENDIX B. Communities and Education: An Analysis of Variance

1. Alexander James Inglis, *The Rise of the High School in Massachusetts* (New York, 1911), p. 36.

2. See *ibid.,* pp. 35–37.

3. See, *e.g., Winchendon, 1852–53,* p. 15.

4. See, *e.g., Eighteenth Report,* p. 134.

5. From the Brookline school committee report, cited in *Eight-*

eenth Report, p. 205. For details of curricula see Inglis, *Rise of the High School,* pp. 71–78; and Emit Duncan Grizzell, *Origin and Development of the High School in New England Before 1865* (Philadelphia, 1923), pp. 296–330.

6. Inglis, *Rise of the High School,* p. 8.

7. *Ibid.,* pp. 24–34.

8. *Ibid.,* p. 8.

9. George H. Martin, *The Evolution of the Massachusetts Public School System* (New York, 1894), pp. 92–93. See *Law of the Commonwealth of Massachusetts Providing for the Instruction of Youth,* passed March 10, 1827.

10. B. A. Hinsdale, *Horace Mann and the Common School Revival in the United States* (New York, 1913), pp. 16–17.

11. Raymond Culver, *Horace Mann and Religion in the Massachusetts Public Schools* (New Haven, 1929), pp. 21–28.

12. Inglis, *Rise of the High School,* p. 12.

13. *Ibid.,* pp. 65–70.

14. Population and dependency rate (computed as the number of children under fifteen divided by the total population) were taken from the general censuses. From the 1840 census came also the total employed in manufacturing, agriculture, commerce, navigation, and professions; these measures were used to derive the total employed in non-agricultural occupations and the ratio of this figure to the number employed in agriculture. From the 1865 census came the number of foreign born. The state census of industry for 1875 contained data compiled from the state census of industry for 1865, which merely listed but did not compile information on each town. From the 1875 census were taken the 1865 figures for total employed in manufacturing, agriculture, and "other occupations" (a category comprising navigation, commerce, and a number of trades). In addition, the 1875 census provided information concerning the number of women employed a decade earlier in manufacturing and, finally, the number of manufacturing establishments. The last measure was divided by the number of people employed in manufacturing and the result used as a variable. Unfortunately, there is no source for the number of professionals in each town in 1865 nor for a separate consideration of commerce and navigation.

To determine whether or not a town had established a high school by 1865 Alexander Inglis' results in *The Rise of the High School in Massachusetts* (New York, 1911) were used. All of Inglis' results were not checked; but spot checking revealed accuracy. The school return abstracts of both years contain the number of incorporated academies; the numbers of unincorporated academies and private schools (in 1840 this category also included schools kept to prolong the common schools); the average monthly salary, including board, of both male and female teachers; per-pupil expenditure; and mills per dollar of valuation raised through taxation for school support. This last variable will hereafter be termed school tax rate. The data in the returns were used to compute the percent of females teaching in the winter, hereafter referred to as feminization. Population figures from the census and valuation figures from the school reports were used to determine per capita valuation. The use of valuation is open to the objection that towns assessed their property differently, and that hence the recorded valuation of two or more towns of actually similar real valuation might be different. However, Charles J. Bullock, in *Historical Sketch of the Finances and Financial Policy of Massachusetts from 1780 to 1905* (New York, 1907, pp. 13, 54), has pointed out that the valuation of towns was determined at ten-year intervals. A special valuation committee was appointed for this purpose. The committee recognized that towns might undervalue their property, and consequently the committee tried to correct for inaccuracies and to arrive at a uniform standard. Therefore, the valuation reported is a reasonably accurate figure to employ.

The 1840 abstract contained a category of the number of students over sixteen attending public school; by 1865 the category had been changed to the number of students over fifteen. Miles from Boston, another measure used, was derived partly from a gazetteer of Massachusetts published in 1828 (Jeremiah Spofford, *A Gazetteer of Massachusetts,* Newburyport, 1828); in part from atlases; and in a few cases through measurements made directly from a map. A final measure of considerable importance was density, computed as population divided by square miles of territory. The earliest figures for square mileage that could be located were in the Massachusetts census of 1915. Towns were created and various boundaries altered between 1865 and 1915, but fortunately the state government published an excellent pamphlet listing in great detail all name and boundary changes in towns and cities. (See Secretary of the Commonwealth of Massachusetts, *Historical Data Relating to Counties, Cities and Towns in Massachusetts,* Boston, 1920). This pamphlet was used to determine both certain necessary alterations that could be made with reasonable accuracy in the 1915 figures and certain situations in which the town had to be dropped from the sample because of boundary changes. The density figures are not absolutely accurate since small boundary changes could not be measured, but it is assumed that most boundary adjustments were not large enough to invalidate the results. The variables measuring differences between 1840 and 1865 were computed.

15. Inglis, *Rise of the High School,* pp. 2–5; Hinsdale, *Horace Mann and the Common School Revival,* pp. 13–14; Robert Middlekauff, *Ancients and Axioms: Secondary Education in Eighteenth-Century New England* (New Haven, 1963), pp. 128–137.

16. Inglis, *Rise of the High School,* pp. 42–45.

17. On the problem of the definition of urbanism see John Burchard, "Some Afterthoughts," in Oscar Handlin and John Burchard, eds., *The Historian and the City* (Cambridge, Mass., 1963), pp. 254–257.

18. For an additional discussion of factor analysis see the thesis version of this study, same title, Harvard University, 1966. See also I. L. Thurstone, *Multiple-Factor Analysis: A Development and Expansion of the Vectors of the Mind* (Chicago, 1947), p. 57; William W. Cooley and Paul R. Lohnes, *Multivariate Procedures for the Behavioral Sciences* (New York, 1962), pp. 151–172; and J. P. Guilford, *Psychometric Methods* (New York, 1954), pp. 470–535.

Index